Talk That Counts

Talk That Counts

Age, Gender, and Social Class Differences in Discourse

RONALD K. S. MACAULAY

OXFORD
UNIVERSITY PRESS

2005

OXFORD
UNIVERSITY PRESS

Oxford   New York
Auckland   Bangkok   Buenos Aires   Cape Town   Chennai
Dar es Salaam   Delhi   Hong Kong   Istanbul   Karachi   Kolkata
Kuala Lumpur   Madrid   Melbourne   Mexico City   Mumbai   Nairobi
São Paulo   Shanghai   Taipei   Tokyo   Toronto

Published by Oxford University Press, Inc.
198 Madison Avenue, New York, New York 10016

www.oup.com

Oxford is a registered trademark of Oxford University Press

Library of Congress Cataloging-in-Publication Data
Macaulay, Ronald K. S.
Talk that counts : age, gender, and social class differences in discourse / Ronald K. S. Macaulay
p. cm.
Includes bibliographical references and index.
ISBN 0-19-517381-3; ISBN 0-19-517382-1 (pbk.)
1. Scots language—Social aspects—Scotland—Glasgow.   2. Scots language—Spoken
Scots—Scotland—Glasgow.   3. Scots language—Variation—Scotland—Glasgow.   4. Scots
language—Dialects—Scotland—Glasgow.   5. Language and social
status—Scotland—Glasgow.   6. Glasgow (Scotland)—Social conditions.   7. English
language—Discourse analysis.   8. Urban dialects—Scotland—Glasgow.   9. Glasgow
(Scotland)—Languages.   10. Discourse analysis.   11. Sociolinguistics.   I. Title.

PE2274.G57M33 2004
306.44'0941443—dc22   2003059247

9 8 7 6 5 4 3 2 1

Printed in the United States of America
on acid-free paper

ACKNOWLEDGMENTS

This work has been a long time in preparation and gone through many transformations. Parts of the material have been presented in conference papers and journal articles over several years. During this period I have received comments and suggestions from many people, including the anonymous reviewers for Oxford University Press. To all of them I here express my gratitude. However, there are two people who deserve special mention. One is Jane Stuart-Smith, whose excellent recordings provided the material for the Glasgow sample. The other is Lee Munroe, whose counsel and advice, particularly in the area of statistics, have sustained me through the lengthy process. To both of them I am deeply grateful. My thanks also to Peter Ohlin, Christi Stanforth, Robert Milks, and my copyeditor, Susan Ecklund, for seeing the work through the press in a timely and efficient manner.

CONTENTS

Talk That Counts

Discourse Variation

$\mathbf{F}$or almost 50 years now, quantitative methods have been used to investigate the correlation between variation in language and certain extralinguistic categories. Table 1.1 lists some of these quantitative studies of language variation and the major extralinguistic variables that have been examined.

TABLE 1.1. Extralinguistic factors in quantitative studies of language variation

	Social class	Gender	Age	Other factors
Fischer 1958	yes	yes	no	personality
Labov 1963	no	no	yes	ethnicity, ambition
Labov 1966	yes	yes	yes	ethnicity
Wolfram 1969	yes	yes	yes	racial isolation
Fasold 1972	yes	yes	yes	race of interviewer
Trudgill 1974	yes	yes	yes	rurality
Macaulay 1977	yes	yes	yes	religion
Feagin 1979	yes	yes	yes	ethnicity, locale
Milroy 1980	no	yes	yes	religion, social network
Cheshire 1982	no	yes	no	peer group status
Coupland 1988	yes	yes	no	education
Macaulay 1991b	yes	no	no	none
Haeri 1996	yes	yes	yes	education
Eckert 2000	yes (?)	yes	no	peer group status
McCafferty 2001	yes	yes	yes	ethnicity, religion
Labov 2001b	yes	yes	yes	social network

In table 1.1 the extralinguistic factors have been cited as *yes* where they have been correlated with the linguistic variables. Thus, since Milroy 1980 deals only with working-class speakers, there is no social class comparison; similarly, Cheshire 1982 deals with adolescents but does not contrast their behavior with that of other age-groups, so age is not an extralinguistic variable.

Table 1.1 shows that sociolinguists employing quantitative methods have generally been interested in a wide range of factors, but the emphasis has shifted over the years. Given the prominence of social class in early sociolinguistic investigations (e.g., Labov 1966; Macaulay and Trevelyan 1973; Trudgill 1974; Wolfram 1969), it is perhaps surprising that the topic seems to be less visible in current research. For example, *The Handbook of Language Variation and Change* (Chambers, Trudgill, and Schilling-Estes 2002) allocates less than 3% of its 787 pages to a chapter on social class, with scattered references to social class in another 3%. The chapter on social class in the handbook by Sharon Ash cites only one major work (Haeri 1996) later than 1982. Whatever attention has been paid to social class differences in recent years has been overshadowed by a focus on other topics, such as ethnicity (Labov 1972), networking (Milroy 1980), and gender (Coates 1996). Recent studies of social class differences (e.g., Foulkes and Docherty 1999; Labov 2001b) have been concerned primarily with the role of social class differences in language change. This is particularly true of discourse studies, even in works that come into the category of critical discourse studies. As Grimshaw concedes, "The study of the discursive reproduction of class has been rather neglected in this perspective" (2001: 764). Table 1.2 shows the kind of variables that have been examined in these studies.

The most salient differences are phonological and morphological. These features often are diagnostic of social differentiation in communities (Coupland 2001a: 189), so it is hardly surprising that they have received the most attention. Nevertheless, a skeptical observer might wonder whether these studies have fully investigated what

TABLE 1.2. Sociolinguistic variables in quantitative studies of language variation

Fischer 1958	*-ing/in* alternation
Labov 1963	2 phonological variables
Labov 1966	5 phonological variables
Wolfram 1969	4 phonological variables, 4 grammatical variables
Fasold 1972	2 phonological variables, 2 grammatical variables
Trudgill 1974	16 phonological variables, 1 grammatical variable
Macaulay 1977	5 phonological variables
Feagin 1979	6 grammatical variables
Milroy 1980	9 phonological variables
Cheshire 1982	16 grammatical variables
Coupland 1988	6 phonological variables
Macaulay 1991b	8 phonological variables, 4 morphological variables, syntactic and discourse features
Haeri 1996	2 phonological variables
Eckert 2000	6 phonological variables, 1 grammatical variable
McCafferty 2001	5 phonological variables
Labov 2001b	9 phonological variables, 1 grammatical variable

Milroy (1979: 91) calls "the sociolinguistic complexity" of the communities. The most prominent example of going beyond phonological and morphological features ("dialect features," in Coupland's 2001a: 189 sense) was Bernstein (1962, 1971), and the reaction to his views was so extreme that it probably discouraged sociolinguists from exploring the kind of questions he raised (Edwards 1987). As Bernstein himself rather ruefully remarked on recalling his contribution to the study of language differences, his distinction between an elaborated and a restricted code "became a means of bestowing ideological purity on those who denounced it" (1997: 47).

However, apart from the adverse reaction he provoked, Bernstein's work had little impact on most sociolinguistic investigation. As he observed in his chapter in *The Early Days of Sociolinguistics* (Paulston and Tucker 1997), "My contribution to the origins and development of sociolinguistics is at best tangential or perhaps even negative" (1997: 43). A possible explanation for this resistance not only to Bernstein's ideas but also to the questions he raised will be presented in a later chapter.

In my own work (Macaulay 1977, 1991a) the principal focus has been on social class differences among Scottish speakers, but I am less interested in what is changing than in what stays constant (Macaulay 1988). Despite considerable social mobility in Britain (Argyle 1994), there is also great stability in the composition of the two major social classes, the middle class and the working class. As Argyle observes, "Your chance of being the director of a bank is 200 times more if your father was one" (1994: 177). All the adults I interviewed in Glasgow (Macaulay 1977) were from a similar background to that of their parents, and this was true (with one exception) of the speakers I interviewed in Ayr (Macaulay 1991b). In both locations, it was possible to identify features of speech that were indexical of social class membership, and Stuart-Smith's more recent study (1999) of Glasgow speech found that the distinction remained. Rather than a continuum of language variation with gradations between, the situation in Scotland seems to be one of a polarized society with basically two groups identified by their speech: the middle class and the working class (Stuart-Smith 2003). This is consistent with the results of a survey in Britain cited by Argyle (1994: 5) showing the responses to a question regarding which feature is "the most important in being able to tell which class a person is" (Argyle 1994: 4). The response given by the largest number of respondents (33%) was "the way they speak." It is a hundred years since George Bernard Shaw's *Pygmalion*, but the way you speak is still important in Britain.

Just as Labov's interest in language variation has focused largely on linguistic change, my interest has been on the distribution and effects of stable differences within the community, and my concerns have been in many ways similar to those expressed in Bernstein's early work (e.g., Bernstein 1962). In my first investigation of Glasgow speech (Macaulay and Trevelyan 1973; Macaulay 1977), I interviewed teachers at primary, secondary, and tertiary levels, and also a sample of employers, in addition to what I called "the community sample," a balanced sample of 10-year-olds, 15-year-olds, and mature adults. The phonological analysis showed quite clearly that there was social stratification in the use of the five variables. The interviews with the teachers and employers suggested that "accent" was not a major concern but that the problem for many of the working-class adolescents was their ability to express themselves effectively. Of course, my survey of their speech had uncovered limited useful information about how the working-class spoke other than the use of the phonological variables I had studied. It was clear that the social class dichotomy in Scotland indexed by "the way they speak" involved more differences than the relatively salient phonological and morphological variables that are the usual topic of sociolinguistic research. My analysis of 12 less structured interviews recorded in Ayr (Macaulay 1991b) was an attempt to go beyond dialect features to other aspects of language use. The present volume is an extension of that work based on conversations recorded in Glasgow in 1997 (Stuart-Smith 1999).

One of the major innovations in analyzing the Ayr materials was to consider the interviews as a whole, as speech events (see Macaulay 2001a for some comments on the notion of genre). This required transcribing the tapes in their entirety and tabulating all the tokens of a particular feature in each interview. A similar procedure was followed in dealing with the 1997 Glasgow conversations. The methodology employed will be described in chapter 2. In Ayr all those I interviewed were adults, and the sample was unbalanced in gender terms, so the only comparisons possible were of social class. The Glasgow sample is balanced in social class, gender, and age categories, so it is possible to make comparisons in all three categories.

One of the aims of the present volume is to demonstrate the use of quantitative measures in the investigation of discourse features that cannot be treated in the same way as the kinds of features analyzed as linguistic variables in variationist sociolinguistics. The assumption that underlies the notion of a linguistic variable is that the individual variants are equivalent in their function and meaning, so that, for example, the choice between a glottal stop and an alveolar stop is not considered to be semantically motivated. With discourse features, such as *you know* and *I mean*, there is no similar alternation of variants. The quantitative investigation of discourse features, consequently, cannot look at the proportional distribution of variants. It is possible, however, to investigate the frequency with which a feature is used, and that is the method employed here. Obviously, the frequency with which a particular feature is used will depend upon all the characteristics of the speech event (Hymes 1974; Macaulay 2001a), but this is true also of all variation studies.

The second aim is to explore the kinds of conclusions that can be drawn from the difference in the frequency with which categories of speakers use a discourse feature. Recently, Finegan and Biber (1994, 2001) have presented claims based on the differential use of a number of discourse features. One of their suggestions is that education has a major effect on speech styles. Their position has been interpreted as offering support for Bernstein's distinction (1971) between restricted and elaborated codes, though Finegan and Biber reject this association.

Bernstein remains the salient figure in claims about social class differences in language, despite the fact that all his empirical work on language use was done more than 25 years ago. The present work examines Bernstein's claims on a more extensive sample of speakers, with a more adequate sample of speech from each of them. It will be shown in subsequent chapters that there is little to support most of the specific claims Bernstein made, and, equally important, that he seems to have misinterpreted the significance of those features (e.g., adverb use) for which support is found.

The examination of the frequency with which certain discourse features are used will show that there are age, gender, and social differences in speech styles in the sample groups. Interpreting these differences and estimating their significance remains a challenge that will require a more comprehensive investigation, but the evidence presented here may provide a suitable base from which to explore these questions further.

The study of language is replete with dichotomies: *langue* versus *parole* (Saussure 1922), competence versus performance (Chomsky 1965), linguistic competence versus communicative competence (Hymes 1974), transactional versus interactional (Brown and Yule 1983), text versus discourse (Stubbs 1983), elaborated code versus restricted code (Bernstein 1962), formalism versus functionalism (Leech 1983), and monologism versus dialogism (Linell 1998).

Underlying several of these dichotomies is a contrast in methodology. On the one hand, those who seek to investigate the structure of language as an abstract system are generally content to examine decontextualized examples, many of them based on written materials (Linell 1982, 1998, 2001), or invented to illustrate a point. On the other hand, those who are interested in the use of language, and particularly in variation in the use of language, examine examples of language recorded in a specific context. Most sociolinguistic investigations of language variation are based on audio-recorded samples of connected speech, collected in a manner that with luck provides a legitimate sample of the speaker's everyday speech. However, where there is an interest in obtaining comparable samples of individual sounds, recourse may be had to reading out lists of separate words.

This latter technique will not work for the study of discourse variation, where it is necessary to have samples of talk in action with speakers interacting with one another. Many studies of discourse concentrate on specific occasions of communication, focusing on what is being communicated and how that communication is achieved (e.g., Goodwin 1981; Eggins and Slade 1997; Linell 1998). These studies come under the general rubric "functional" (Coupland 2001a: 187; Linell 2001), since they are concerned with how language is used to achieve the ends of one particular interaction. However, there is no a priori reason that the study of discourse should always be from a functional perspective in this sense; it is also possible to study discourse from a more formalist position, looking at the language employed by speakers without focusing on what is being communicated in each particular instance. This approach has been taken by a number of scholars interested in the grammatical structure of discourse (e.g., Scheibman 2002; Tao 2001; Thompson and Hopper 2001) and is similar to the approach employed in this volume. In Linell's terms, I am dealing with "structure-in-focus" rather than "dynamics-in-focus" (Linell 2001: 121). In Rampton's terms, this is an example of the "linguistics of community" rather than of the "linguistics of contact" (2001: 276). Although all speech is dialogic (Bakhtin 1981; Markova and Foppa 1990) and speakers may be influenced by their audience (Bell 1984; Duranti 1986), there are characteristics of speech that correspond to membership in certain social categories. Nobody would dispute this with regard to pronunciation or such salient features as negative concord (e.g., Labov 1972; Smith 2001), but there have been fewer studies of discourse variation (Macaulay 2002a).

It needs to be emphasized that this is not a book exemplifying the aims and methods of discourse analysis (e.g., Schiffrin 1994; Johnstone 2001; Weihun He 2001). On the contrary, the aim of the analysis here is similar to that of most variationist investigation: to determine to what extent variation in the use of certain linguistic features correlates with extralinguistic categories, in this case, age, gender, and social class. Just as membership in a particular category may correlate with the use of a phonological variant, so speakers in one category may use discourse features differently from those in a contrasted category. This will be illustrated for a number of discourse features in subsequent chapters. The measure used is frequency of occurrence on the grounds that high versus low frequency is one indication of a difference in discourse style. This is appropriate for what is a study of *parole*. Saussure contrasts the structure of *langue* with its absence in *parole*: "Il n'y a donc rien de collectif dans la parole; les manifestations en sont individuelles et momentanées. Ici il n'y a rien de plus que la somme des cas particuliers" (Saussure 1922: 38) ("Thus there is nothing collective about speech. Its manifestations are individual and ephemeral. It is no more than an aggregate of particular cases" [trans. Harris 1986: 19]).

Even if he had wanted to investigate this side of language, Saussure would have faced immense methodological problems, but the invention of tape recording has made it possible to collect "the sum of individual cases" in samples of *parole* by different speakers and compare them to find out if there are interesting patterns of use. However, since the amount of speech recorded will vary for each speaker, it is not the total number of tokens that is significant but the relative frequency with which an item is used. In the present work, the frequency used is the number of tokens per 1,000 words. Some investigators have reported only the total number of tokens for individuals or groups without controlling for the amount of speech recorded; this may distort the results if, for example, the males have produced more speech in that situation than the females.

Anyone attempting to write about discourse is faced with a daunting task, given the many definitions and approaches that have been developed (Schiffrin 1994; Macaulay 2002a). As Tannen asserted/complained/admitted about discourse analysis: "The goal of a homogeneous 'discipline' with a unified theory, an agreed upon method, and comparable types of data, is not only hopeless but pointless" (Tannen 1989: 7–8). There is also no agreement as to the definition or even labeling of key elements that have been studied under the aegis of discourse analysis. Jucker and Ziv summarize the situation as follows: "A variety of terms are used to refer to these elements. Among them are discourse marker (e.g. Schiffrin 1987), pragmatic marker (e.g. Fraser 1996; Brinton 1996), discourse particle (e.g. Schourup 1985; Abraham 1991; Kroon 1995), pragmatic particle (e.g. Östman 1981), pragmatic expression (e.g. Erman 1987) or connective (Blakemore 1987, 1988)," (1998b: 1). Each of these terms (and others not cited here) has been chosen for practical or theoretical reasons by those conducting the research, and their precise definition has often proved problematic. For a variety of reasons, I do not want to enter into this debate about terminology. Partly this is because I do not want someone to complain that some feature I am investigating is not really a discourse marker or a pragmatic particle, and so forth. In this work I am less concerned with the definition of such items than with their distribution in socially stratified samples of speech. Moreover, this is not a study in discourse analysis; it is an attempt to find out if there are differences in discourse style that correlate with social class, age, and gender. Accordingly, I will examine the frequency of use of various discourse features, some of which would be labeled differently by various scholars as discourse markers or pragmatic particles, and others that are not often considered in examples of discourse analysis.

Another reason for avoiding a commitment to any of the competing labels is that I will be adopting a rather ascetic view of the function of these features. Specific examples will be mentioned in later chapters, but here I simply wish to make clear my own concern about some of the work done on the use of discourse features. There is an understandable desire to show that a certain feature (e.g., *like* or *you know*) has a unitary meaning in which a wide range of uses can be subsumed. Schourup writes of "the seemingly irresistible temptation to 'import' meaning" (1999: 251) into discourse markers and also the tendency to look for "extremely general 'one-size-fits-all' meanings" (253). Although investigators such as Fraser (1990), Östman (1982), Redeker (1991), Schiffrin (1987), and Schourup (1985) have stressed the multifunctionality of discourse markers, there is also the attraction of Bolinger's dictum that "the natural condition of language is to preserve one form for one meaning, and one meaning for one form" (Bolinger 1997: x). So there is a temptation to interpret examples of *like* as having some connection with the notion of similarity and examples of *you know* as referring to knowledge of some kind. While I admire this goal and the ingenuity with which some scholars have tackled the problem, I have far too often remained unconvinced by the arguments. The basic problem is that most (all?) discourse features of these kinds are multifunctional, and which function a particular example illustrates can often be judged only from the context in which it occurs. Unfortunately, when the ascribed meaning of the feature can be assessed only by the context in which it occurs, it is often unclear just what contribution the feature adds to the meaning. In too many cases, it seems to me, it would be equally plausible to say that a feature takes its meaning from the surrounding context rather than to argue that the discourse item creates that meaning. For example, Svartvik (1980) did not find the correlation between prosody and meaning that Crystal and Davy (1975) report in their discussion of *well*. He argues that Crystal and Davy did not identify differences in the meaning of *well* itself but rather "differences in the intonational meaning, which they then attribute to *well* itself" (Svartvik 1980: 172). It is probably more accurate to say that discourse features and the context in which they occur are mutually reinforcing in the sense that Firth (1935) maintained was true of all linguistic meaning.

There is another problem with attributing significant meaning to features such as *like* and *you know*. It is clear from a variety of studies, including the present one, that speakers are highly idiosyncratic in their use of these features. Some speakers use them very frequently and others seldom, if at all. If these items carry a heavy semantic or pragmatic load, it would be necessary to identify the alternative means by which speakers who do not use them convey the same information. For example, Watts (1989: 204) claims that "discourse markers are an *essential* means by which speakers achieve coherence in the developing discourse" (emphasis added), but this implies that speakers who do not use discourse markers are incoherent. There is no evidence that this is so, even though Even-Zohar (1982), Déjean le Féal (1982), Östman (1982), Brinton (1996), and Dailey-O'Cain (2000), among others, have argued that the use of discourse markers or pragmatic particles can have many positive aspects. This consequence is hardly surprising if these items have lost most of their original lexical meaning, since they can then be used as optional stylistic markers along with the paralinguistic features of pitch, voice quality, and speech rate that contribute to individual speech characteristics.

There is also a serious problem of identifying the meaning of discourse features in context. Jucker and Smith, in their analysis of three discourse markers, state the need to take into consideration assumptions not only "about explicitly stated information that is assumed to be shared but also about the inferences the partner is expected to draw from this information" (1998:173). This requires a willingness to enter the minds of the participants and identify what they know and what they understand. With respect to this aim, it is pertinent that Andersen and Fretheim quote Hans Kamp: "People have attributed propositional attitudes to other people (as well as to many kinds of animals) as long as anyone can remember, and those who have engaged in the practice have been no better informed about the inner workings of the mind than we are at present" (Kamp 1990: 32, cited by Andersen and Fretheim 2000a: 3).

Andersen and Fretheim cite this passage in support of a relevance-theoretic approach to discourse, but it can also be understood as a warning against trusting our ability to attribute such propositional attitudes to those speakers whose words we are examining, especially when those speakers differ from ourselves in age, gender, or other attributes, such as social class or ethnicity. Of course, it is always possible for each one of us to interpret a given utterance and feel fairly confident about the interpretation, but that is no guarantee that others will arrive at the same conclusion, and it is not uncommon to find such interpretations questioned. When dealing with a corpus of material in which it would be tedious (if not impossible) to justify every individual interpretation, the less appeal there is to subjective judgments the better.

Overstreet (1999:73) has a cautionary example of two women talking. Crystal has just told Julie that she had tried the drug Ecstasy, and Julie is curious about it. Crystal's response is given in (1). (I have modified the transcription.)

(1)

> CRYSTAL: it's kind of like—it's just like really mild acid
> JULIE: oh is that what it is?
> CRYSTAL: that's what I felt
>   that's what it made me feel you know
>   just the colors and the—
>   you know uh the way it makes you think and stuff
> JULIE: mhm

Overstreet points out that Julie gives the impression of understanding exactly what Crystal means, but it turns out that Julie has never tried acid. Overstreet (1999: 74) discusses the reasons that Julie might have indicated that she understands Crystal's comparison, despite never having tried either of the drugs, but the example illustrates how dangerous it can be to draw inferences about comprehension or about shared knowledge from an exchange such as this. Interpretations of the kind made by Overstreet and others are justifiable when the intent is to determine the function of a discourse feature in a specific speech event, where the total context can be considered. Such a procedure is more hazardous in a work, such as the present one, concerned with quantitative measures of a large number of differences in speech style.

It is, however, often necessary to distinguish different functions and meanings (Tao 2001), but any classification based on the analyst's interpretation inevitably brings with it the risk of bias or misinterpretation. The best way to guard against this bias is to be as explicit as possible in justifying the assignment of examples to one category or the other. This becomes particularly difficult where the items are complex (e.g., modal auxiliaries), and the classification is unlikely to please everyone. In general, quantitative methods work best when items can be identified with a minimum of advance interpretation.

My position in this book is similar to that set out by Vincent and Sankoff (1992) in their analysis of 13 interviews from the Sankoff-Cedergren sample of French speakers in Montreal. Vincent and Sankoff examined the interviews for the frequency of what they call "punctors," for example, *la* 'there', *tu sais*, *vous savez* 'you know', and *n'est-ce pas* 'isn't it so'. According to Vincent and Sankoff (1992: 205–6), punctors are assimilated prosodically to the preceding phrase, are almost never preceded by a pause, show a high degree of phonological reduction, and have lost their original meaning or function. Vincent and Sankoff found that "the rate of punctor use increases with the length of the interview, that is, with loquacity or fluency of speech" (212), They also show that "punctors are not frequent in simple answers or when utterances are short, objective, and without much speaker involvement" (212), and claim that the use of punctors is linked to fluency and expressivity. They conclude that the distribution of punctors "is conditioned by factors such as prosodic rupture [i.e., a break in the melody of the sentence], context, and genre of discourse; only the choice of individual punctors seems to be conditioned by social class" (214). Several (but not all) of the discourse features that are examined in later chapters are similar to Vincent and Sankoff's category of punctors.

It does not follow from this that no inferences can be drawn from the differences in discourse style that emerge. On the contrary, as will be shown, it is possible to provide tentative explanations for differences in the frequency with which categories of speakers use various discourse features. Given the nature of the data on which these interpretations are based, these conclusions cannot be taken as firmly established. However, they do provide hypotheses about discourse variation that can be tested on other samples. When such corroboration (or refutation) is undertaken on other samples, we may come closer to understanding the sociolinguistic nature of discourse variation.

2

Methodology

Quantitative methods have been employed in sociolinguistic investigations ever since Labov's pioneering work on Martha's Vineyard (Labov 1963) and in New York (Labov 1966). For the most part, quantitative methods have been used to investigate phonological variation (e.g., Trudgill 1974; Macaulay 1977; Milroy 1980; Eckert 2000), but there have also been studies of morphological and syntactic variation (e.g. Wolfram 1969; Feagin 1979; Cheshire 1982). It is only recently, however, that quantitative methods have been used to investigate variation in the use of discourse features. Usually these have been focused on gender differences (e.g., Holmes 1986).

Schiffrin was the first to use quantitative measures of discourse markers in a corpus of recorded speech showing how they often "bracket units of talk" (1987: 31) and help speakers to produce coherent discourse. The discourse markers she examines include *oh*, *well*, *you know*, and *I mean*. Schiffrin, however, does not examine the differential use of the discourse markers by speakers of different social categories. This would have been difficult given the restricted nature of the sample, which was recorded as part of the Philadelphia Neighborhood Study (Labov 2001b) where the speakers were from similar backgrounds.

To investigate social variation in the use of discourse features, it is necessary to have extended samples of speech recorded under similar circumstances from individuals belonging to different social categories, such as age, gender, or social class. The materials examined in this work come from two sets of recordings. In a study of interviews with 12 speakers in the town of Ayr in southwest Scotland (Macaulay 1991b), I tabulated the use of 12 discourse features, showing some social class variation in their use. Because of the nature of the sample, it was impossible to make gender or age comparisons. These materials will be referred to as the Ayr interviews. In 1997, Jane Stuart-Smith recorded 33 speakers for her study of language change in Glasgow (Stuart-Smith 1999). She recorded both adults and adolescents using the methodology developed for the Newcastle/Derby study (Docherty, Foulkes, Milroy, Milroy, and Walshaw 1997). The sample was balanced by age (adolescents 13–14 and adults 40+), social class (middle-class and working-class), and gender (Stuart-Smith 1999: 204). Participants were asked to choose a friend or acquaintance with whom they would be willing to talk for half an hour in the presence of a tape recorder, without the investigator being present.

This latter method of data collection avoids many of the problems associated with speech accommodation (Giles and Powesland 1975; Bell 1984), since there are no power differentials between the speakers. The pairs of speakers share the same age, gender, and social class classifications. If one of the participants turns out to be dominant in the recording situation, it is not because of a preassigned role, as, for example, in interviews or gatekeeping interactions (Erickson and Shultz 1982). The interaction meets Wilson's (1989) criterion for conversation that the speakers had equal rights to introduce topics. The resulting conversations provide comparable samples that allow the investigation of age, gender, and social class differences in the use of various discourse features. These materials will be referred to as the Glasgow conversations.

The working hypotheses for the quantitative analysis of discourse features are as follows:

1. All speakers have the same opportunity to use certain discourse features in the recording sessions.
2. Variation in the frequency of use of any of these features reflects a different discourse style.
3. Differences in using a discourse feature that correlate with membership of a social category such as age, gender, or social class show that such variation is not simply idiosyncratic.

Since all the recordings were made under similar conditions, all the speakers whose language is analyzed had the same opportunity to speak. In Ayr, I interviewed all 12 speakers myself. Some were more talkative than others (Macaulay 1991b), and the length of the interview largely depended upon how much the interviewee wished to talk. I did not impose any time limit on the interview, and my questions were open-ended. In this sense, the Ayr recordings are consistent with hypothesis 1. In Glasgow, the participants knew each other and were free to talk about any topic. There was a time limit of just over half an hour, but that was the same for all pairs. Again, some speakers spoke more than others, but the opportunity to speak was available equally to all the participants. The Glasgow sessions thus also meet the assumptions of hypothesis 1. While there is no guarantee that either in Ayr or in Glasgow the participants perceived the situation in similar ways (Macaulay 2001b), the conditions in each case are consistent with hypothesis 1.

The methodology employed to investigate frequencies requires a complete word count. For both corpora the tapes were transcribed in their entirety, both as dialogues and with the contribution of each speaker separated. A simple count of word forms constitutes the base figure for each speaker. Frequencies for the speaker are calculated by dividing the number of occurrences of a given feature by the total number of word forms produced by that speaker during the session. These frequencies are expressed as the number of occurrences per 1,000 word forms. Excluded are hesitation phenomena such as *um* and *er*. Included as word forms are minimal responses such as *mhm* (mmm) and *uhuh*. These forms are regularly used as acknowledgment or agreement markers in ongoing feedback responses that do not constitute full turns in the sense of gaining the floor. Even these items can show differences in the frequency of use, and this variation can be used as an illustration of the kind of patterns that may emerge.

The four most common minimal responses in the Glasgow sessions are *mhm*, *uhuh*, *yes/yeah*, and *aye* (the Scottish equivalent of *yes*). The frequencies for the adult speakers are shown in figure 2.1. It is obvious from the figure that *aye* and *yes* are more or less in complementary distribution for the two social classes. *Aye* is used a total of 491 times by the working-class adults and only 12 times by the middle-class adults, but with the exception of two middle-class men, all the middle-class adults have at least one occurrence of *aye*.

The figures for the adolescents are shown in figure 2.2. The only one of these minimal responses that the working-class adolescents use at all frequently is *aye* with 125 instances, compared with 62 in the middle-class conversations. The most surprising finding is that the working-class adolescents do not use *mhm* and *uhuh* in these sessions.

In addition to social class and age differences, these forms also show gender differences. As can be seen in figure 2.3, in the middle-class it is the female speakers who use more minimal responses of this kind, while in the working-class it is the males.

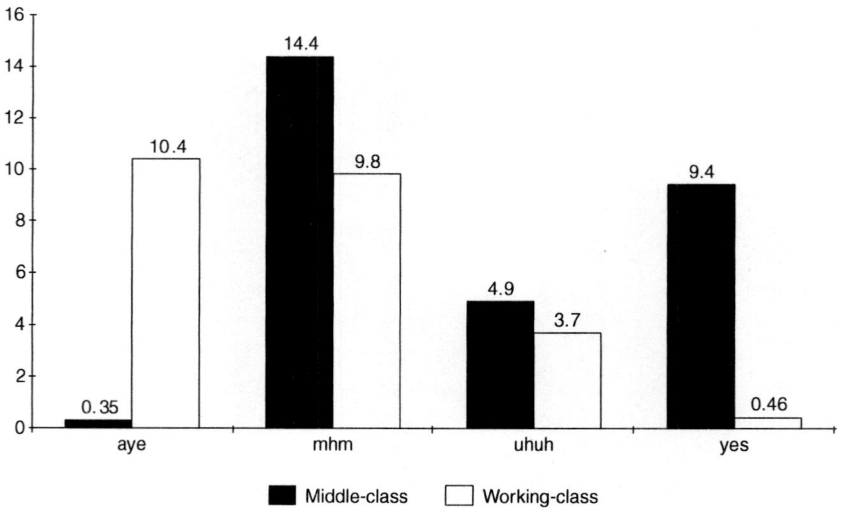

FIGURE 2.1. Minimal responses: Glasgow adults (frequency per 1,000 words)

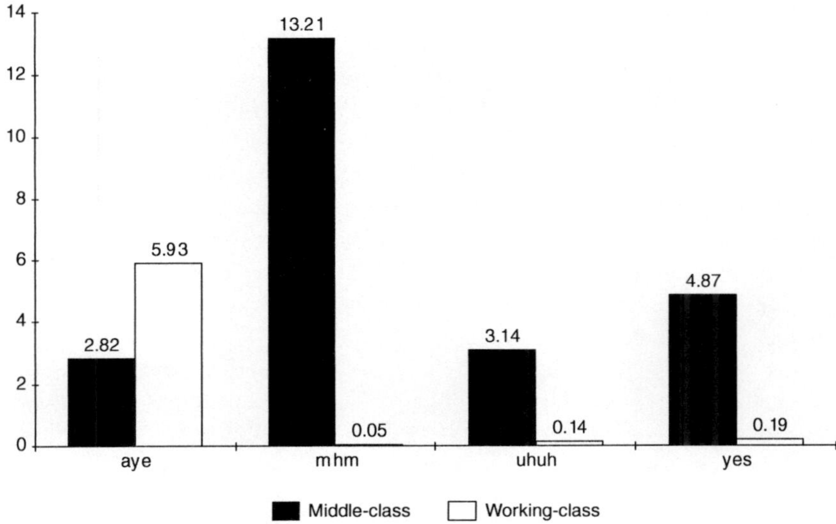

FIGURE 2.2. Minimal responses: Glasgow adolescents (frequency per 1,000 words)

Figures 2.1 through 2.3 illustrate the kind of information that can be obtained from counting tokens of discourse features. The frequencies alone do not give any clue as to their importance. The use of *aye* for *yes* is an example of a traditional Scottish dialect feature. All middle-class Scots will be familiar with the term *aye* and may use it occasionally, just as all working-class Scots are familiar with the form *yes* and also may use it occasionally. What figure 2.1 shows is that under similar conditions

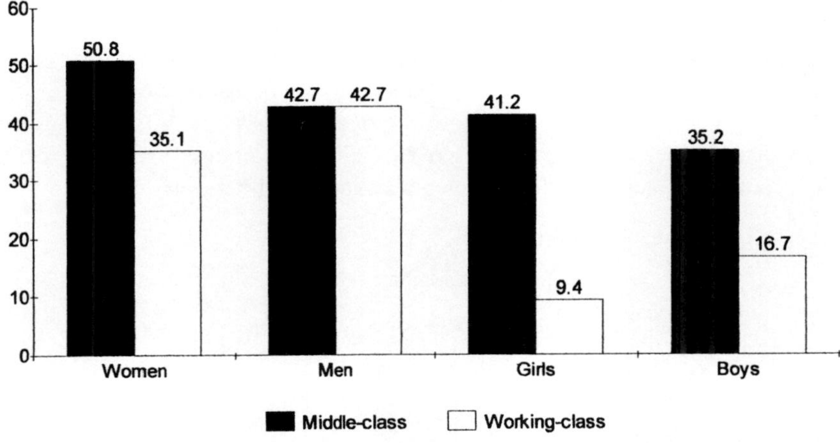

FIGURE 2.3. Minimal responses: Gender differences in Glasgow adults and adolescents (frequency per 1,000 words)

the middle-class adults in Glasgow exhibit a different pattern of usage of the two familiar forms from the pattern displayed by the working-class speakers. A similar distinction can be found in the Ayr interviews. In Ayr, the middle-class speakers use *yes* with a frequency of 3.75 per 1,000 words and *aye* with a frequency of 0.29, while the lower-class speakers use *yes* with a frequency of 0.33 and *aye* with a frequency of 3.76. Although the overall frequencies are much lower than in Glasgow, which is not surprising given the different nature of the speech events, the same social class pattern is revealed. Figure 2.2 shows that the adolescents do not display the adult difference between the two social classes, though the pattern is similar. Figure 2.3 shows that it may be necessary to take gender into consideration when considering any putative differences of this kind.

Later chapters will examine the frequency of several discourse features to discover whether there are class, gender, or age differences in their use. It may be worth pointing out at this stage that a failure to find a substantial difference in the use of a feature does not mean that the exercise was futile. While it is always more interesting to report on differences, it may sometimes be even more important to draw attention to similarities. Neglect of this principle has possibly distorted the evidence on gender differences in language (Brenneis and Macaulay 1996: 75). In dealing with social class differences it is even more important to report similarities as well as differences to guard against giving an impression of linguistic deficit.

There are now sophisticated computer programs that can extract items from texts (e.g., some of the methods illustrated in Baker, Francis, and Tognini-Bonelli 1993), but there are still important decisions to make. Since even the most sophisticated program will not be capable of the kind of judgments that human beings make, ideally the identification of tokens should as far as possible be carried out with minimal recourse to the kind of subjective criteria that require human interpretation. In practice, this is impossible because so many criteria enter into the identification and classification of linguistic items. As Scheibman observes, in her exemplary chapter on coding and classifying conversational data: "The difficulty of having to stipulate one-to-one relations between unit and value when the data did not easily lend themselves to such linear organization was an issue that was prominent during coding of clause types and apparent throughout the coding process" (Scheibman 2002: 33).

Most researchers who have worked with spontaneous speech will endorse Scheibman's view. However, in selecting discourse features to count, several distinctions are worth making, and the following classification may be useful.

Types of discourse features

   I. Unambiguous forms
      1. Invariant forms
         a. Consistent use
            i. Function
            ii. Meaning
         b. Variable use
      2. Minimally variant forms
   II. Ambiguous forms
   III. Complex forms

I. 1. a. i. Invariant forms, consistent
in function and meaning

Unambiguous forms are those that can be found by a simple word search through the transcript. An example of an unambiguous form that is consistent in function and meaning is *very*. It is possible to make a simple frequency count of the use of *very* without taking into account the linguistic context in which it occurs.

I. 1. a. ii. Invariant forms, consistent in form
but varying in meaning

An example of an invariant form that is consistent in function but varies in meaning is *quite*. It can be used as a maximizer (Quirk, Greenbaum, Leech, and Svartvik 1985: 590), for example, "but I think clothes-wise we're *quite* different." It can also be used as a downtoner (Quirk et al. 1985: 597–99), for example, "it is actually *quite* nice." In collecting tokens of *quite*, it is therefore necessary to note the context in which it occurs and to interpret its meaning.

I. 1. b. Invariant forms, varying in both
function and meaning

An example of an invariant form that varies in both function and meaning is *oh*. *Oh* can be used by itself as an acknowledgment marker or as part of an agreement marker, such as *oh right* or *oh yeah*. It can also be used as part of an exclamation of emotion, usually dismay, as in *oh no, oh God*, or *oh shit*. It can also be used to introduce a question that is often a kind of other repair, e.g., *oh were you there? oh it goes on without you even touching it? Oh* can also be used to introduce statements, often expressions of personal feeling, *oh I hate him, oh I'm so tired*. Finally, *oh* may occur in quoted dialogue to mark a change of speaker:

(1)   (Glasgow working-class woman)
    a. I says to them "Your new phone number's in"
    b. "Oh! Was it the day?"

The speaker is reporting an exchange. Her remark is quoted in (1a) and the response in (1b). This is part of a narrative concerning her aunt and uncle, the referent of *them* in (1a). One of them is reported as having given the response in (1b). This is an example of a zero quotative (see chapter 12), where the change of speaker is indicated by intonation and the use of the discourse marker *oh*. The tabulation of *oh* forms consequently requires an examination of the context in which the token occurs (see chapter 6).

I. 2. Minimally variant forms

Examples of minimally variant forms include the personal pronouns. It is reasonable to treat as one lexical item the forms *I, me, mine, my,* and *myself*. Since the number of variant forms is small, it is quite easy to identify all the forms of the pronoun used by a speaker. There is one personal pronoun that is more complex, and that is *it*. This is because *it* has other functions than that of an anaphoric pronoun:

(2)
> a. It is raining
> b. It is your turn
> c. It is clear that he is lying

Identifying only the anaphoric uses of *it* thus requires more detailed study of the linguistic context than for the other personal pronouns.

II. Ambiguous forms

Many discourse features cannot be identified by their form alone. For example, the discourse use of *well* has been studied by Schiffrin (1987) and Svartvik (1980). However, the form *well* can also be an adverb ("he did it well") or a noun ("he went to the well too often"). To investigate the use of *well* as a discourse feature, it is necessary to separate out the other uses. A more complex example of an ambiguous discourse feature is *you know* (Östman 1981; Schourup 1985; Holmes 1986; Schiffrin 1987; Macaulay 2002c). It is complex because it is necessary to distinguish the use of *you know* as a discourse feature (as in "I could see *you know* the hunted look on his face") from its basic meaning (as in "not what *you know* who you knew"). In the first case, *you know* is not an integral part of the syntax, whereas it is in the second. It is usually fairly easy to distinguish these uses, but some investigators have not always done so consistently (Macaulay 2002c). To study variation in the use of a discourse feature such as *you know*, it is necessary to look at each example in context.

III. Complex forms

Complex variables, such as the use of passive voice, questions, or quoted dialogue, obviously require careful examination of the context, and thus extraction becomes even more time-consuming.

In addition to the difficulties in identifying what to count, there are other problems. It may turn out that there are too few tokens of a feature in the corpus to make comparisons meaningful. With the Ayr corpus I tabulated the tokens of *anyway, in fact, of course,* and *now,* but there were too few examples to make analysis rewarding. In the Ayr interviews, however, speakers used *you see* as a discourse feature with an overall frequency of 2.83 per 1,000 words (3.74 in the lower-class interviews, 1.57 in the middle-class interviews). In the Glasgow sessions, on the other hand, there are only 13 examples (a frequency of 0.10 per 1,000 words). Consequently, it is not possible to chart the use of *you see* in Glasgow on the basis of the recorded sessions, although there is other evidence that this discourse marker occurs in Glasgow speech. Of the other discourse features tabulated in the Ayr materials, the distribution of *oh*, *well*, *you know*, and *I mean* in the Glasgow sessions will be examined in later chapters.

Since the Glasgow sessions provide an opportunity for age, gender, and social class differences, most of the analysis will be devoted to this corpus. The Ayr materials allow only social class comparisons, and most of these have been presented elsewhere (Macaulay 1991b). The details of the two corpora are set out in chapter 3.

3

The Sample

$\mathbf{A}$s stated earlier, the principal method employed in this work is to correlate the use of some feature in the tape-recorded material with the membership of the speaker in some social category. The categories are socioeconomic class, gender, and age. It is undeniable that class is still a salient aspect of Scottish society, with certain forms of speech indexical of class membership. For example, many working-class Scots will variably use a monophthong rather than a diphthong in words such as *down*, *house*, and *out*, conventionally transcribed as *doon*, *hoose*, and *oot*. They may also use a front vowel in words such as *hame* 'home' and *flair* 'floor'. (There are other salient differences, but these two will be enough for illustrative purposes.) The routine use of forms such as *doon* or *hame* in everyday exchanges marks the speaker socially, although all Scots, regardless of class, are familiar with the forms, and middle-class speakers may use them at times for comic or imitative purposes (Macaulay 1987b). Socioeconomic class is therefore an unignorable aspect of language variation in Scotland, since so many common forms are unmistakably indexical of class membership.

Gender membership is another salient aspect of speech. It is usually possible to identify the sex of adult speakers on the basis of pitch and voice quality. The transcripts, however, do not give any indication of these differences, so the speakers are identified as male or female. One aim of the analysis will be to discover whether there are features of language shown in the transcripts that are more characteristic of one gender.

The third category is age. Most of the speakers represented in the recorded materials are mature adults in early to late middle age, but the Glasgow sample includes adolescents, who were recorded under similar circumstances to those of adults and whose transcripts provide suitable material for comparison. Apart from this group, differences in age will not be considered.

Since the nature of the language recorded will be affected by the circumstances under which the sample was collected, it is important to make clear what those circumstances were. The most commonly used method for collecting information on language variation has been the "sociolinguistic interview" (Labov 1966, 1981). Wolfson (1976) and Milroy and Milroy (1977) criticize the quality of speech recorded in interviews. I have argued against this negative view (Macaulay 1984, 1991b) by showing that useful samples of speech could be recorded under these circumstances. Schiffrin (1987) also shows that important discourse features can be studied on the basis of interview data.

Despite the criticism they have received, sociolinguistic interviews can provide valuable evidence of more than phonetic or phonological features, particularly where the same interviewer conducts all the interviews so that there is some consistency in the approach to the interviewee. The role of the interviewer, however, is heavily biased in favor of being a receptive listener rather than an equal partner in the conversation between "intimate strangers" (Gregersen and Pedersen 1991: 54). In a successful sociolinguistic interview the interviewee is often almost a monologuist, telling stories, reminiscing, offering opinions, and so on. Clearly, individuals differ in the ways in which they take advantage of this opportunity (Macaulay 1984, 1991b, 1999), and one of the important factors will be how the interviewee perceives and reacts to the interviewer (Eisikovits 1989; Macaulay 1991b; Schilling-Estes 1998; Dubois and Horvath 1993; Laforest 1993). This is not simply a matter of "audience design" (Bell 1984), since the contribution of both participants is critical, and the interviewer's interest in and rapport with the interviewee can have an important effect on the quality of speech recorded (R. Macaulay 1990, 1991b, 2001a). Such factors will affect any findings on the use of discourse features, as they do other aspects of speech.

One alternative is to set up group interviews (Labov, Cohen, Robins, and Lewis 1968; Labov 1972; Gregersen and Pedersen 1991; Eckert 1990). In group sessions, however, there is a much greater chance of extraneous noise, and unless each speaker is recorded on a separate track from an individual microphone, there is always a risk that it may be difficult to separate out the speakers' contributions unless their voices are clearly distinct. It is also difficult to arrange a systematic set of group interviews by a stratified sample, and the results may be disappointing because of the unnaturalness of the speech event (Gregersen and Pedersen 1991: 56). This makes it difficult to obtain comparable samples of speech.

There is a form of data collection that lies between the monologues of individual interviews and the polyphony of group sessions. This is to set up a situation in which two speakers, who know each other and are from the same kind of background, talk to each other in unstructured conversations in optimal recording conditions. This avoids the danger of accommodation (Giles and Powesland 1975) to the speech of an interviewer, perhaps from outside of the community (Douglas-Cowie 1978) or from a different sector of the community (Rickford and McNair-Knox 1993). Naturally, speakers may react differently to the artificiality of the situation, but the method permits the systematic collection of extended samples of speech from a selected sample of the population. The resulting data set will provide materials for comparison between categories of speakers recorded under similar conditions and therefore appropriate for an analysis of any differeces that may emerge.

The chapters that follow contain examples of speech recorded under two of the three kinds of situation just mentioned. The first is in interviews, mostly those I conducted myself. The second is in same-sex dyads where the speakers know each other and have agreed to talk by themselves in the presence of a tape recorder.

In 1973, in order to investigate the relationship between language and education and their impact on employment (Macaulay and Trevelyan 1973; Macaulay 1977), I interviewed sixteen 10-year-olds, sixteen 15-year-olds, and sixteen adults, in four socioeconomic groups, with equal numbers of males and females, for what I called the community sample. The socioeconomic status was determined by the occupation of the principal wage earner in the family and was based on the registrar-general's classification of occupation. For the sample of teachers, I interviewed 32 teachers at primary, secondary, and tertiary levels, and for the employers' sample, 28 individuals involved in making hiring decisions in a variety of businesses.

The children and adults were identified through the schools that the children attended and contacted by letter, informing the parents that the purpose of the survey was to collect information on attitudes toward changes that had taken place in Glasgow. In interviewing, a different questionnaire was used for each age-group. The language used by the speakers was "careful, rather formal speech" (Macaulay 1977: 21) and therefore produced limited information on the use of discourse features; the interviews were not transcribed in their entirety.

As a follow-up I decided to do a comparative study of urban speech in Scotland and chose as sites Aberdeen, Dundee, and Ayr. (I omitted Edinburgh, since it was the subject of a survey being conducted by Suzanne Romaine and later Paul Johnston.) In the summers of 1978 and 1979, I carried out interviews at all three sites, following the pattern of the Glasgow survey by interviewing 10-year-olds and 15-year-olds as well as adults; however, I obtained most of the adult sample through network contacts rather than using the schools as the main source. This project was not brought to completion, but I used a balanced sample of 12 speakers from Ayr, 6 middle-class and 6 lower-class, to investigate possible patterns of difference between the two groups (Macaulay 1991b). As an experiment, I transcribed the tapes of the Ayr interviews in their entirety and then wondered what would emerge from analyzing them. I decided to look at phonological, morphological, syntactic, lexical, and discourse features. I did not know what to expect, other than the obvious phonological and morphological differences that distinguish the two social classes. I spent a great deal of time coding all the syntactic structures in the corpus, and in some ways the most interesting result was that syntactic differences between the two classes of speakers were not as great as those (e.g., Bernstein 1971) who have expressed negative views about lower-class speech would have predicted. More interesting differences occurred in the use of discourse features, including narrative style, and these interviews provide some of the material that will be analyzed in later chapters.

In 1997, Jane Stuart-Smith recorded 33 speakers for her study of language change in Glasgow Stuart-Smith 1999, 2003). She recorded both adults and adolescents using the methodology developed for the Newcastle/Derby study (Docherty et al. 1997).

The sample was balanced by age (adolescents 13–14 and adults 40+), social class (middle-class and working-class), and gender (Stuart-Smith 1999: 204). Participants were asked to choose a friend or acquaintance with whom they would be willing to talk for half an hour in the presence of a tape recorder, without the investigator being present. When I heard excerpts of the tapes, I realized that they provided excellent samples of speech between two individuals without the effect of an interviewer. I asked Stuart-Smith if I could use the tapes for discourse analysis, and she agreed. The tapes were transcribed in their entirety, both as dialogues and with the contribution of each speaker separated; the transcripts provide the basis for several of the chapters that follow.

It must be repeated at this stage that none of the materials were recorded as part of an investigation of discourse features, and there was no preliminary hypothesis about the use of such features. Their availability, however, allows the investigation of discourse variation using quantitative methods. The quantitative analysis of discourse features requires that the total sample of speech be transcribed, because raw numbers are misleading unless the total amount of speech is reported and the relative frequency of occurrence is calculated. It is therefore not surprising that few quantitative studies of discourse variation have been undertaken, since the investment of time and resources in producing complete transcripts is considerable. The results presented in this volume will, however, give other investigators examples of the kinds of variation that can be charted using these methods.

There is a fundamental question in all empirical investigation: How solid is the evidence for the conclusions drawn from it? For the work of others, we must usually take the answer on trust, since we are seldom given more than a distant glimpse of the data. For our own work, however, it is a question we must constantly ask ourselves because science has a major stake in honesty, and honesty, like charity, should begin at home. For the study of spoken language, some awareness of the limitations of the evidence is paramount, because we know that any manageable sample of speech cannot cover the range of styles and registers controlled by any mature speaker. This is particularly important for the investigation of language variation, since the validity of the results depends upon having comparable samples of speech. For the two corpora that are used in this book, the claim for comparability lies in two different directions. In one, the continuity is based on a single interviewer (myself). In the other, it is based on the fact that the sessions were conversations between individuals of roughly the same age, of the same sex, and from the same social class, who knew each other and who were recorded under similar circumstances. Thus in both cases the situations were similar for the speakers whose language was being recorded. This does not guarantee comparability, but it reduces the number of confounding factors.

The quantitative analysis in this book is based on two small corpora. The first is the set of interviews I conducted myself with 12 adults in the small town of Ayr, in the west of Scotland. (Details of the speakers are given in Macaulay 1991b.) The sample is shown in table 3.1. The sample is balanced for social class but not for gender.

The second corpus consists of the adults and adolescents recorded by Jane Stuart-Smith for her study of language change in Glasgow. The sample was balanced by age (adolescents 13–14 and adults 40+), social class, and gender. Participants were

TABLE 3.1. Sample of Ayr speakers

	Lower-class	Middle-class
Men	4	5
Women	2	1

asked to choose a friend or acquaintance with whom they would be willing to talk for half an hour in the presence of a tape recorder, without the investigator being present. In the Ayr study I used the term *lower-class*, but following Stuart-Smith (1999), I have used the term *working-class* for the Glasgow sample. No theoretical distinction is implied by this difference. The Ayr speakers are referred to by pseudonyms, the Glasgow speakers by the number of their session and the channel on which they were recorded (e.g., 2L = the speaker recorded on the left channel in session 2). The Glasgow sample is shown in table 3.2.

For technical reasons three sessions were recorded with working-class women; one speaker was recorded twice, with different interlocutors. As a result the number of participants in each social class/age/gender category is not totally consistent, but since the results are presented in terms of frequencies, the difference in absolute numbers need not materially affect any conclusions. The raw figures for working-class women, however, cannot be used in direct comparison with those for the other groups.

The Ayr interviews and the Glasgow sessions were transcribed in their entirety. This is a painstaking process and one that requires constant revision of the transcript. (For the Glasgow materials I am grateful to Jane Stuart-Smith, who organized the project, and to her assiduous assistants who transcribed the tapes: Cerwyss Ower, Claire Timmins, Kathryn Allen, Lesley Eadie, and Susan Bannatyne, especially the first two.) I then separated out the contribution of each speaker so that the total amount of speech produced by that individual could be tabulated. As stated earlier, the quantitative analysis of discourse features requires that the total sample of speech be transcribed, because raw numbers are misleading unless the total amount of speech is reported and the relative frequency of occurrence is calculated. The word totals for the Ayr speakers are given in table 3.3, and those for the Glasgow speakers in tables 3.4 and 3.5.

TABLE 3.2. Sample of Glasgow speakers

	Working-class	Middle-class
Adolescent boys	4	4
Adolescent girls	4	4
Men	4	4
Women	5	4

TABLE 3.3. Individual word totals in Ayr interviews

Lower-class	No. of words	Middle-class	No. of words
Ritchie (f)	4,373	Muir (m)	4,573
Rae (m)	5,030	Menzies (f)	5,110
Gemmill (m)	9,761	MacGregor (m)	7,673
Laidlaw (f)	13,189	Gibson (m)	8,510
Lang (m)	16,255	MacDougall (m)	9,764
Sinclair (m)	21,163	Nicoll (m)	15,268
All lower-class	69,771	All middle-class	50,898

It can be seen from table 3.3 that the speakers varied greatly in their response to the interview situation. The nature of the individual interviews is described in Macaulay (1991b: 205–55). It may be a confounding factor that the lower-class speakers were generally more willing to talk at length than the middle-class speakers, but by hypothesis 1 (see chapter 2) all the speakers had the same opportunity to tell me about themselves.

Table 3.4 gives the total number of words for the adolescent speakers in the Glasgow sample. It can be seen from table 3.4 that, while there is great individual variation in the amount of speech produced, the total amount from each social class group is roughly similar. The pattern is more clearly seen in figure 3.1, which shows that while there is considerable variation within each group, it is the working-class boys who produce the least speech in the time allotted. Table 3.5 shows the number of words produced by each speaker in the Glasgow adult sample. Once again there is considerable difference in the individual contributions, as can be seen in figure 3.2. Again, there is great variation within each group. The amount of speech recorded for each of the groups is set out in table 3.6.

Since there are six contributions by working-class women, it is the average number of words per speaker that can be used for comparison. Looking at the average

TABLE 3.4. Individual word totals in Glasgow adolescent sessions

Working-class	No. of words	Middle-class		No. of words
6-L (m)	1,827	2-L	(f)	2,313
6-R (m)	2,528	2-R	(f)	3,681
7-L (f)	2,356	3-L	(m)	1,978
7-R (f)	4,608	3-R	(m)	2,985
8-L (f)	3,430	4-L	(m)	2,420
8-R (f)	3,284	4-R	(m)	4,149
9-L (m)	1,754	5-L	(f)	2,703
9-R (m)	1,306	5-R	(f)	1,724
All	21,093			21,953

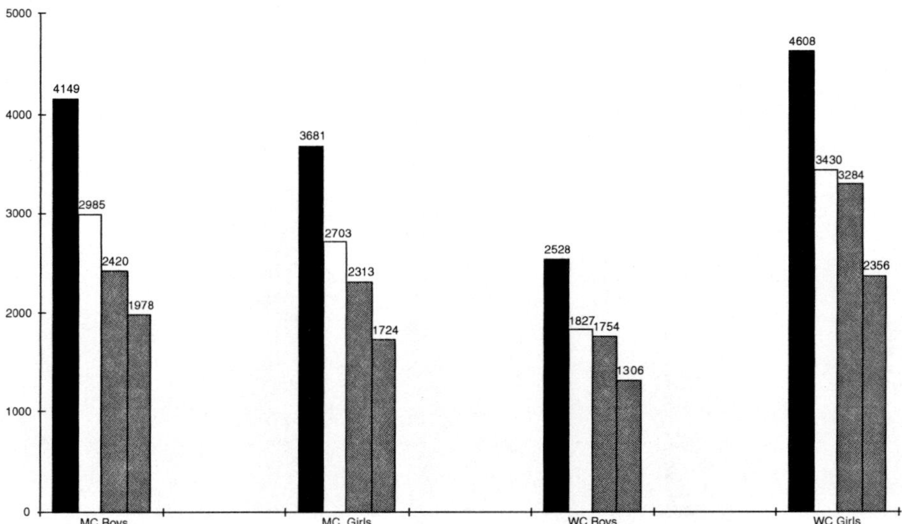

FIGURE 3.1. Individual word totals: Glasgow adolescents. *Note*: Each bar represents a single speaker.

per speaker, it can be seen that the Glasgow adults produce almost twice as much speech (as measured in total number of word forms) as do the adolescents ($p < .001$), and that the working-class adults are rather more talkative than their middle-class counterparts, while the reverse is true of the adolescents, though minimally so. The females talk considerably more than the males, though this is not quite statistically significant, and the difference between the two categories is much less than that between the two age-groups. With the exception of the middle-class boys, who are slightly more talkative than the middle-class girls, in each category the females out-talk the males, but these are trends rather than clear differences.

TABLE 3.5. Individual word totals in Glasgow adult sessions

Working-class	No. of words	Middle-class	No. of words
13-L (f)	4,109	10-L (f)	4,582
13-R (f)	5,164	10-R (f)	7,265
14-L (f)	4,314	11-L (m)	5,195
14-R (f)	7,860	11-R (m)	2,681
15-L (f)	7,372	12-L (f)	4,375
15-R (f)	4,306	12-R (f)	2,492
17-L (m)	1,870	16-L (m)	4,686
17-R (m)	6,276	16-R (m)	3,033
18-L (m)	4,633		
18-R (m)	4,403		
All	50,307		34,309

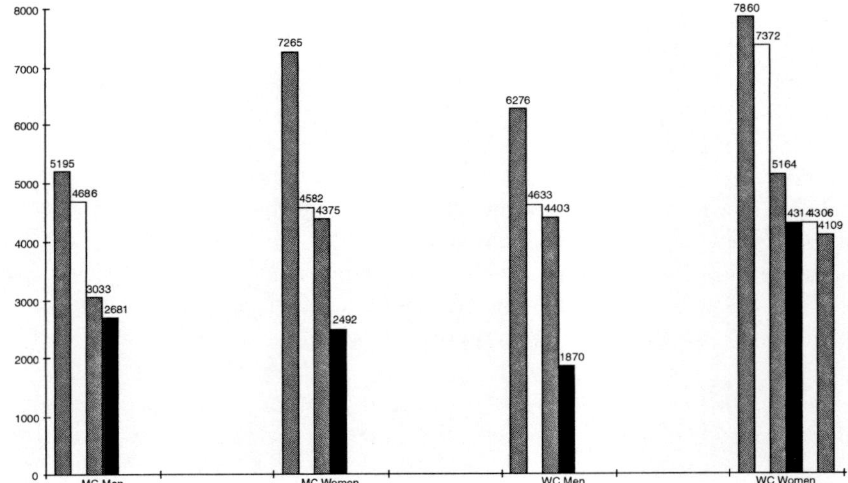

FIGURE 3.2. Individual word totals: Glasgow adults. *Note*: Each bar represents a single speaker.

In 15 cases out of 17, one of the participants dominated, contributing from 57% to 77% of the exchange. Only in one of the conversations between working-class girls (conversation 8) and one between working-class men (conversation 18) were the contributions roughly equal. The range of participation is from one working-class boy who contributed 1,306 words (during a session in which the two boys uttered about 90 words per minute) to one of the working-class women who produced 7,860 words in a conversation that proceeded at a rate of approximately 345 words per

TABLE 3.6. Combined word totals in Glasgow conversations, by gender and social class

	Words	*Average per speaker*
Working-class girls	13,678	3,420
Working-class boys	7,415	1,854
Middle-class girls	10,421	2,605
Middle-class boys	11,532	2,883
Working-class women	33,125	5,521
Working-class men	17,182	4,296
Middle-class women	18,714	4,679
Middle-class men	15,595	3,899
All adolescents	43,046	2,690
All adults	84,616	4,700
All females	75,938	4,219
All males	51,724	3,233
All working-class	71,400	3,966
All middle-class	56,262	3,516

minute. Thus, although all the speakers have the same opportunity to speak (hypothesis 1), they do not all take equal advantage of the opportunity.

The two corpora are clearly different in many ways. In the Ayr interviews the speakers were telling a stranger about their lives, and in the Glasgow conversations the speakers were talking to someone they knew who was already familiar with at least some aspects of their lives. In the Glasgow conversations, both participants were equally entitled to ask questions (and to introduce new topics), and many of the questions were about specific points or situations. In the Ayr interviews, I was responsible for most of the questions, which tended to be open-ended questions designed to elicit extended responses. Obviously, these differences affected the dynamics of the exchanges and the kind of topics covered in the recordings, but there are also similarities.

In both corpora, individuals give narrative accounts of things that have happened to them. In the Ayr interviews, some of these narratives are quite long and deal with important events in the speaker's life (see Macaulay 1985, 1991b, 1997, to appear, for examples). These narratives illustrate many of the characteristics of the oral narratives analyzed by Labov (Labov and Waletzky 1967; Labov 1972). In the Glasgow conversations, the narratives refer mainly to recent events that make tellable stories, even though they are not of major importance in the speaker's life. Here is an example from the conversation between two middle-class women.

(1)   (Conversation 10—Middle-class women [simplified transcription])
       R: and you went all that way down yourself
       L: I was very proud of that
           driving all that way with mother and two children in torrential rain in November
           [2 lines omitted]
           oh it was funny because I'm hopeless with directions
           and I'm saying, "How am I going to find my way there?"
           he says "Look, once you're on the motorway
           you don't hit a traffic light till you get to Exeter
           you just keep going"
       R: I know but that's what worries me about motorways
           you can't stop at a traffic light and grab the map
           and say "Where the heck am I?" you know
           just got to keep going and preferably—
       L: no what I found the most frightening was that it being November
           and the roads were wet
           I've never seen so many lorries in my life
           and here's me tootling along in this wee Nova
           and you looked in your mirror
       R: uh huh
       L: and you just saw a line of lorries across all three carriages behind you
           bearing down on you with the light
       R: [*laughs*]
       L: and you thought [*laughing*] "Oh my God" you know you'd nowhere to go

R: uh huh

L: it was awful

R: uh huh

L: and then in Somerset it chucked it down
    and you couldn't see a foot in front of you

R: and then you lose the motorway
    and then you go onto the wee roads
    which are better in some ways and yet

L: Cornwall was brilliant
    once you left the motorway in Exeter you got onto
    I can't even remember what it is em
    but being November there was nothing on it
    and they'd improved the road down there so much
    that that part of the journey

R: it was okay

L: was a dawdle [i.e., easy]

R: I bet you were glad to see your brother [*both laugh*]
    "For once in my life I'm glad"

This is typical of the kind of narratives that occur in the Glasgow conversations. In response to 10R's comment *you went all that way down yourself,* 10L describes the experience in dramatic terms while 10R intersperses encouraging remarks or back-channel signals. In calculating the proportion of the transcript that consists of narrative, only the narrator's words are counted (i.e., 10R's contribution would not be included in the word count for 10L's narrative).

Overall, the proportion of narratives in the two corpora is roughly similar. It is about 25% in the Ayr interviews and about 33% in the Glasgow conversations, though in both cases there is great individual variation among the speakers. Table 3.7 gives the proportion of narrative in the Ayr interviews.

Included in this category are only those sections where the speaker was describing an event or events that occurred at a specific time and place. Reminiscences referring to typical kinds of events that occurred in the past are not included. The proportion of the Glasgow sessions devoted to narrative in each group is shown in tables 3.8 and 3.9.

TABLE 3.7. Proportion of narrative in the
Ayr interviews

Lower-class		*Middle-class*	
Ritchie (f)	5%	Muir (m)	0%
Gemmill (m)	15%	Menzies (f)	0%
Rae (m)	20%	MacDougall (m)	2%
Sinclair (m)	25%	MacGregor (m)	25%
Laidlaw (f)	30%	Gibson (m)	25%
Lang (m)	50%	Nicoll (m)	45%
All lower-class	29%	All middle-class	22%

TABLE 3.8. Proportion of narrative in
Glasgow adolescent conversations

Working-class girls	60%
Working-class boys	5%
Middle-class girls	28%
Middle-class boys	27%
All girls	46%
All boys	18%
Working-class adolescents	40%
Middle-class adolescents	27%
All adolescents	34%

It can be seen from tables 3.8 and 3.9 that the proportion of the sessions devoted to narrative is similar for the adolescents and the adults taken as groups, but the overall figures mask the gender difference that occurs in the working-class conversations. The working-class women show a proportion of narrative that is 3 times higher than that of the working-class men, and among the working-class adolescents the proportion of the sessions that the girls devote to presenting narratives is 12 times the amount in the boys' conversations. There are no parallels among the middle-class speakers, where the proportions are roughly similar for both genders. With two striking exceptions, the speakers tend to reciprocate; where one of the speakers tells many stories, the other speaker also does, and in one conversation neither of the boys tells any.

A feature of oral narrative is the use of quoted dialogue (Labov 1972; Tannen 1989). Table 3.10 gives the proportion of quoted dialogue in the Ayr interviews. Table 3.11 gives the equivalent figures for the Glasgow sessions.

The Ayr and the Glasgow corpora thus contain fairly similar amounts of narrative, though there are, differences in the kinds of narrative told. As pointed out earlier, in the Ayr interviews there were more vivid narratives about early experiences (see Macaulay, to appear), while in the Glasgow conversations the narratives tended to be about relatively recent events. This is probably because of the difference between talking to a stranger and talking to a friend. It is impossible to separate out all the effects of interlocutor, topic, and setting on the language used in these samples,

TABLE 3.9. Proportion of narrative
in Glasgow adult conversations

Working-class women	44%
Working-class men	13%
Middle-class women	32%
Middle-class men	35%
All women	39%
All men	23%
Working-class adults	33%
Middle-class adults	33%
All adults	33%

TABLE 3.10. Proportion of narrative
in the Ayr interviews that is quoted
dialogue

Lower-class	23%
Middle-class	35%

but there is enough material to permit quantitative analysis of certain features, and this makes possible comparison with other studies of similarly recorded speakers. Despite the considerable achievements of sociolinguistic investigation to this date, it remains a massive task to map out the kinds of variation that we all know exist in every community. Every careful study adds a tiny piece to the mosaic that one day may provide a clearer picture of the use of language. It is in this hope that the information in the following chapters is presented.

A note on the transcriptions

Transcriptions function in two ways. One is for the researcher, the other is for the reader. As I have argued elsewhere (Macaulay 1991a), different transcripts are appropriate for different purposes. I also believe that transcripts, as far as is possible, should be user-friendly. The transcripts in this book are designed for readability. The excerpts quoted are presented in lines that roughly correspond to clauses, but not in any rigid fashion. The aim of this kind of division is to present to the eye linguistic units that make sense in terms of the structure of the utterance. No attempt is made to represent the timing and pausing that occur on the tapes. The eye and the ear process information differently, and transcripts that give details of prosody and paralinguistic features can make very difficult reading. Such transcripts are necessary if the purpose is to illustrate such features, but if the analysis focuses on other aspects, then such information is a distraction, and consequently counterproductive. The transcripts in this volume are designed to draw attention to the kind of features analyzed and consequently omit details (such as pauses, tempo, pitch, and features of voice quality) that would be distracting. Some of the line divisions may appear to be inconsistent with decisions taken elsewhere, but the decisions are always local and no theoretical issues depend upon these differences. Some of the transcripts differ in

TABLE 3.11. Proportion of narrative
in the Glasgow conversations that is
quoted dialogue

Working-class adolescents	14%
Middle-class adolescents	9%
Working-class adults	25%
Middle-class adults	14%

minor ways from their appearance in earlier publications. Again, no theoretical implications should be drawn from these differences. False starts and hesitation phenomena are generally shown, but in some cases they are omitted in the interests of readability.

The policy of providing readable transcripts should not be interpreted as reflecting a cavalier attitude toward the transcripts. Great care has been taken to ensure that the transcripts accurately reflect what was said on the tape, to the extent that this is possible. Anyone who has transcribed tapes of connected speech will know that frequently there are difficulties in determining what the speaker actually said. Repeated hearings may result in an apparently satisfactory reading, but anyone who claims that a lengthy transcript is 100% accurate is either dealing with deviant data or exaggerating the success. Those of us who have spent hours on transcribing a tape know that on playing it to an audience (often on a different machine), we will often hear something that is inconsistent with what we thought was an accurate transcript. Usually, the errors are minor, but it is also possible to mishear a whole chunk (R. Macaulay 1990). The transcripts in this book are thus presented as being accurate with the proviso that few human products are perfect.

A note on statistics

Kretzschmar, Meyer, and Ingegneri raise the basic methodological question about corpus studies: "Have the texts included in the corpora been selected in a manner that makes them truly representative of the speech and writing of the general population from whom the texts in the corpus have been selected?" (1997: 168). Kretzschmar et al. discuss the "near-impossibility" of obtaining "a truly representative sampling of speakers of American English" (170). They then address the need for a sample of adequate size: "Suffice it to say, if linguists are going to move toward quantitative, statistically sound methods for addressing research questions and hypotheses, they will have to strive to create much larger corpora than have traditionally been created" (173). Kretzschmar et al. say that the British National Corpus "comes close to providing a truly representative sample of written and British English" (168); elsewhere they refer to a sample of more than 4 million words as being adequate. The corpora on which the present analysis is based are minuscule in comparison. Moreover, far from being examples of probability sampling (Kalton 1983), they are judgment samples chosen by a method that better fits Kalton's characterization as "haphazard, convenience, or accidental sampling" (1983: 90). There is no way in which either sample could be considered "truly" representative of any population. Consequently, there is no justification for generalizing from the sample to the population at large. At best, the results of the analysis can only provide hypotheses that could be tested on a truly representative sample. This is true, as far as I can tell, of almost all the work that has been done on discourse variation.

As Lavandera (1978) pointed out, the notion of the linguistic variable does not extend easily beyond phonological variation. Most of the features that are examined in the present volume cannot be treated as variables with a choice between variants.

Instead, the measure that is employed is the frequency with which a feature is used in the recorded speech of each individual. As pointed out in the previous chapter, the working assumptions are that all the speakers have equal opportunity to use these features and that differences in the frequency of use may be meaningful. Since I am interested in how certain categories of speakers differ in their usage, I report the frequency for a particular group, for example, working-class women. However, as will be obvious from the individual figures given in the Appendix, there is often great intragroup variation. As a result, group differences that appear large may not prove to be statistically significant, but I report them as indicative of a possible trend.

The dependence on statistically significant results may be misleading because it focuses attention on certain results and deflects attention from others. Kretzschmar et al. point out that when a distribution fails the test of significance: "The distribution may still be interesting, might still be worth explaining, but the statistical test will not be one of the grounds for finding it so. On the other hand, the fact that a statistical test has had a significant result does not mean that the distribution is necessarily 'important'" (1997: 175).

The statistical measure that is most appropriate for these kind of data is the Mann-Whitney nonparametric test, which is considered one of the most powerful nonparametric statistical tests (Woods, Fletcher, and Hughes 1986; Davis 1990; Elifson, Runyon, and Haber 1990). All statistical results given in this volume refer to this test unless otherwise stated. It has been said that God is as much in love with .06 as with .05, and in borderline cases a marginally significant difference may not be more interesting than one that marginally failed a test of significance. My concern is that a narrow focus on statistical significance may distract attention from the raw frequencies, which I believe can be interesting in themselves and suggest questions for further exploration.

Many factors affect the language speakers use in the recording situation, including all those set out by Hymes (1974) in his characterization of a speech event. Yet certain patterns appear in the transcripts of one social category that differ from those of another. Does it make sense to ask which patterns might have occurred by chance, according to some statistical measure? For many people the answer is obviously yes, but I believe that this is to attach the wrong significance (no pun intended) to the data. So many features of the transcripts occur literally "by chance" that even a finding of strong statistical significance may not provide any indication that this result would occur with a different sample. In the absence of probability sampling the best way to establish the generality of the results will be through comparison with other studies because it is only through convergence of results from replications of earlier studies or evidence from studies using different samples or different methodology that we can have any confidence in the results (Campbell and Fiske 1959).

Because investigation of discourse variation must examine samples of talk in action, the use of a specific feature is locally determined, and thus any conclusion from a specific data set may not generalize to other situations. For this reason, any conclusions drawn from a single study may give an unreliable indication of a more widespread difference. Donald Campbell, an American psychologist, points out the need for replication: "Because we social scientists have less ability [than physical scientists] to achieve experimental isolation, because we have good reason to expect our treatment effects to interact significantly with a wide variety of social factors many of which we have not yet mapped, we have much greater needs for replication experiments than do the physical sciences" (1969: 427–28).

It is my hope that the results presented in the following chapters will stimulate other investigators to examine the distribution of some of these discourse features in other corpora and in this way come to a better understanding of discourse variation.

4

Social Class

Despite receiving considerable attention in recent years by a range of scholars (e.g., see the references in Crompton, Devine, Savage, and Scott 2000), social class remains a controversial subject on which there are many conflicting views. Williams berates sociolinguists (in particular Labov) for their deficiencies in matters of sociological theory and for "a tendency to treat social structure merely as background information" (1992: 66), but sociologists have provided few models that seem helpful, and it is not easy to know which sociological theory it would be best to follow. As Rampton (2001: 266) has pointed out, references to work outside of one's own area of expertise can often seem simplistic to those more knowledgeable about the other discipline. Coupland (2001b), in the introduction to a volume entitled *Sociolinguistics and Social Theory* (Coupland, Sarangi, and Candlin 2001), suggests that "the future theoretical shape of sociolinguistics will be determined by how sociolinguists orient to integrationist social theories" (Coupland 2001b: 15). The integrationist social theories Coupland refers to include those of Foucault (1980), Bourdieu (1991), Giddens (1987, 1990, 1991), and Habermas (1972). Unfortunately, the chapters that follow Coupland's introduction, despite the well-intentioned efforts of several scholars, do not offer clear guidance as to how social theories can help to ground sociolinguistic investigation. The sociologist who proves to be most useful to several investigators is Goffman (1974, 1981), a scholar not known for his overall theory of social structure. Coupland et al.'s volume illustrates the difficulties of attempting to borrow concepts from other disciplines, and it may be more useful for sociolinguists simply to be explicit about the categories they employ and how they identify membership in them.

Social stratification may be nearly as universal as language, but, like language, social stratification takes different forms in different societies. Similarly, what kinds of social differences receive overt attention may vary from country to country. Milroy (2004: 167) observes that race and ethnicity are salient in American language ideology, in contrast to the situation in Britain, where social class is more salient. Argyle points out that as regards the situation in Britain: "Part of the evidence that there *is* a class system is that about 95 per cent of the population think there is, and can say which class they belong to themselves" (1994: 3). In 1973 in Glasgow I found that the adults I interviewed were willing to discuss the situation in Glasgow and generally to say where they would put themselves (Macaulay 1976, 1977).

Argyle (1994: 4) cites figures from Reid (1989) showing that 36% of a national sample in Britain rated themselves middle-class and 46% working-class, showing a clear polarization. Reid (1998: 32) reports that the British Social Attitudes survey found that two-thirds of the respondents classified themselves as working-class or upper-working-class and the rest as middle-class. In Glasgow, I started out with an assumption that four categories of social class would be necessary. My conclusion, after looking at the linguistic results and the self-reports, was that there were only three classes, corresponding roughly to upper-middle-class, lower-middle-class, and working-class, though I did not label them in this way (Macaulay 1976). In dealing with the smaller sample of speakers in Ayr I used a simple distinction between middle-class and lower-class. Stuart-Smith chose her sample to give equal representation to "Glasgow Standard English, spoken by most middle-class speakers," and "Glasgow vernacular, the dialect of many working-class speakers" (1999: 203), but she did not ask her speakers to identify their social class.

Given the desire to use social class as an extralinguistic variable, it is necessary to have some basis on which to choose the sample. Labov (1966) was able to make use of an earlier survey that had been designed by the New York School of Social Work for the Mobilization for Youth survey, with a team of 40 interviewers. He was able to draw a subsample from the 988 individuals who had been interviewed as part of this survey. Probably no other sociolinguist has had such a large randomly chosen sample to work with.

Labov made use of a 10-point socioeconomic class index developed for the Mobilization for Youth survey by John Michael (Labov 1966: 211–17). Michael's scale is based on measures of occupation, education, and income. Labov points out that Michael gave "considerable attention to the problem of dividing the continuum of social class" (Labov 1966: 216), and this was a problem for Labov, too. Labov did not only correlate use of the linguistic variables with speakers from each of the 10 points on the scale. Instead, he usually grouped the speakers into three or four social class groups and illustrated the difference this can make (220–48). The most interesting of these is the difference between Labov's figure 1 for the class stratification of the variable (*r*) (22) and his figure 11 (241) for the same variable. In figure 1, Labov has three groups: 0–2 (the lowest group), 3–5 (the middle group), and 6–9 (the highest group). The three groups show the same stylistic stratification. In figure 11 (which is the most frequently cited example of hypercorrection), there are six groups (0, 1, 2–3, 4–5, 6–8, and 9). The separation of 9 from 6–8 shows that the speakers in the latter group use more /r/ in reading aloud than the speakers in the highest group. This difference was concealed by the grouping in figure 1. The example illustrates one of the problems with "dividing the continuum of social class." There is clearly a linguistic justification for the grouping in figure 11, but is there other evidence that the speakers in, for example, category 8 belong with those in categories 6 and 7 rather than with those in category 9?

I was able to get some information from the speakers in Glasgow as to where they would put themselves in the class structure (Macaulay 1976, 1977) because social class, as Milroy points out, is a salient feature of identity in Britain. Labov's questionnaire does not include any question of this sort, either because he did not think it was appropriate or because he thought his respondents might have difficulty in answering it, but it would have been interesting to see what kind of answers they gave.

Labov (2001b) followed a similar strategy in the Philadelphia Neighborhood Study. On the basis of education, occupation, and residence value, he developed a 16-point scale, which he then divided into six social classes, as shown in table 4.1.

Labov uses regression analysis to tease out the different effects of occupation, education, and residence value on the use of the variables (2001b: 183–86). He concludes:

> The predominance of occupation for the most recent changes suggests that the combined index [i.e., the six social classes] is preferable only for those changes that have become engaged in the processes of sociolinguistic differentiation which extend over large portions of the speaker's life span. For young people growing up, the occupation of the breadwinner(s) of the family is the strongest determinant of their linguistic behavior. (185)

This is consistent with Labov's earlier comment that "it is generally agreed that among objective indicators, occupation is the most highly correlated with other conceptions of social class" (2001b: 60). The other factors are perhaps more relevant to notions of social prestige in general than to categories of social stratification. It is hard to be sure from Labov's charts, but there would appear to be a major difference between his first three groups (the working-class groups) and the other three (the middle-class and upper-class groups). In terms of social class differences, a two-way division would probably have provided very clear evidence of the difference between the two. Would this have been a more accurate picture of social class differences in

TABLE 4.1. Social class in Labov's Philadelphia Neighborhood Study

	SEC categories	No. in group
Lower working-class	2–3	5
Middle working-class	4–6	48
Upper working-class	7–9	16
Lower middle-class	10–12	13
Upper middle-class	13–15	15
Upper-class	16	15

speech than the one that Labov presents? In the absence of any corroborating evidence, it is impossible to tell, but the question would be worth exploring if Labov's primary concern were with linguistic indicators of social class identity rather than with the process of linguistic change.

Trudgill (1974) also selected a quasi-random sample from the local register of electors from four of Norwich's electoral wards. He then developed a social class index on the basis of six separate indicators: occupation, father's occupation, income, education, locality, and housing. Trudgill scored each of these indicators on a 6-point scale and added them together, giving a range from 0 to 30 (1974: 38–44). One problem with this approach is that each of the indicators is taken to have an equal effect on social class (Macaulay 1976: 185), and that assumption may not be justified. In Warner's Index of Status Characteristics (Warner, Meeker and Eells 1949), occupation was weighted 4, income 3, housing 3, and dwelling area 2. These weightings were developed on the basis of local research, but the results have been criticized as not measuring class (Argyle 1994: 5).

Like Labov, Trudgill then, on the basis of linguistic data, grouped the scores on the 30-point range into groups that he labeled middle middle-class, lower middle-class, upper working-class, middle working-class, and lower working-class. Trudgill was able to show fine stratification in these five categories, but a skeptic might wonder whether the separation of the working-class speakers into three categories is justified. Like Labov, Trudgill did not ask his speakers about social class or where they would put themselves, but as a native of Norwich Trudgill may have felt confident that they would have identified themselves according to the categories he established, even though they might not have used the same labels.

Labov's and Trudgill's methods are worth examining closely because they are scrupulously honest and make it quite clear how they arrived at their categories. However, they also illustrate the difficulties that sociolinguists face in employing categories such as social class. Williams (1992: 79) mocks Lyons's assessment of Labov's work as having employed "rather more sophisticated sociological concepts and techniques than have been applied hitherto," finding Labov's sociological input "limited." Williams may not be representative of all sociologists, but his strictures show the type of criticism that sociolinguists may face. My own view, as stated earlier, is that sociolinguists should not worry too much. It is unlikely that we shall ever employ methods and techniques that will satisfy the standards of sociological research. But there is no reason that we should attempt to mollify sociologists unless they can show how their methods will improve our results. We deal with a very different aspect of human behavior, and their methods and techniques would not work for our goals. It is enough if we are explicit about our methods and our data. We are dealing with an important aspect of human behavior, and what we have to say is worth saying.

Consequently, in the chapters that follow I will not be concerned about whether the way the categories of social class that I use have been determined would satisfy a sociologist. I have every reason to believe that the speakers themselves and those who know them would agree with their identification in the broad social class categories used, though in neither project was this question asked. I base my belief in this on the usual criteria of occupation, education, and residence without any need to develop a numerical scale.

In the Ayr study, I argued that "on the basis of family background, education, occupation, residence, interests, and attitudes" (Macaulay 1991b: 16), there was a clear division between the middle-class speakers and the lower-class speakers. In the Glasgow study that is the primary focus of the present work, Stuart-Smith chose her speakers on the basis of residence. The working-class speakers were chosen from "Maryhill, a working-class inner-city area," and the middle-class speakers from "Bearsden, a leafy suburb . . . inhabited mainly by the middle classes" (1999: 204). Such a method might not satisfy the criteria of survey research, but in practice it produced a polarized sample in which the two groups of speakers were distinguished by a number of critical characteristics, including occupation, education, and almost certainly income. As someone very familiar with Glasgow, I am confident that the sample does represent two distinct groups, though obviously neither set of speakers could be said to represent the wide range of individuals who belong to either class. The middle-class speakers come from the ranks of professionals, and the working-class speakers are in service occupations. A wider range of speakers might have presented a different picture. As the present work represents an exploratory study rather than a comprehensive survey of speech differences in the city, such limitations in the sample may have a less significant impact.

In the following chapters, reference will be made to the middle class and the lower class or working class. No significance should be attached to the difference between the labels lower and working class. I have used the former to be consistent with Macaulay (1991b) and the latter to be consistent with Stuart-Smith (1999).

In a similar fashion, I refer to adults and adolescents, and to males and females, without treating these categories of age or gender as problematic, though both categories are quite complex (Eckert and McConnell-Ginet 1992, 1999; Coupland 2001a). The adults in the Glasgow data are in their early 40s and thus are younger than most of the Ayr speakers. The adolescents are mostly aged 14 and therefore represent early adolescence. In no way could the adolescents and adults in the Glasgow sample be taken as representative of *all* adolescents or *all* adults in Glasgow. Any general statements about adolescent or adult speech in the chapters that follow refer only to these two age-groups.

All three categories, age, gender, and social class, are thus crude measures that can be criticized from various perspectives, but they provide an operational basis on which to examine examples of variation in the use of certain discourse features.

Decoding Bernstein

It is probably safe to say that no studies of linguistic variation have proved more controversial than those of Basil Bernstein (Atkinson 1985). Bernstein was in fact a pioneer in discourse analysis, but his efforts in this respect have received less recognition because of the controversy that arose over the implications of his interpretation of his findings into restricted and elaborated codes (Rosen 1972; Trudgill 1975). Yet, as Milroy (2001: 254) points out, Bernstein's views have been extremely influential in teacher training programs, both in Britain and in the United States, and Bernstein continues to receive favorable mention in sociolinguistic reviews (e.g., Grimshaw 2001). Because I will be making reference to some of Bernstein's claims in later chapters, it may be worth examining in detail here the basis for those claims.

As a young man working with boys' clubs in the East End of London and later teaching adolescents at a day college, Bernstein was struck by the difference between the boys' verbal skills and their performance skills (Bernstein 1971: 2–5). He later demonstrated this by comparing the results of two polarized groups on tests of verbal and nonverbal intelligence. He was able to show that the verbal scores of the working-class boys were depressed in comparison with their nonverbal scores, while there was no difference for the middle-class subjects (Bernstein 1960). For the next 10 years Bernstein and his colleagues at the Sociological Research Unit at the University of London Institute of Education explored the implications of this finding.

Bernstein's first formulation (1958) of the difference between working-class speech and middle-class speech was in terms of a distinction between what he called *public language* and *formal language*, as shown in (1).

(1)
> if the words used are part of a language which contains a high proportion of short commands, simple statements and questions where the symbolism is descriptive, tangible, concrete, visual and of a low order of generality, where the emphasis is on the emotive rather than the logical implications it will be called a *public* language.
>
> The language use of the middle class is rich in personal, individual qualifications, and its form implies sets of advanced logical operations; volume and tone and other non-verbal means of expression, although important, take second place. This mode of language-use will be termed *formal*.
>
> (Bernstein 1971: 28 [1958])

The page references to Bernstein are to the collected papers in the 1971 volume with the date of original publication in brackets.

The paper begins by drawing a clear distinction between the middle class and the working class on the basis of educational and occupational criteria. This is uncontroversial, though Lawton (1968: 82) finds the definition of social class unsatisfactory. Bernstein then goes on to say:

(2)   The groups are fundamentally distinct because the first [i.e., the middle class] possesses:
   (1) An awareness of the importance of the relationships between means and ends and of the relevant cognitive and dispositional attributes.
   (2) A discipline to orient behavior to certain values but with a premium on individual differences within them.
   (3) The ability to adopt appropriate measures to implement the attainment of distant ends by a purposeful means-end chain. (Bernstein 1971: 25 [1958])

By implication the working class possesses none of these attributes. The sole linguistic illustration of these qualities (and of the distinction between a formal and a public language) is that the middle-class mother says to her child, "I'd rather you made less noise, darling," while the working-class child has been brought up only to respond to "Shut up!" (1971: 26 [1958]).

In his next paper, Bernstein (1959) sets out the characteristics of both public and formal language. It is worth repeating them here because they present a more testable set of assumptions.

(3)   Characteristics of a public language:
   1. Short, grammatically simple, often unfinished sentences, a poor syntactical construction with a verbal form stressing the active mood.
   2. Simple and repetitive use of conjunctions (*so, then, and, because*).
   3. Frequent use of short commands and questions.
   4. Rigid and limited use of adjectives and adverbs.
   5. Infrequent use of impersonal pronouns (*one, it*).
   6. Statements formulated as implicit questions which set up a sympathetic circularity, e.g., "Just fancy?" "It's only natural, isn't it?" "I wouldn't have believed it."

   7. A statement of fact is often used as both a reason and a conclusion, or more accurately, the reason and conclusion are confounded to produce a categoric statement, e.g., "Do as I tell you" "Hold on tight" "You're not going out" "Lay off that."

   8. Individual selection from a group of idiomatic phrases will frequently be found.

   9. Symbolism is of a low order of generality.

  10. The individual qualification is implicit in the sentence structure, therefore it is a language of implicit meaning. *It is believed that this fact determines the form of the language.* (Bernstein 1971: 42–43 [1959])

Since Bernstein 1959 is a paper about the sociological implications of a public language, Bernstein relegates the characteristics of a formal language to a footnote. They are more or less the mirror image of the characteristics of a public language, but they are worth citing in full to show the wording:

(3)   Some characteristics of a formal language:

   1. Accurate grammatical order and syntax regulate what is said.

   2. Logical modifications and stress are mediated through a grammatically complex sentence construction, especially through the use of a range of conjunctions and relative clauses.

   3. Frequent use of prepositions which indicate logical relationships as well as prepositions which indicate temporal and spatial contiguity.

   4. Frequent use of impersonal pronouns (*it, one*).

   5. A discriminative selection from a range of adjectives and adverbs.

   6. Individual qualification is verbally mediated through the structure and relationships within and between sentences. That is, it is explicit.

   7. Expressive symbolism conditioned by this linguistic form distributes affectual support rather than logical meaning to what is said.

   8. A language use which points to the possibilities inherent in a complex conceptual hierarchy for the organizing of experience. (Bernstein 1971: 55 [= 1959])

The quantifier *some* in the heading is Bernstein's and implies that there may be more characteristics of a formal language. There is no such implication in the listing of the characteristics of a public language.

    Given the obvious bias in the wording of (2) and (3) (e.g., "rigid" versus "discriminative"), not to mention the views expressed in Bernstein 1958, cited above, it is hardly surprising that linguists and others reacted negatively to Bernstein's ideas (e.g., Bisseret 1979; Labov 1969; Rosen 1972; Trudgill 1975), and in his introduction to the collected papers, Bernstein admits the shortcomings of these descriptions: "The list of attributes of a public or formal language are a rag-bag, possessing no linguistic respectability, as so many critics have so rightly pointed out, yet for me they were critical focusing points in order to explore an intuition" (Bernstein 1971: 2).

    Yet Bernstein's pioneering insight was to set out a number of hypotheses about social class differences in speech that in principle could be tested.[1] It should be remembered that at the time Bernstein was engaged in this work, there were few studies of talk in action and no accounts of the features of speech events such as those provided by Hymes (1974). It became increasingly obvious that Bernstein did not have an adequate methodology to investigate these speech differences, and he backed off from making claims about actual language. He later acknowledged that the restricted and elaborated codes were "not directly observable" (1971: 15), though he continued to make occasional reference to notions such as "a wide range of syntactic alternatives" (1971: 145 [1972]).[2]

Not all of Bernstein's characteristics are amenable to quantitative analysis. For example, "symbolism" and "the possibilities inherent in a complex conceptual hierarchy"[3] are difficult to count, and it is not surprising that Bernstein does not include them in his major empirical study of what he was now calling a restricted code (= public language) and an elaborated code (= formal language) (Bernstein 1962). This study is easy to criticize (Lawton 1968; Dittmar 1976), but it was the first attempt to investigate quantitative differences in a wide range of linguistic features.

Bernstein's methodology in this study is so suspect that it was unfortunate that anyone took his results as being more than indicative of possible differences. He had two groups of five middle-class boys and three groups of working-class boys, aged 15 to 18. He held what he called "a tape-recorded, relatively undirected discussion" (1971: 83 [1962]) on the abolition of capital punishment, but because he was worried that "the working-class group would find the test situation threatening" (1971: 84), he held two practice sessions (one a week) with them before the recorded sessions. It is impossible to know what impact these practice sessions may have had on the speech recorded. It is also unclear how much Bernstein's own contribution affected the results: "As far as possible the boys set the level of discussion and the research worker [i.e., Bernstein] intervened when a particular sequence was exhausted, when a boy was monopolizing the discussion or when voluntary contributions came to an end. The number of such interventions was considerably greater for the working-class groups for the last-mentioned reason" (Bernstein 1971: 84 [1962]). This suggests that the working-class boys were less comfortable in the recording situation, raising the possibility that the two samples were not equivalent.[4]

Bernstein extracted samples of approximately 1,800 words from each of the five recorded sessions, but just over 9% of the words were excluded from the analysis, including repeated words, false starts, question tags, parentheticals, and discourse markers such as *I mean* and *you know*. The total number of words analyzed was 8,027, of which the 10 middle-class boys produced an average of 329 words each, and the 12 working-class boys an average of 395. The sample of speech analyzed is thus very small, and since Bernstein, with one exception, gives only the results of his statistical analysis, there is no way of knowing how many tokens of each feature were produced.[5] This is frustrating, since it would have been interesting to see the actual frequencies of the items even in such a small sample. It is depressing, not to say alarming, to recall the vast exposure Bernstein's views have had, given the slender empirical base for his claims.

Bernstein's example, however, provides a useful starting point for the quantitative analysis of discourse. It is not necessary to get involved in the controversy over his views (Atkinson 1985) to find the questions Bernstein raised interesting (Macaulay

1986). I have never had the slightest doubt about the sincerity of Bernstein's motives or his ethical values. However, he was hampered by the lack of any model for the analysis of discourse variation and by the unwillingness of the Department of Education at the University of London to fund the kind of research he proposed (Bernstein 1971: 10). He was also probably influenced by his view of the standard language, seeing it very much in terms of written language.[6] It will be clear in the following chapters that many of the questions raised by Bernstein about social class differences in speech have not been fully explored, far less satisfactorily answered.

Given the restricted nature of Bernstein's sample, adolescent boys, it is unfortunate that many of those who apparently paid attention only to his overall conclusions seem to assume that his claims would generalize to adult class differences. It will be obvious in the following chapters that adolescent boys differ in their speech patterns both from adolescent girls and from adults. This is no surprise to sociolinguists (e.g., Labov 1966; Trudgill 1974; Horvath 1985; Eckert 1997, 2000), who know that there is a complex interaction between the membership categories of social class, gender, and age. However, too many teachers, most of them in the United Kingdom but also some in the United States, seem to have accepted Bernstein's claims as well-established facts about social class differences in language. The following chapters will examine some of the features Bernstein considered and show to what extent some people may have been misled.

Talk in Action

Unless we are surreptitiously recording friends and acquaintances (e.g., Tannen 1984; Coates 1996), there must always be some compromise in the kind of talk recorded. For the analysis of talk in action, Labov's Observer's Paradox (Labov 1972) is even more frustrating because there are so many uncontrolled and uncontrollable aspects of the situation. For this reason, it is important to determine the degree to which the quality of speech recorded is adequate for the purposes of analysis.

At the end of the analysis of the Ayr interviews, I argued that the recordings were a legitimate sample of the speakers' language because of the wide variety of conversational skills they had displayed: "They use discourse markers, introduce direct speech, initiate topics, perform narratives, and maintain both a global coherence and local cohesion in their speech. They reminisce, tell stories, express opinions, and ask questions" (Macaulay 1991b: 266).

As explained earlier, the Glasgow recordings were made under very different conditions. Instead of being interviewed by an academic researcher, the speakers were talking with someone they knew quite well. However, it is obvious that the conversations are not samples of naturally occurring interactions. The speakers knew that they were being recorded and that they were expected to talk for at least half an hour, and in some cases there were overt signals that they were trying hard to find a suitable topic. There are clear indications that some speakers (e.g., the working-class girls) found the situation easier than others (e.g., the working-class boys), but they all persevered and produced substantial amounts of talk-in-action. However, the analysis depends upon the samples meeting the conditions of hypothesis 1 (see chapter 2):

All speakers have the same opportunity to use certain discourse features in the recording sessions.

What evidence is there that the samples meet this condition?

A number of features show how the speakers are actively interacting with each other. For example, it is clear from the work of the conversation analysts (e.g., Sacks, Schegloff, and Jefferson 1974; Goodwin 1981; Schegloff 1982) that listeners must indicate by some means that they have been paying attention to what the speaker is saying. One way to do this is by a minimal response such as *uhuh* or *mhm*. In chapter 1 it was shown that there was variation in the use of the minimal responses *mhm* and *uhuh*, which are regularly used as acknowledgment or agreement markers in ongoing feedback responses that do not constitute full turns in the sense of gaining the floor. Other forms used in this way include *aye, I know, no, oh yes, right, that's right,* and *yeah/yes*. The social class differences in the frequency of all types of minimal responses are shown in figure 6.1.

With one exception, there are no significant differences in the use of minimal responses by any of the groups. Both middle-class and working-class men use minimal responses with an average frequency of 42.7 per 1,000 words (with a range of 12.7 to 122.7 for the middle-class men and from 6.7 to 137.9 for the working-class men). The middle-class women, however, use minimal responses with an average frequency of 50.8, much higher than the average frequency of the working-class women of 35.1. The range for the middle-class women is 32.9 to 91.5, and for the working-class women from 12.7 to 67.1. The two adult speakers with the highest number of minimal responses are both men, one middle-class and one working-class. Since none of the group differences is statistically significant, the important point is that all adult groups are using minimal responses in similar ways.

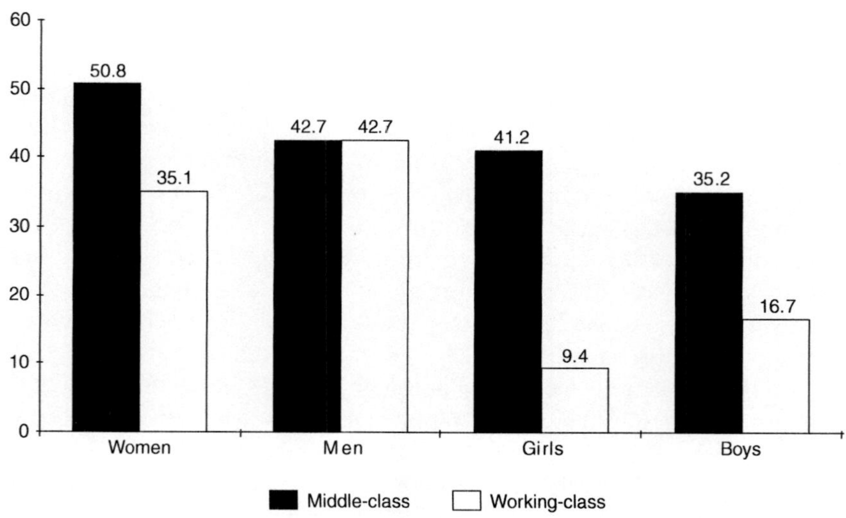

FIGURE 6.1. Minimal responses: Glasgow adults and adolescents (frequency per 1,000 words)

The middle-class boys use minimal responses with an average frequency of 35.2 per 1,000 words (with a range of 11.6 to 86.4), and the middle-class girls with an average frequency of 41.2 (with a range of 20.4 to 66.1). The working-class boys use minimal responses with an average frequency of 16.7 (range 6.3 to 32.2), while the working-class girls have an average frequency of only 9.4 (range 3.2 to 27.9). The only statistically significant finding is that the middle-class adolescents use minimal responses more frequently than the working-class adolescents ($p < .01$). Although the middle-class women and girls use minimal responses more frequently than the middle-class men and boys, this difference is not significant, and it is clear from both the adult and the adolescent figures that there is no simple gender distinction in the use of minimal responses. This is contrary to reports that such usage is more common among females (e.g., Coates 1988: 105–7; Roger and Nesshoever 1987: 252). However, the adults use minimal responses more frequently than the adolescents, though this difference falls just short of significance. The working-class girls use fewer minimal responses because they allow each other to tell extended narratives with little in the way of comment or sustaining responses. Since the working-class girls have the highest proportion of narrative in their conversations, the lower frequency of minimal responses is probably a consequence of this.

Another obvious form of interaction is to ask questions. There are age, social class, and gender differences in the frequency with which the participants ask each other questions, as can be seen in figure 6.2. Questions in quoted dialogue are not included in these figures, since such questions are not part of the dyadic interaction.

Figure 6.2 shows that the adolescents ask questions of each other much more frequently than do the adults, and this is highly significant ($p < .001$). With the exception of the girls, the working-class speakers ask more questions than do the middle-class. The exact figures are given in tables 6.1 and 6.2. It can be seen from the tables that the

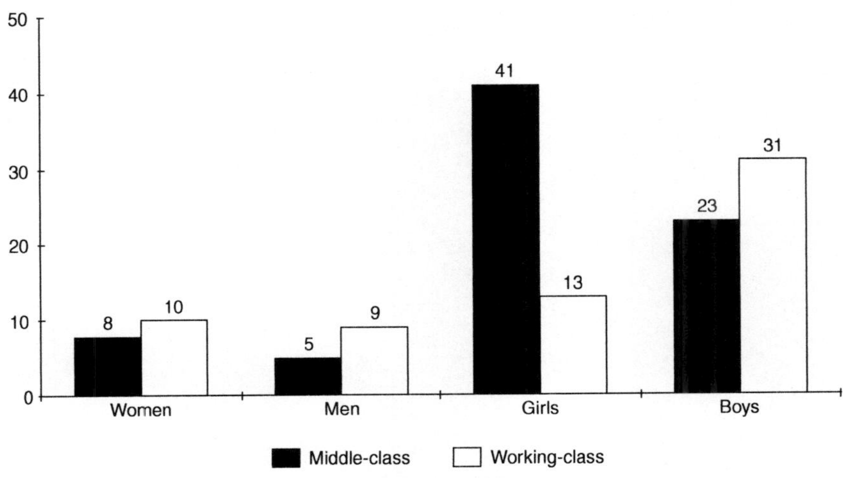

FIGURE 6.2. Frequency of questions asked by Glasgow adolescents and adults (frequency per 1,000 words)

adolescents employ questions almost three times more frequently than do the adults and that this is characteristic of their interactional style, with the exception of the working-class girls, though even their frequency is higher than that for any of the adults. The lower frequency of questions in the working-class girls' conversation again may be related to the higher proportion of narratives in their conversations. Since narratives are extended turns, the need or opportunity for questions is reduced.

Questions are generally of one of two kinds. Questions formed by inverting the verb and the subject (e.g., *Has she got no family?*) can be answered by a simple *yes* or *no* and are often referred to as Yes/No questions. Questions introduced by one of a class of question words (e.g., *Where did they come from? Who died?*) cannot be answered by a simple *yes* or *no*. They are usually known as WH-questions. Yes/No questions can be used to elicit new information (e.g., *Did they say what they thought of the new people?*), but they can also be used to check that the listener is following what is being said (e.g., *You know the ones that fold in?*). WH-questions, however, are almost always used to elicit new information. Tables 6.1 and 6.2 show the proportion of WH-questions for each group of speakers. The social class, age, and gender differences are shown more clearly in figure 6.3.

It can be seen that the working-class boys, girls, and men, and the middle-class girls have a higher proportion of WH-questions than the other groups. This suggests an interest in obtaining new information and may reflect sense of "involvement" (Tannen 1989). However, the more important point is that all the speakers are engaged in interacting with each other through the use of questions. None of the speakers is a passive respondent simply acknowledging what the interlocutor has said.

Coates (1996: 174–202) examines the use of questions in her corpus of women's conversations. She found that her speakers used questions to obtain information, for conversational maintenance, to instigate stories, for topic initiation, for topic development, as a hedging device, as rhetorical questions, and to avoid playing the expert. All these functions are found in the Glasgow conversations, with the exception of the last, though there are few rhetorical questions. The most frequent use is for

TABLE 6.1. Frequency of questions in adolescent conversations

	All Qs		Y/N Qs		WH Qs	
	[a]*Freq.*	*(n)*	*Freq.*	*(n)*	*Freq.*	*(n)*
Working-class girls	13	(177)	7	(101)	6	(76)
Working-class boys	31	(226)	14	(107)	16	(49)
Middle-class girls	41	(425)	25	(257)	16	(168)
Middle-class boys	23	(264)	16	(190)	6	(74)
All girls	25	(602)	15	(358)	10	(244)
All boys	26	(490)	16	(297)	10	(193)
All working-class	19	(403)	10	(208)	9	(195)
All middle-class	31	(689)	20	(447)	11	(242)
All adolescents	25	(1092)	15	(655)	10	(437)

[a]per 1,000 words

TABLE 6.2. Frequency of questions in adult conversations

	All Qs		Y/N Qs		WH Qs	
	[a]Freq.	(n)	Freq.	(n)	Freq.	(n)
Working-class women	10	(348)	8	(275)	2	(73)
Working-class men	9	(146)	5	(84)	4	(62)
Middle-class women	8	(159)	7	(125)	2	(34)
Middle-class men	5	(84)	4	(65)	1	(19)
All women	10	(507)	8	(400)	2	(107)
All men	7	(230)	5	(149)	2	(81)
All working-class	10	(494)	7	(359)	3	(135)
All middle-class	7	(243)	6	(190)	2	(53)
All adults	9	(737)	6	(549)	2	(188)

[a]per 1,000 words

conversational maintenance, followed by requests for information. There are no marked differences between males and females in these two uses of questions.

There is one other syntactic form that directly impinges on the addressee (i.e., is conative, in Jakobson's (1960) sense), namely, the imperative. There is a striking difference between the two age-groups and between males and females in their use of imperatives addressed to the other speaker, as can be seen in table 6.3.

The adolescents address each other with direct imperatives more than 25 times as frequently as do the adults ($p < .001$). In fact, the adults rarely use imperatives. The gender difference is caused principally by the working-class boys, as figure 6.5 shows.

The extract in (1) illustrates this use of imperatives. The boys are exploring the files in the teacher's office where they are being recorded.

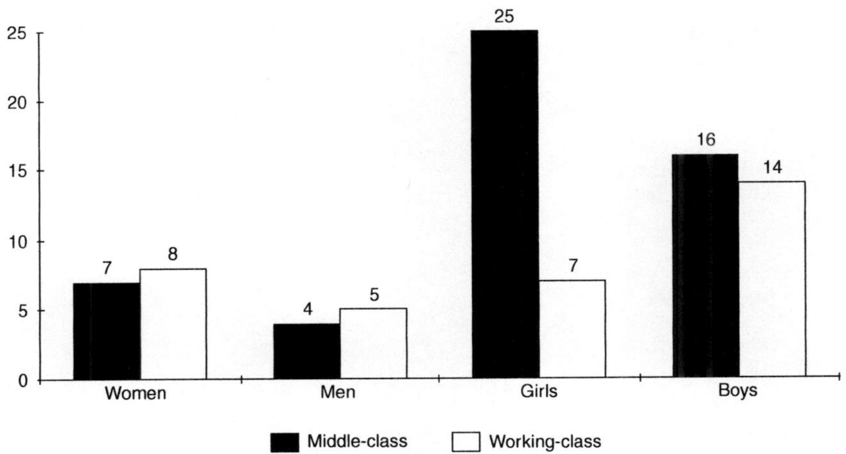

FIGURE 6.3. Frequency of yes/no questions in Glasgow (frequency per 1,000 words)

FIGURE 6.4. Frequency of WH-questions in Glasgow (frequency per 1,000 words)

(1)   (Conversation 6—Working-class boys)
    L: get us one by the way   ⇐
        get us one   ⇐
        and I'll bag it.
    R: hold that.   ⇐
    L: No don't   ⇐
        keep it on.   ⇐
    R: I cannae
    L: You can
        it'll reach
    R: no
        it won't reach anyway
    L: no
        don't bother Alex   ⇐
        HOLD ON   ⇐
    R: (............)
    L: every day is a winding road
    R: here
    L: (............)
    R: rip this off man   ⇐
        in the bag

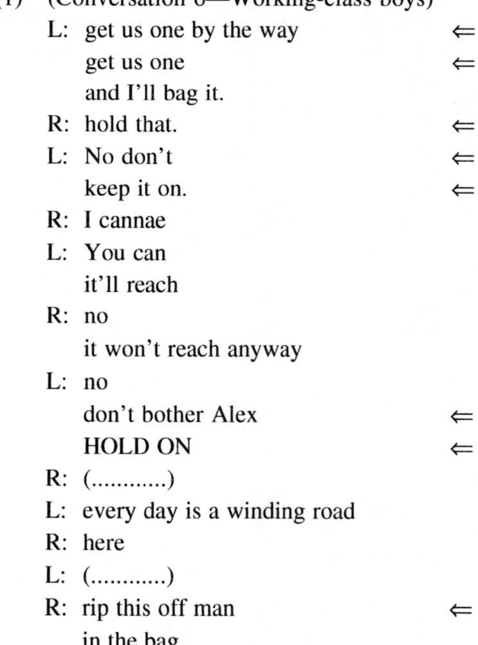

TABLE 6.3. Use of imperatives

	Freq.	*No.*
Adolescents	3.3	141
Adults	0.06	5
Females	0.57	43
Males	3.07	103

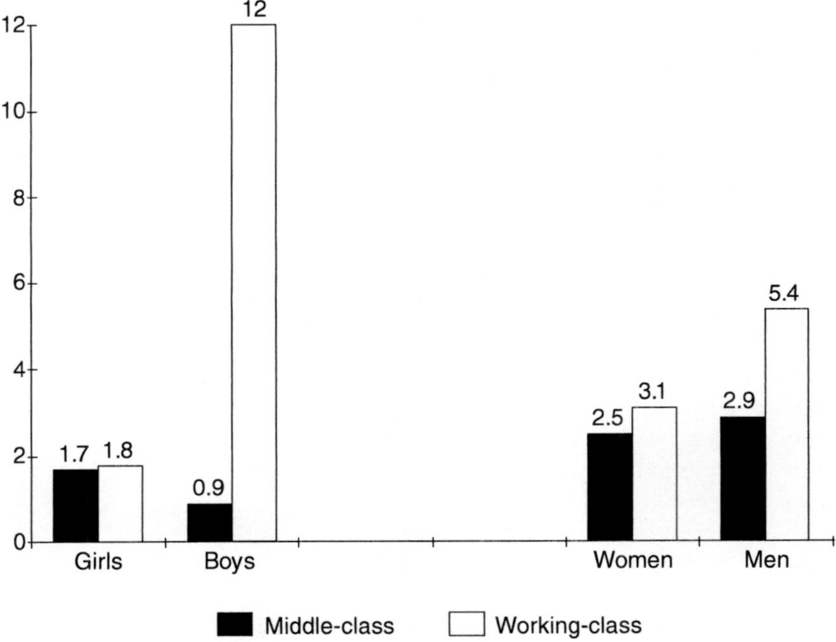

FIGURE 6.5. Frequency of imperatives in Glasgow (frequency per 1,000 words)

In this short extract there are eight imperatives. It is the working-class boys who are repeatedly telling each other what to do. This is similar to the difference between boys and girls that Goodwin (1980) found in her study of African-American children playing in single-sex groups, where it is the boys who use unmitigated directives. Although in many ways (e.g., in the amount of speech produced, and in frequent references to how slowly the time is passing), the working-class boys are the least comfortable in the recording situation, the use of imperatives shows one of the ways in which they are actively engaged in communicating with each other.

There is also a very wide range of topics covered. The middle-class women talk about holidays, visiting friends and relatives, education, jobs, their children, decorating the house. The middle-class men talk about their professional work, traveling, and sports (including waterskiing, golf, and rugby, but not football). The working-class women talk about their families, shopping, bingo, and drinking. The working-class men mainly reminisce about the past and how things have changed. The middle-class and working-class girls mostly talk about their peers, and the working-class girls talk a lot about drinking. Two of the middle-class boys talk about school, travel, and sports (including football); the other two middle-class boys talk mainly about computer games. The working-class boys talk about their peers, school, football, and about objects in the teacher's room where they are being recorded. In short, all the speakers talk about the kinds of things that interest them; they are not being pushed into talking about abstract subjects such as the death penalty or corporal punishment or the kind of questions that figure on many questionnaires.

The conversations in this set of recordings are examples of what Enkvist (1982) and others have called "impromptu speech," in that they are spontaneous, minimal in planning, and not affected by larger frameworks, such as classroom exchanges or doctor-patient interviews. Östman has claimed that certain discourse features characterize impromptu speech: "One line of approach is to argue that impromptu speech is, partly at least, created by the occurrence of pragmatic particles. Or, to make the statement more plausible, the occurrence of pragmatic particles in a discourse implies that the discourse is of an impromptu nature" (1982: 165). By "pragmatic particles" (154), Östman means such items as *I mean*, *you know*, *like*, *well*, and *oh*. By looking at the frequency of use of these features in the Glasgow conversations, we can confirm that they deserve to be considered examples of impromptu speech, since all five are widely used, though not equally frequently by all speakers. This chapter will illustrate this point by looking at the use of *well* and *oh*. All five features will be examined in greater detail in the next chapter.

The discourse marker *oh* has been investigated as to its functions in discourse (Heritage 1984; Schiffrin 1987; Aijmer 1987), but its differential use has not been investigated. The Glasgow materials provide an opportunity to see whether there are age, gender, and social class differences in the use of these markers. There are 742 tokens of *oh*, an average of 22 per speaker, if they were equally distributed, which of course they are not. However, if Östman is correct, the frequency of its use is one indication that the conversations represent samples of impromptu speech.

Figure 6.6 shows that there are social class differences. The middle-class adults use *oh* with a frequency of 7.23 per 1,000 words, the working-class adults with a

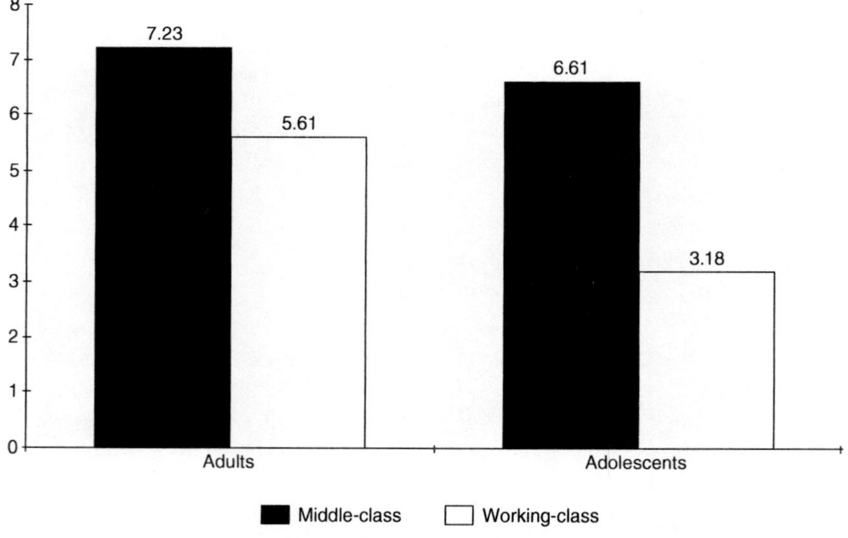

FIGURE 6.6. Frequency of *oh* in Glasgow (frequency per 1,000 words)

frequency of 5.61. The difference is even greater in the adolescents, with the middle-class adolescents using *oh* with a frequency of 6.61, compared with a frequency of 3.18 among the working-class adolescents. This social class difference is the reverse of that found in the Ayr interviews, where the lower-class speakers used *oh* with a frequency of 7.04, compared with the middle-class speakers at 2.69. In Glasgow the adults use *oh* with a higher frequency (6.26) than the adolescents (4.92).

Figure 6.6 conceals the fact that there is also a gender difference. Figure 6.7, in contrast, shows that females use *oh* with an overall frequency of 7.31, compared with 3.62 for males, and that this is true of both adults and adolescents (women 7.62 versus men 4.12; girls 6.64 versus boys 2.74). This difference is statistically significant ($p < .005$). However, neither figure 6.6 nor figure 6.7 gives the complete picture of the situation, which can be seen more clearly in figure 6.8.

Figure 6.8 shows that it is the middle-class women (9.67) and middle-class girls (10.84) who are the most frequent users of *oh*. Differences in the ways in which *oh* is used will be examined in the next chapter.

The discourse marker *well* has also received attention (e.g., Schiffrin 1987; Svartvik 1980), but as with *oh* there has been no attempt to determine whether there are differences in the extent to which it is used by different speakers. There are 497 tokens of *well* in the Glasgow conversations, equivalent to 15 per speaker if they were equally distributed, which again they are not. However, the frequency reinforces the notion of impromptu speech.

Figure 6.9 shows that among the adults, it is the working-class speakers who use *well* more slightly frequently, while the reverse is true among the adolescents, but the differences are not significant. *Well* is used twice as frequently by the adults (3.65) compared with the adolescents (1.50), and here the difference is significant ($p < .005$). The gender differences are shown in figure 6.10.

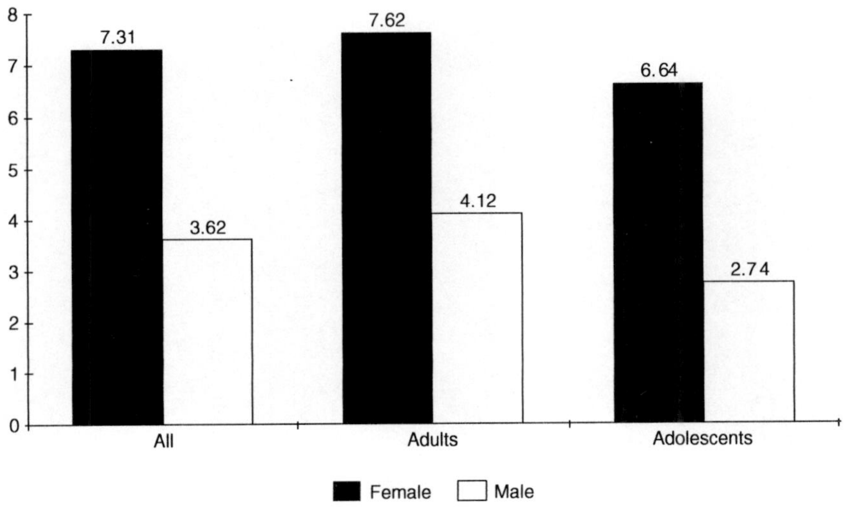

FIGURE 6.7. Gender differences in the use of *oh* in Glasgow

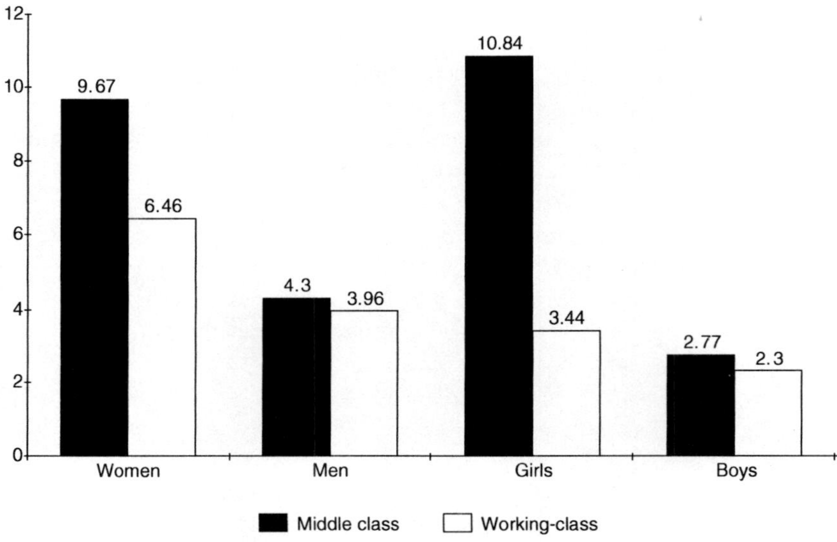

FIGURE 6.8. Age and gender differences in the use of *oh* in Glasgow

The men use *well* slightly more frequently than the women, while the reverse is true of the boys and girls, but the differences are not significant. The situation is clearer in figure 6.11, which shows that among the adults it is the working-class men who use *well* the most, while among the adolescents it is the middle-class girls. As with *oh*, there are different ways in which *well* is used in the Glasgow sessions, and these will be examined in the next chapter.

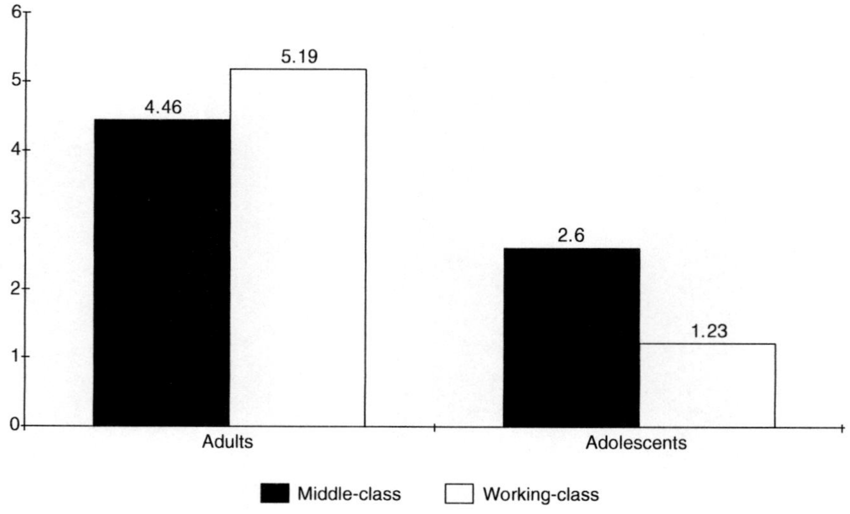

FIGURE 6.9. Frequency of *well* in Glasgow (frequency per 1,000 words)

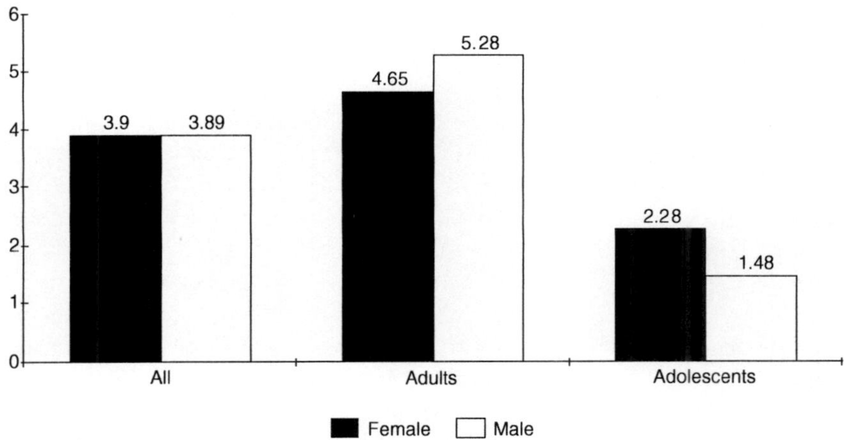

FIGURE 6.10. Gender differences in the use of *well* in Glasgow

The examination of the use of *oh* and *well* in the Glasgow recordings has shown that while there are patterns of use that correlate with membership in categories of age, gender, and social class, there are more similarities than differences. All groups make some use of both discourse features, *oh* being somewhat more frequently used by the middle-class speakers and *well* by the working-class speakers. There is also an interaction with gender, since *oh*, which is used more frequently by the middle-class speakers, is also used more frequently by women, whereas *well*, which is used more frequently by working-class speakers, is used more frequently by men. Among the adults, the most frequent users of *oh* are middle-class women and the most fre-

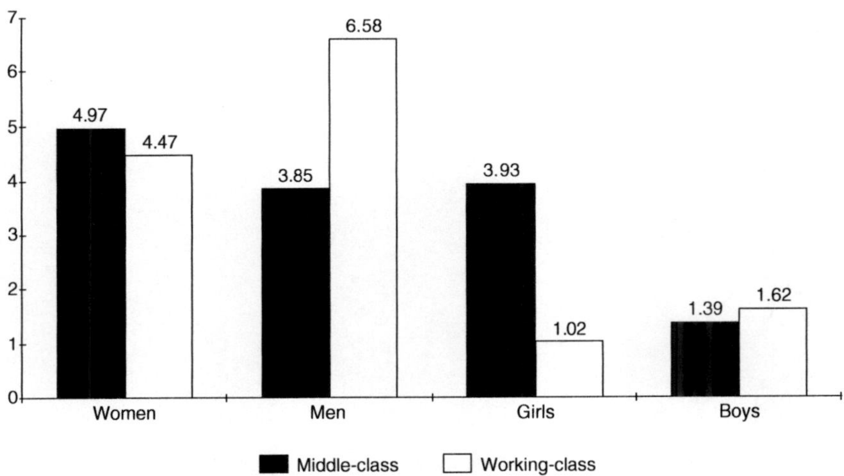

FIGURE 6.11. Age and gender differences in the use of *well* in Glasgow

quent users of *well* are working-class men. The adolescents, with one noticeable exception, show less frequent use of both discourse markers than do the adults.

In some ways, the most interesting group are the middle-class girls, who show high use of both *oh* and *well*. Since both markers are common in adult speech, the results suggest that of the four groups of adolescents it is the middle-class girls who are closest to developing adult patterns of speech. Their use of *oh* parallels that among the middle-class women, so that the middle-class girls appear to be adopting the speech style of their mothers' generation.

Although the numbers are too small to be significant, it is also interesting that the working-class boys use *well* with a slightly higher frequency (1.62) than either the middle-class boys (1.39) or the working-class girls (1.02), although their use of *oh* is the lowest of all the groups. Since *well* is most frequent in the sessions with the working-class men, it may be the case that the working-class boys are beginning to pattern their speech on that of their fathers' generation.

This chapter has attempted to demonstrate that the Glasgow recordings are appropriate examples of spontaneous conversation, despite the constraints of the recording situation. In their use of minimal responses, questions, imperatives, and the items *oh* and *well*, the speakers have shown themselves interacting in much the way we would expect them to do under other circumstances. In their use of *oh* and *well*, they meet one of Östman's criteria for impromptu speech. The next chapter will investigate in greater detail the use of all five of Östman's pragmatic particles, *oh*, *well*, *you know*, *I mean*, and *like*.

Some Common Discourse Features

In the previous chapter, it was shown that there were age, gender, and social class differences in the use of the discourse features *oh* and *well*. This chapter will examine some other differences in the use of these two items and then go on to explore differences in the use of *you know*, *I mean*, and *like*.

As has been pointed by others (e.g., Heritage 1984; Schiffrin 1987; Aijmer 1987), *oh* has several functions. It is important to show how *oh* is used in the Glasgow conversations.

The use of *oh*

Acknowledgment

One use is as a simple acknowledgment marker as in (1).

(1) (Conversation 12—Middle-class women)
     12L: I'm doing a writing course this week in Kilmoredinny
     12R: *oh*
     12L: you know
            do you know Kilmoredinny?
     12R: I've never actually been there

In (1), 12R's use of *oh* is simply an acknowledgment that she has heard 12L's statement, but it does not indicate anything further in the way of surprise or enthusiasm.

Agreement

In other cases *oh* can be part of a signal of agreement, as in (2).

(2)   (Conversation 12—Middle-class women)
       12L: it's a fascinating library
       12R: *oh* yes

It generally indicates a degree of enthusiastic agreement, as in (3).

(3)   (Conversation 16—Middle-class men)
       16R: the Gulf is—is pretty warm
       16L: yeah
       16R: but em if you get on to the other coast the—the Atlantic coast
       16L: *oh* yes yes
       16R: then you've got the breakers and the wind

Emotion

Another use of *oh* is to express a strong reaction, often dismay or approval, as in the examples in (4).

(4)
       a. *oh* dear (10L, middle-class woman)
       b. *oh* God (10L, middle-class woman)
       c. *oh* wonderful (12L, middle-class woman)
       d. *oh* shit (2L, middle-class girl)
       e. *oh* fuck (9L, working-class boy)

Similar in many ways is the use of *oh* before a strong statement of opinion or feeling as in (5).

(5)
       a. *oh* her face would have been a picture (10L, middle-class woman)
       b. *oh* it was dreadful you know (10R, middle-class woman)
       c. *oh* it's just out of this world (12L, middle-class woman)
       d. *oh* he's a wee arsehole (8L, working-class girl)
       e. *oh* I could strangle her (5L, middle-class girl)

Quoted dialogue

Oh is also common in quoted dialogue, as in the examples in (6).

(6)
       a. and I'm going "*Oh* I don't know" (10R, middle-class woman)
       b. also thought "*Oh* this'll be no problem" (16L, middle-class man)

   c. And I went "*Oh* I need to bring my pyjamas then?" (14R, working-class woman)

   d. she's like em "*Oh* I'll get off with him after school today" (5L, middle-class girl)

   e. and she went like that "*Oh* right" (7R, working-class girl)

Questions

Finally, *oh* can be used to introduce questions, usually asking for confirmation or elaboration, as in (7).

(7)

   a. *oh* Ian?   (10L, middle-class woman)

   b. *oh* does she? (12R, middle-class woman)

   c. *oh* doon to Crosslands? (13L, working-class woman)

   d. *oh* were you there? (2R, middle-class girl)

   e. *oh* are they not bad man? (9R, working-class boy)

Figure 7.1 shows the distribution of the 742 tokens of *oh* in the Glasgow recordings, both adults and adolescents. All adult categories of speaker use *oh* most frequently when signaling agreement, with the exception of the working-class women, who use *oh*, most often in quoted dialogue. Of the other uses of *oh* the most interesting is for the expression of emotion, as can be seen in figure 7.2.

    The important figures here are those for middle-class women (22%) and middle-class girls (31%), since these are the two groups with the highest frequency of use of

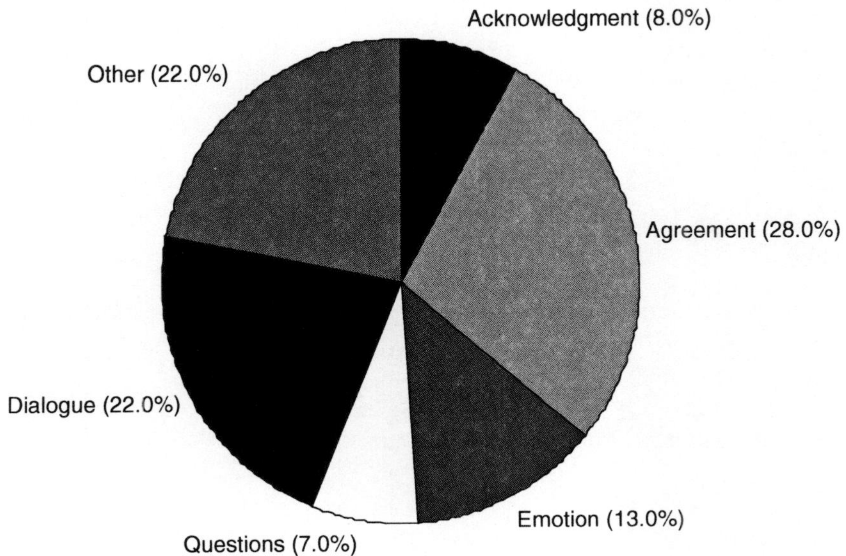

FIGURE 7.1. Uses of *oh* in Glasgow

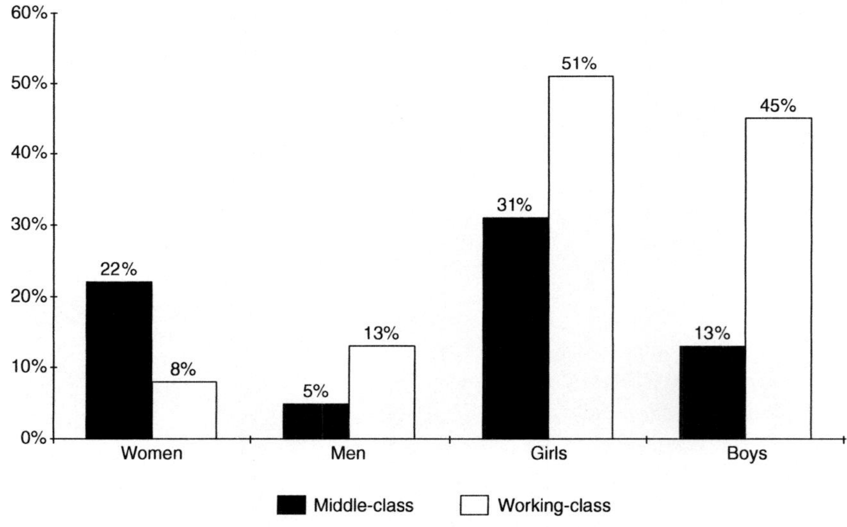

FIGURE 7.2. Use of *oh* to express emotion in Glasgow

oh, as was shown in figure 6.7. (The percentages for the working-class adolescents are less important because their overall use of *oh* is so low.) One possible explanation for the higher frequency of use of *oh* by the middle-class women and girls is that they are expressing their personal feelings more strongly. Evidence from other features will be needed to test whether this hypothesis is valid.

To sum up, there is evidence from the Glasgow recordings of differential use of the discourse marker *oh*. It is used more frequently by adults than by adolescents, by females more than males, and by middle-class speakers more than working-class speakers. The two groups with the highest use of *oh* are middle-class women and middle-class girls. These two groups also are most likely to use *oh* in expressing personal feelings.

The use of *well*

As with *oh*, the discourse feature *well* can be used in a number of functions.

Agreement

Well can be used as part of a signal of agreement, as in the examples in (8).

(8)

    a. (Conversation 15—Working-class women)
       15R: it's like your own house isn't it really I mean
       15L: *well* that's right

    b. (Conversation 11—Middle-class men)
       11R: because they'll be on full-time training and you know
       11L: *well* that's true

Responses

As Schiffrin (1987) has pointed out, *well* is quite often used in response to questions, particularly WH-questions. This is found in the Glasgow sessions, though sometimes the question is implied rather than explicitly stated.

(9)

    a. (Conversation 15—Working-class women)
       15R: how long have you been in there?
       15L: *well* I was pregnant when I moved in there
    b. (Conversation 10—Middle-class women)
       10R: so you'll have a fortnight all on your own?
       10L: mhm yes with Ian working and me working
       10R: and saying "Hi" as you pass each other
       10L: *well* we do that anyway Helen

Elaboration

Well is often used in the Glasgow recordings to amplify or elaborate an earlier statement.

(10)

    a. (Conversation 11—Middle-class man)
       11L: I—I made a mistake in cheques recently
             well sometime this—this year
    b. (Conversation 15—Working-class woman)
       15L: see if you went up to the next street and turned left
             well you would just go along until you get to roughly the first street
             well she would be right facing that on Raebury Street

Repair

Well is also used in self-repairs. I have restricted this category to those examples where there is a break in the intonation pattern, although some of the examples of elaboration (e.g., 10a) could also be considered repairs.

(11)

    a. (Conversation 11—Middle-class man)
       11R: one of the things I've noticed about em my—my—*well* my two
             daughters now was that when they started er secondary school
    b. (Conversation 17—Working-class man)
       17R: but I mean *well* when I—when I got married in 67 as I said

Quoted dialogue

As with *oh*, it is common to find *well* used at the beginning of quoted remarks, as in the examples in (12).

(12)
    a. (Conversation 15—Working-class woman)
      15L: so I decided "*Well* it's just junk food"
    b. (Conversation 10—Middle-class woman)
      10R: and I said "*Well* maybe it's in the fridge Elizabeth"

Topic switch

Occasionally, *well* is used when the speaker is changing the topic, usually to begin a narrative.

(13)
    a. (Conversation 10—Middle-class women)
      10L: I mean about size twelve in the little black dress you know
          and I thought grr
      10R: oh I know
          hate her I hate her
          well there's a girl at Bearsden Primary who's got seven children
    b. (Conversation 15—Working-class women)
      15R: I'm getting hungry
      15L: oh I know
          stomach
          well I was down in that—
          that's what I was going to tell you
          I was down in that em community centre

The distribution of the 497 tokens of *well*, for both adults and adolescents, is shown in figure 7.3. Most of the examples in quoted dialogue (84%) come from the sessions with the adult women. Since this is a reflection of the amount of quoted dialogue in the narratives and not all sessions have narratives, in order to compare groups of speakers on the other uses the figures have also been calculated without those for quoted dialogue. When this is done, the most interesting comparison is the gender differences between the adults, as shown in figure 7.4. The most interesting difference here is that the men use *well* for repair and elaboration (combined 64%) more than the women (combined 46%), whereas the women use *well* in agreement and response (combined 41%) more than the men (combined 26%). What this shows is that the men are twice as likely to use *well* within an utterance (i.e., a monologic function) as they are in response to an interlocutor (i.e., a dialogic function). The women do not show this bias to the same extent.

To sum up, the most frequent users of *well* are working-class men and middle-class girls. Other than by the middle-class girls, *well* is rarely used by the adoles-

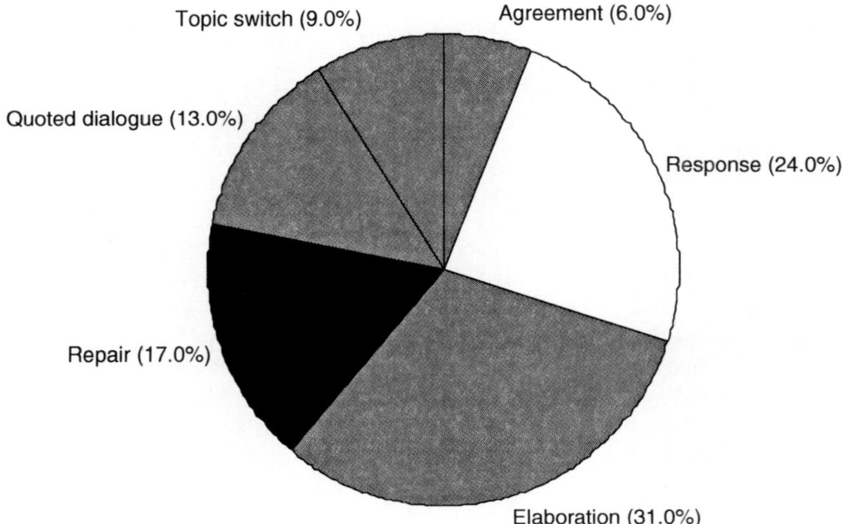

FIGURE 7.3. Uses of *well* in Glasgow

cents (freq. 1.29) compared with the adults (freq. 4.89).[1] Men are more likely to use *well* in self-repairs and for elaboration than as a response to another speaker. This is not the case with women.

The discourse feature *you know*

The one place where Bernstein (1971: 98 [1962]) gives numbers of tokens rather than simply reporting the results of statistical tests is with the features *I mean, I think,*

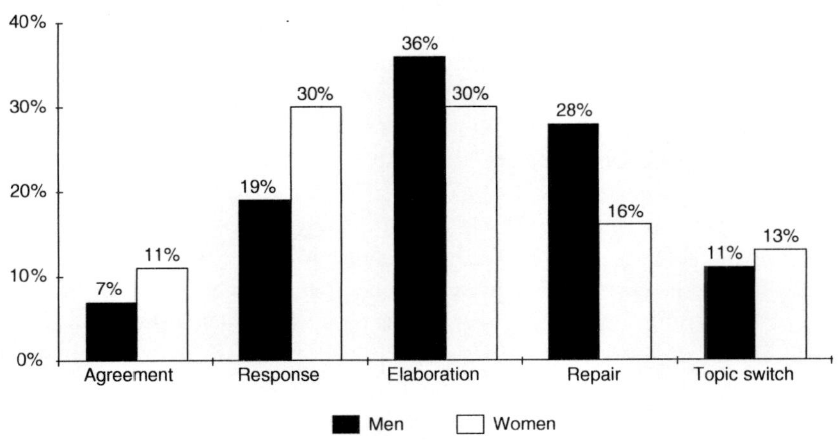

FIGURE 7.4. Uses of *well* by Glasgow adults

and what he calls "sympathetic circularity sequences" (1971: 97 [1962]). The latter
are "terminal sequences such as 'isn't it,' 'you know,' 'ain't it,' 'wouldn't he,' etc."
(1971: 96–97 [1962]). Bernstein attaches great importance to sympathetic circularity (S.C.) sequences because high frequency of their use is one of the important characteristics of a restricted code (earlier public language). Bernstein contrasts the use
of S.C. sequences with the use of "I think":

> The S.C. sequences, which are generated basically by uncertainty, invite implicit
> affirmation of the previous sequence then they tend to close communication in a
> particular area rather than facilitate its development and elaboration. The sequences
> tend to act to maintain the reduction in redundancy and so the condensation of mean-
> ing. The "I think" sequence, on the other hand, allows the listener far more degrees
> of freedom and may be regarded as an invitation to the listener to develop the com-
> munication on his own terms. The sequence facilitates the development and elabo-
> ration of the communication and so the logical development and exploration of a
> particular area. (1971: 114 [1962])

I may not be the only one to be unsure of exactly what Bernstein is saying here or
how he could possibly support it, but the message is clear: "I think" is good; S.C.
sequences are bad.

Bernstein reported the results of the analysis of his very small corpus of about
8,000 words and gave the figures of 8 S.C. sequences for the middle-class boys and
67 for the working-class boys. These convert to frequencies of 2.53 for the middle-
class boys and 14.14 for the working-class boys. Bernstein interpreted these results
as symptomatic of the "restricted code" used by the working-class boys:

> The meanings signaled in this code tend to be implicit and so condensed, with the
> result that there is less redundancy. A greater strain is placed upon the listener which
> is relieved by the range of identification which the speakers share. The S.C. se-
> quences may be transmitted as a response of the speaker to the condensation of his
> own meanings. The speaker requires assurance that the message has been received
> and the listener requires an opportunity to indicate the contrary. It is as if the speaker
> is saying "Check—are we together on this?" On the whole the speaker expects af-
> firmation. At the same time, by inviting agreement, the S.C. sequences test the range
> of identifications which the speakers have in common. (1962: 235/1971: 111)

This notion that S.C. sequences are "addressee-oriented" will be discussed later.

The S.C. sequence that will be examined in this chapter for comparison with
Bernstein's claims is *you know*, though unfortunately Bernstein does not give separate figures for its use. Another discourse feature in this chapter is the sequence *I
mean*, which Bernstein excluded from his general analysis because "it was considered a simple reinforcing unit of the previous or subsequent sequence and likely to
be an idiosyncratic speech habit" (Bernstein 1971: 98 [1962]). As we shall see later,
this is a reasonable summary of its function. The final discourse feature to be examined in this chapter is the use of *like*, but it does not feature in Bernstein's list.

Of Bernstein's S.C. markers, the one that has received the greatest amount of
attention is *you know*, in relation to both social class and gender. It is clear from various

references (e.g., O'Donnell and Todd 1980; Francis 1983; Schourup 1985; Huspek 1989; Watts 1989) that *you know* is both a stigmatized form and one associated, not surprisingly, with lower-class speech. It has also been claimed that women are more likely to use *you know* than men (e.g., Östman 1981; Fishman 1978, 1980), though this view has been challenged by Holmes (1986) and Stubbe and Holmes (1995). *You know* has also been studied from a functional perspective (Schiffrin 1987; Erman 1987, 1992, 2001; Fox Tree and Schrock 2002). The only study that examines age differences in the use of *you know* is Erman (2001), though she does not present her results in terms of frequency of occurrence.

The following section reports the results of the quantitative analysis of *you know* in the Ayr interviews and Glasgow conversations. Some of this material is covered in Macaulay 2002c and will be presented in more summary form here. First it is necessary to define the feature, as some investigators (e.g., Schiffrin 1987; Erman 2001), include examples of *you know* where the verb is in construction with other elements in the clause, as in the examples in (1).

The examples in (14) and (15) are from the Ayr interviews.

(14)

    a. well *you know* how we're di—we're different
    b. if *you know* somebody who's there *you know* if you're going to stay
    c. whether *you know* it or not
    d. *you know* Jim Sellars the M.P.
    e. not what *you know* who you knew

In all these cases, the construction *you know* forms part of the syntax of the clause and could not be omitted. In the examples in (15) this constraint does not hold.

(15)

    a. you didnae offer her money *you know*
    b. I could see *you know* the hunted look on his face
    c. than I would be if I was actually *you know* out
    d. than if I was *you know* working nine till three
    e. I maybe always *you know* didnae back the winner

The examples (15b–e) are the clearest illustrations of *you know* as a discourse feature, since, far from being part of the syntax of the clause, they actually separate constituents that are usually contiguous. There are, however, examples that are potentially ambiguous in that it would be possible to claim that there is a syntactic role for the construction. Identifying *you know* as a discourse feature in such examples is based on prosodic features because the sequence is generally uttered as a single unit with a falling intonation and often at a slightly lower pitch and volume than the surrounding speech. For the present analysis, occurrences of *you know* are treated as examples of discourse features if they are not crucially part of the syntax of the clause and/or they are marked prosodically as separate units. In practice, it is usually not difficult to identify *you know* in its role as a discourse feature.

TABLE 7.1. Frequency of *you know*
in Ayr and Glasgow (adults only)

	No.	[a]*Freq.*
Ayr interviews	261	2.16
Glasgow conversations	548	6.48

[a]per 1,000 words

Table 7.1 gives the total number of tokens in the two corpora. These figures suggest that *you know* is more likely to occur in conversations between peers who know each other than in interviews with a stranger, since the frequency is three times as high in Glasgow. There may be other reasons (see later text).

The Glasgow adults have a total of 548 instances, with a frequency of 6.48 per 1,000 words; the adolescents have 37 instances, with a frequency of 0.86, a difference that is highly significant ($p < .001$). Whatever it is that might lead to the use of *you know* in peer conversations of this kind does not seem to be well established in Glasgow at the age of fourteen. The frequency for the Glasgow adults is almost identical to that found by Holmes (1986: 13) for informal contexts, namely, 6.9 per 1,000 words (calculated from her table 3). Although Holmes's New Zealand corpus is much smaller (30,000), the similarity of frequency is interesting. In Stubbe and Holmes (1995: 71) the frequency for another New Zealand corpus of 75,000 words is only 3.78 per 1,000 words (calculated from their table 2).

Social class differences in the use of *you know*

The first extralinguistic variable to be examined here is social class. In the total sample the working-class speakers produced 493 tokens for a frequency of 3.49 per 1,000 words and the middle-class speakers 353 tokens for a frequency of 3.29.[2] This is clearly equivalent to no difference and is consistent in both the Ayr and Glasgow samples; it is hardly the kind of social class difference that Bernstein (1962) claims. Dines (1980: 16) reports that two unpublished Australian studies, Poole (1973) and (Brotherton 1976), found "a higher frequency of *you know* in lower-working-class speech" but does not give any more information. In New Zealand, Stubbe and Holmes (1995: 73) found *you know* to be significantly more frequent in working-class speech. In Ottawa, Woods (1991: 146–47) found "the use of phrases signaling Sympathetic Circularity" (*you know, eh,* [*isn't that*] *right,* and *don't you think*) to be more common in the interviews with working-class speakers, but he does not give separate figures for *you know*. Huspek (1989: 665) found *you know* to be frequent in the speech of the workers he interviewed, but since he reports the tokens only in relation to the number of sentences, it is impossible to calculate the frequencies per thousand words. Huspek did not interview middle-class speakers, so there are no comparative figures.

The Ayr and Glasgow figures showing no social class difference are therefore at odds with other studies of social class differences in the use of *you know*. In the case of Bernstein and Woods, we do not know the figures for *you know* by itself; thus there is no direct comparison. Moreover, Woods (1991: 146) reports "that the percentage of speakers who use signals of sympathetic circularity is high in all socioeconomic classes." Huspek's figures show that *you know* is used quite frequently by the workers, but without a middle-class comparison group, or even a frequency count, his results do not address the question of greater use by working-class speakers. The most important contrasting study is that by Stubbe and Holmes (1995), where the figures showing greater working-class use are strong and robust. Stubbe and Holmes (1991: 67) admit that in New Zealand research "social class divisions are fluid, and the concept must be used with caution," but this need not weaken the contrast with the Scottish results. However, until more extensive investigation has been made into social class differences in the use of *you know*, it might be safest to avoid any assumption that it is more common in working-class speech.

Gender differences in the use of *you know*

In Ayr and Glasgow, social class is much less of a determinant than age, gender, or recording situation. Table 7.2 gives the figures for the social class and gender differences. The females use *you know* with a frequency of 4.92 per 1,000 words and the males with a frequency of 2.41.[3] Since the adolescents are less frequent users, the gender difference is shown more clearly in the figures for the adults alone. The Glasgow women use *you know* with a frequency of 7.64 in contrast to the Glasgow men's frequency of 4.48, a difference that is marginally significant. This gender difference is consistent with results reported by Fishman (1978, 1980) and Östman (1981) but not with Holmes (1986) or with Stubbe and Holmes (1995). Holmes (1986: 13) found no differences in the use of *you know*, while Stubbe and Holmes (1991: 76) found that male working-class speakers used the phrase four times more frequently than the middle-class speakers. This, like the social class difference, is just the opposite from that found in Glasgow. However, there may be an additional factor. Holmes (1986: 14) and Erman (1994: 228) found a greater use of *you know* in same-sex interactions than in mixed-sex ones. The Glasgow sessions were all same-sex. In the nine conversations from the London-Lund Corpus[4] analyzed by Svartvik and Stenström (1985: 346), the frequency was 4.49, and not all of these were same-sex.

TABLE 7.2. Social class and gender differences in the use of *you know*

	Ayr		Glasgow	
	Freq.	*(No.)*	*Freq.*	*(No.)*
Middle-class women	4.11	(21)	8.07	(151)
Middle-class men	1.88	(86)	4.36	(68)
Working-class women	2.33	(41)	7.40	(245)
Working-class men	2.16	(113)	4.59	(79)
Middle-class girls	—	—	1.73	(18)
Middle-class boys	—	—	0.35	(4)
Working-class girls	—	—	0.66	(9)
Working-class boys	—	—	0.81	(6)

The transcribed portions of the London-Lund Corpus (Svartvik and Quirk 1980) are not easy to analyze in terms of individual speakers because the contribution of each speaker is not tabulated separately. Instead, Svartvik and Quirk present 5,000 word samples of 34 sessions, which may contain from one to six speakers. It is, however, possible to separate out the contributions of men and women, with an approximate estimate of the number of words contributed by each gender. There is a gender imbalance, with men providing approximately 107,500 words (63%) of the total (170,000) and women approximately 62,500 (37%). There are 10 sessions in which only men speak and 4 in which the speakers are women. The remainder are mixed-sex. The overall frequency of *you know* is 4.28,[5] but the men use *you know* with a frequency of 3.35, compared with a frequency of 5.87 for the women. This is a significant difference ($p < .05$).

A closer analysis of the 34 conversations of the London-Lund Corpus confirms the view that *you know* is more likely to occur in same-sex sessions. In the 20 mixed-sex sessions the frequency of *you know* is only 3.79, compared with 5.06 in same-sex sessions. However, the gender difference persists. In mixed-sex sessions the men use *you know* with a frequency of 3.14, compared with the women's frequency of 4.75. In the same-sex sessions the differences are even greater, with the men using *you know* with a frequency of 3.64 and the women using it with a frequency of 8.25. The London-Lund sessions thus support the notion that *you know* is used more frequently by women than by men.

Position of occurrence of *you know*

Erman (2001) analyzed two corpora to explore age differences in the use of *you know*. The adolescent sample was extracted from the Bergen Corpus of London Teenager Language (COLT),[6] and the adult sample from the London-Lund Corpus (LLC). She examined the position of *you know* in the speaking turn and found that "the LCC speakers use *you know* more often in the middle of a speaking turn as compared to the COLT speakers" (2001: 1349). The LCC speakers used *you know* 84.6% of the time in medial speaking-turn position, compared with the COLT speakers' 77%. In initial position the COLT speakers used *you know* with a frequency of 9.9%, compared with the LCC speakers' 5%, and in final position the proportion for the COLT speakers was 13.1%, compared with 10.4% for the LCC speakers. While this is reported as an age difference, there may also be a social class factor. The LCC speakers are all middle-class, but the COLT sample may include working-class speakers.

I did not examine the position of *you know* in relation to turn-taking but investigated its position in the clause. In Ayr I found that both social class groups favored final position in the clause, but the preference was stronger in the interviews with the lower-class speakers, while the middle-class speakers had a higher proportion of tokens in medial position. In Glasgow the middle-class speakers showed a definite preference for medial position in the clause. The figures for both corpora can be seen in figure 7.5.

Huspek (1989: 666) found that his workers used *you know* 43.3% of the time at the end of an utterance, 23.9% initially in an utterance, and the remainder in a variety of positions. In an examination of nine dialogues from the London-Lund Cor-

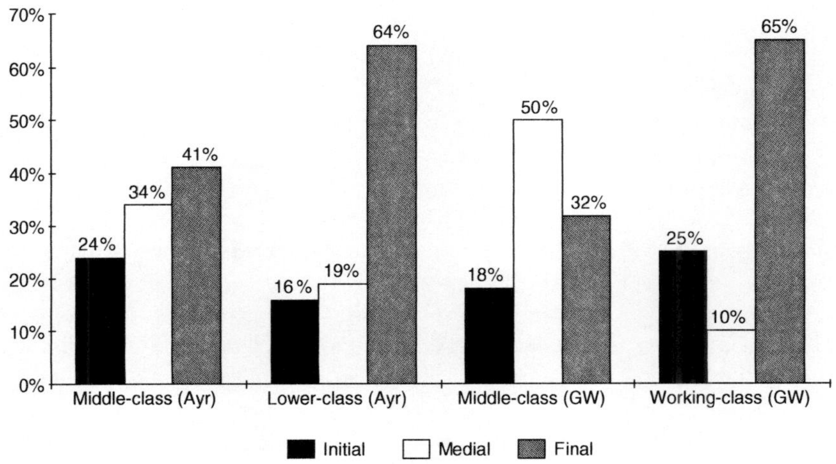

FIGURE 7.5. Position in clause of *you know* in Ayr and Glasgow (adults only)

pus, Stenström (1990b: 226) found that *you know* plus a pause occurred 68% of the time in the middle of a speaking turn (calculated from Stenström's table 8:6) and 64% of the time in the middle of a tone unit (calculated from Stenström's table 8:10, p. 230). It should be emphasized that Erman's, Huspek's, and Stenström's figures are not directly comparable with those in figure 7.5 because the units of measurement are different. Still, Erman's and Stenström's studies support the view that middle-class speakers show a preference for medial position, and Huspek's is consistent with the working-class preference for final position in both Ayr and Glasgow.

Function of *you know*

It has been common in analyzing the use of *you know* to place the emphasis on shared knowledge (e.g., Schiffrin 1987; Quirk et al. 1985; Crystal and Davy 1975; Holmes 1986) or on the effect on the addressee (e.g., Östman 1981; Crystal and Davy 1975; Schourup 1985). For example, Holmes states: "All instances of *you know* allude specifically to the relevant knowledge of the addressee in the context of utterance. This may be genuinely mutual knowledge or it may be knowledge which the speaker (for a variety of purposes) wishes to attribute to the addressee, regardless of her actual knowledge" (1986: 16). However, it is often the case that a speaker will use *you know* when the addressee does not know (and manifestly could not know) what the speaker is about to say or has already said (Östman 1981: 17; Fox Tree and Schrock 2002: 735). (See Macaulay 2002c: 756, for examples.)

It is possible that the insistence on the notion of shared knowledge results from a belief that the words *you* and *know* must retain something of their basic semantic value. The difficulty that this attitude causes for explaining the use of *you know* can be seen in the set of definitions given in the *Oxford Dictionary of Current Idiomatic English* (Cowie, Mackin, and McCaig 1983. 603–4):

(16)

    1. "you know or understand very well; you are a person I don't need to tell,
      explain, things to"
    2. "I am informing, or reminding, you"
    3. "I am giving you my opinion, or advice"
    4. "I am correcting, or contradicting, you"

The incompatibility of informing or correcting someone who knows or understands very well and does not need explanations suggests that these meanings are not signaled by *you know* but by the accompanying discourse. The more obvious interpretation is that *you know* itself is transparent and takes its significance from the context in which it is used. However, it is also common to find suggestions that *you know* is a multifunctional feature. Holmes, for example, argues that *you know* is "a complex and sophisticated pragmatic particle" and that it may act "as a turn-yielding device, as a linguistic imprecision signal, as an appeal to the listener for reassuring feedback, or as a signal that the speaker attributes understanding to the listener" (1990: 189). Erman (2001: 1341) provides a functional analysis of *you know*, distinguishing three categories: textual monitors, social monitors, and metalinguistic monitors. Since in the latter two categories Erman includes examples where *you know* is in syntactic construction with other elements in the utterance, it is only the textual function that is relevant to the analysis here. Of the latter, Erman remarks: "Discourse markers functioning at the textual level are not primarily concerned with the addressee's decoding of the message, but rather with the organization of the discourse" (1343). In other words, Erman found that *you know* in this function is not primarily addressee-oriented.

    Nor is initial *you know* used in the Ayr interviews or Glasgow conversations to claim the floor by introducing a new topic (Fishman 1978, 1980). This may be because the dynamics of turn-taking are different in the interviews and same-sex dyads from those in multiparty conversations. In final position *you know* occurs at what Sacks et al. 1974 call a "transition relevance place," since it usually marks the end of a syntactic unit, but generally in the Ayr interviews and Glasgow conversations the listener does not take advantage of this opportunity to take over the floor, except to contribute feedback in the form of a minimal response such as *uhuh* or *mhm*. This is not surprising, since *you know* usually does not signal a desire or intention to yield the floor. (See examples in Macaulay 2002c: 757.) Oreström (1983: 67), in an examination of material from the London-Lund Corpus, found that for *you know* and *you see* "their turn-yielding force is relatively weak."

    The most interesting uses of *you know* are those that occur medially, that is, potentially within a constituent. It is necessary to include the notion of potential constituents because one of the uses of *you know*, particularly in the middle-class interviews and conversations, is before self-repairs, as in (17).

(17)

    a. and yet it's a shame
      because they—*you know* they do need they need a holiday but
    b. I mean I'm—*you know* a—I—I having gone through it earlier em with Mum
      and Dad

    c. certainly one for the formal situation and one f—*you know* for the more sort of
       relaxed situation

    d. er but em you know Christine was a—*you know* was a good player really

    e. and even then you wouldn't se—*you know* you wouldn't er compare him with
       the—the current back-row forwards

This use of *you know* is what would be described by Brown (1977: 107) as a "verbal filler" and by Edmondson (1981: 153) as a "fumble" in that it allows the speaker time to find the desired expression. Edmondson's term is appropriate here because it suggests that the use of an expression such as *you know* is the result of hesitation or word search. However, this use of *you know* is not the most common and is less frequent in the working-class samples. In Huspek's data only 7.8% of the examples of *you know* are of this kind (Huspek 1989: 666). Schourup points out that these repairs are often "clause internal 'restarts'" (1985: 137).

    In the middle-class Glasgow conversations, *you know* is often used with hedges such as *sort of* and *kind of* as in (18).

(18)
    a. I think that's the sort of feeling that the feeling of guilt that you have *you know*
       when you're—*you know* you—you kind of chuck your children round

    b. and she's a very *you know* neat em kind of gentle person

    c. so there'll be a kind of *you know* they'll avoid em Hilary em

    d. it took me a while to *you know* sort of master it you know

    e. and—and you—you just—*you know* you sort of semi-scramble down to the bay

However, not all medial uses of *you know* are in connection with repairs or hedges. *You know* is often used when the speaker apparently wishes to highlight a constituent or to signal that the expression is not one the speaker would normally use.[7] Some examples are given in (19).

(19)
    a. I'm sometimes actually ending up doing more out and about
       than I would be if I was actually *you know* out

    b. and they demand things
       and they *you know* stomp out

    c. whether they're *you know* into boys or into make-up or into pop or into what
       or whatever

    d. cos they'd cut through some of these *you know* undulating fields

In (19a) the speaker has been talking about just being a housewife and not "out" at work, so *out* here is shorthand for "having a job." In (19b) the speaker uses *stomp out* as a kind of condensed reference to the attitude and behavior of teenagers. In (19c) the speaker is signaling that she would not normally talk about "being into" things but that is appropriate when talking about teenagers. In (19d) the speaker is almost apologizing for using such an unusual word as *undulating*. All these examples come from middle-class speakers.

In other cases, such as those in (20), the speaker is elaborating a preceding item.

(20)
    a. It's just horrendous *you know* absolute madness
    b. there's a lot of pressure *you know* power stuff in the pack
    c. I wondered actually if what we're seeing over the last couple of weeks is end of term *you know* celebrating end of term
    d. because you—you met everybody *you know* all varieties of people
    e. I mean it was all the old-fashioned stuff *you know* the—*you know* the Brown system

Again, these examples all come from the middle-class conversations.

In contrast to these examples of medial use by middle-class speakers in Glasgow, the working-class speakers are more likely to use *you know* in final position, as in (21).

(21)   (Conversation 18—Working-class men)
    L: and all the women would go "Oh we got a murder" *you know*
    R: aye aye
    L: and they—they eh em they'd buy the paper *you know*
    R: aye aye aye
    L: oh it was amazing
        nowadays it's eh *you know*
    R: it's commonplace
    L: murder it's commonplace *you know*
    R: aye aye
    L: you get a snippet of it on the back page of the Evening Times or something like that *you know*

You know in this usage is somewhat similar to the use of terminal tags by some of the working-class speakers in Ayr (Macaulay 1985, 1991b).

You know as a desematicized discourse feature

There does not appear to be any strong evidence that either *you* or *know* retains its basic meaning and function. Edmondson defines "fumbles" as "standardized or fixed formulae, for which reference to the semantic content of the uttered expression seems unhelpful" (1981: 153), and this is a good description of *you know*. Eble (2000) (following Wales (1996: 78–82) comments on the increase in the use of "indefinite *you*" as a general agent, distinct from its use as a second-person addressee form. She cites examples such as those in (22) (emphasis added).

(22)
    1. "It's scary how Hollywood treats *you* like this completely different person when *you*'re thin." (Jennifer Anniston, *McCall's*, June 2000)

2. "*You* dream about it. *You* fantasize about it," [Matt] Doherty said of coaching the Tar Heels. ([Raleigh] *News and Observer*, 12 July 2000)
3. "*You*'ve got three million Palestinian refugees." (Martha Raddatz, *Washington Week in Review*, 21 July 2000)

It is likely that *you* in *you know* is an indefinite pronoun like the examples in (22) more often than it is a reference to the addressee as an individual. If *you* in *you know* has lost its second-person deictic reference, then there is no reason to interpret it as addressee-oriented.

The element *know* also seems to have weakened. There are examples showing little sense of conflict in the use of *you know* in close proximity to the verb *know* in its basic sense, suggesting that its meaning has been at least partly bleached out (see later text). Vincent and Sankoff (1992) examine a set of discourse markers that they call "punctors" in 12 interviews sampled from the Sankoff-Cedergren corpus (Sankoff and Sankoff 1973) of French speakers in Montreal. Among the 10 punctors are the forms *tu sais* and *vous savez*, which correspond to *you know*. Vincent and Sankoff comment that "punctors have lost all or most of their original meaning or function; we can say that they are to a large extent desemanticized" (1992: 206). The same seems to be the case with *you know* in the Ayr and Glasgow materials.

Even-Zohar (1982: 180) identifies a class of desemanticized or "void" features. There is a good case to be made that *you know* has become desemanticized much in the same way as *lets*, for example (Hopper and Traugott 1993), or certain uses of *like* (Romaine and Lange 1991), in which most of the basic meaning has been bleached out. Some examples where *you know* occurs in close proximity to the verb *know* (shown in bold) in its basic function, are given in (23).

(23)

    a. Do you **know** *you know*
       that's what I would have had with me
    b. sort of *you know* not **knowing** what an A.G.M. would be like at a golf-course
    c. but *you know* I think that's the sort of thing that maybe you do when you're
       eighteen *you know* er I don't **know**
    d. *you know* you **knew** at some point
    e. Tim would **know** *you know* (LLC 1.4.92)

Such examples do not prove that the basic meaning has been bleached out of *you know*, but they suggest that the speakers are not anxious about the conflict of homonyms, and there is never any reference to the proximity of the two different uses. It is as if the speaker was unaware of their similarity.

In the Scottish materials *you know* appears to be a feature of the speaker's presentation. This can be seen most clearly in the use of *you know* in final position. As was shown in figure 7.5, two-thirds of the working-class examples in both Ayr and Glasgow are in final position. However, one function is to provide a form of rhythmic pattern in a fluent narrative, or to act as a kind of oral punctuation marker, what

Jefferson has called "an utterance lengthener" (1973: 69). Far from indicating hesitancy, it can be used quite effectively by fluent speakers. It is unfortunate that Edmondson's term *fumbles* should be cited so often. A much more appropriate term would be his alternative reference to "discourse lubricants" Edmondson (1981: 168), since *you know* usually occurs in very fluent utterances.

If the use of *you know* is not to get "the addressee to cooperate and/or to accept the propositional content of his utterance as mutual background knowledge" (Östman 1981: 17), "to allude specifically to the relevant knowledge of the addressee in the context of utterance" (Holmes 1986: 16), to check "Are we together on this?" (Bernstein 1962: 235/1971: 111), or to show a presumption about "some shared ground between the private world and other worlds with respect to what is in the shared world" (Schourup 1985: 109), what is it that motivates the speaker to use it? If the answer is not to lie in the meaning of *you know*, the answer must lie in its contribution to production of the communicative act.[8] Before considering this question further, it may be worth looking at a similar discourse marker *I mean*.

The discourse feature *I mean*

The discourse feature *I mean* shares with the discourse feature *you know* the characteristic that it is homonymous with a form that is not used as a discourse feature, as in the example in (24).

(24)

>   18R: *I mean*—in the times—in your times it was the American pop groups
>   like coming over and eh eh *you know what I mean* and—and it was like
>   Gene Vincent, Chuck Berry and all that

The first example of *I mean* is the discourse feature in which the verb is not in construction with any other constituent. The second example occurs in the construction *you know what I mean*, where *what* is the direct object of *I mean* and *what I mean* is the complement of *you know*. Neither *I mean* nor *you know* is a discourse feature in this latter example. As with *you know*, only examples of *I mean* where the verb is not in construction with another constituent are counted as examples of the discourse feature.

Bernstein (1971: 98 [1962]) gives figures showing that the middle-class boys used *I mean* with a frequency of 4.56 per 1,000 words, compared with a frequency of 8.23 by the working-class boys (calculated from his table 4). However, he excluded this form from the analysis because two-thirds of the working-class examples were contributed by one boy, and another boy was responsible for a fifth. Bernstein commented that this form was "likely to be an idiosyncratic speech habit" (1971: 98).

In the Ayr interviews *I mean* is also much more frequent in the lower-class interviews (3.9 per 1,000 words) than in the middle-class interviews (1.57), while in the Glasgow conversations *I mean* is more frequently used by the middle-class speakers, both adults and adolescents. The gender differences in Glasgow are shown in figure 7.6. The figure shows that in Glasgow it is the middle-class women and girls

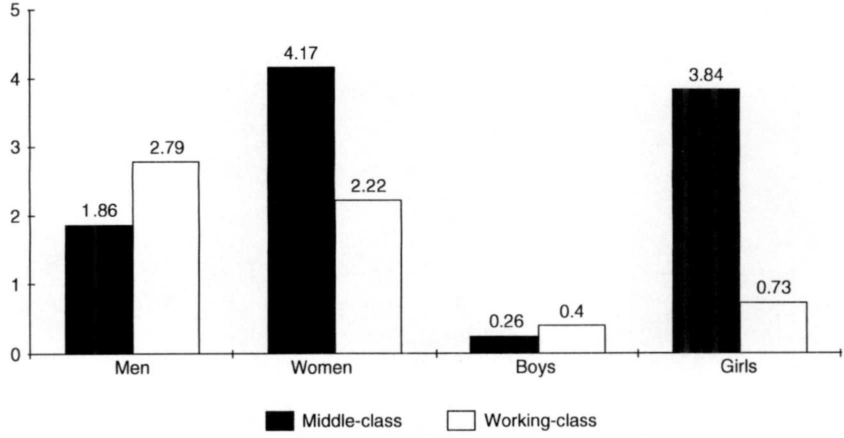

FIGURE 7.6. Frequency of *I mean* in Glasgow (frequency per 1,000 words)

who use *I mean* most frequently, but the only significant difference is that the adults use *I mean* almost twice as frequently as the adolescents ($p < .01$).

In the 34 conversations of the London-Lund Corpus transcribed by Svartvik and Quirk (1980), on the other hand, it is the men who use *I mean* with the higher frequency (3.55 versus 2.16). This difference occurs in both the mixed-sex sessions, where the men use *I mean* with a frequency of 4.18 and the women 2.47, whereas in the all-male sessions the frequency is 2.69 and in the all-female sessions it is only 1.50. In one mixed-sex session two men use *I mean* with a frequency of 14.0, and in one all-male session two men use *I mean* with a frequency of 13.0. The highest frequency by a woman (6.33) occurs in a mixed-sex session.

It is possible to distinguish certain contexts in which *I mean* occurs in the Glasgow conversations. It might be expected that *I mean* would be used most often when the speaker is correcting an error, as in (25).

(25)   (Middle-class man)
    11L: now we—Alison and I have the last couple of days
           last couple of days—*I mean* years
           have gone off on our own

In (25) the speaker realizes that he has said "days" instead of "years" and corrects himself, but this is one of only two examples in the whole Glasgow corpus. However, there is a use of *I mean* that comes close to this.

Elaboration

Sometimes a speaker will expand on something he or she has said, as in the examples in (26).

(26)

    a. 16L: now the other place the temperature that—that is really cold is Capetown
            I mean Capetown is colder than the Clyde

    b. 13L: pure greed
             I mean that's all it is
             it's pure and utter greed

In (26a) and (26b) the speakers are not paraphrasing the *meaning* of what they have just said but making it more emphatic in (26a) by giving a comparison and in (26b) by expanding what she has just said.[9] In neither case can the words *I mean* be interpreted literally, as they can in examples such as (25).

Explanation

Sometimes the elaboration bears little or no direct verbal connection to the previous utterance but constitutes an explanation for something said earlier.

(27)

    a. 10R: [these curtains] go from the ceiling to the floor
             and they've got this big pelmet and things and
             they're they're they're huge
             I mean there's a big bay window

    b. 13L: I'm terrible
             I mean I go to the Co
             I'm walking roond the Co
             and I'm going "What did I come up for?"

In (27a) the speaker is explaining why the curtains are so huge, and in (27b) the speaker is explaining why she is "terrible" (she forgets what she has gone to the store to buy). In neither case can the phrase *I mean* be applied literally to what has just been said.

Adversative

The conjunction *but* is generally used when opposing or contradicting something that has been said. It is therefore odd that it should occur immediately before *I mean*, as in the examples in (28).

(28)

    a. 11L: I don't know ho—when he's developed
             but *I mean* he strikes me as being a guy I wouldn't like to have to try and stop

    b. 15L: she says "Oh, I'll no eat anything tonight"
             but *I mean* she's kidding herself on you know

In this use and in the one examined next it seems as if *I mean* only has a forward-looking significance.

New information

Sometimes *I mean* is used to introduce new information or even to begin a new topic. In these cases there is no sense that *I mean* is referring back to the wording of something that has just been uttered.

(29)

    a. 18R: well as you know eh urban decay
                 I mean you can get right into that politically
                 but at the end of the day *I mean* you walk up Maryhill Road
                 you can see it in—in Maryhill
    b. 11L: as I should do
          11R: *I mean* the friend I'm meeting at half-past one er is in the Labour Party

Examples of this kind are the furthest from any literal meaning of the verb *mean*. In examples (29a) and (29b) the use of *I mean* is totally redundant. It does not in any sense refer to what has been said earlier either as explanation or elaboration.

Repair

Finally, *I mean* may occur, like other discourse markers, at places of prosodic rupture where the normal flow of speech is broken and the intonation interrupted.

(30)

    a. 11L: and I've got—*I mean* I've got no hang-ups about people who speak broad
                 Glaswegian
    b. 13L: well this is like their—*I mean* Mary's left school now
                 so sh-that's another adult and then

The distribution of uses of *I mean* is shown in figure 7.7, which indicates that the most common use of *I mean* in the Glasgow data is to introduce new information and the second most common is to add an explanation. The gender and social class differences are shown in figure 7.8. This figure indicates that in Glasgow the middle-class women differ from the other groups in their use of *I mean*. The most frequent use among the middle-class women is for explanation (45%), whereas for the others it is new information. It has to be remembered that the middle-class women are the most frequent users of *I mean*, so this difference may indicate an important aspect of middle-class women's speech.

Like *you know*, *I mean* seems to have lost most of its precise semantic value and become a "filler" that has a function in the production of the utterance but not in its content. The phrases *you know*, *I mean*, *you see*, and *of course* have an iambic structure, so it is perhaps not surprising that all four should occur frequently as discourse markers, since the iambic foot is such a common part of English rhythm. In the Ayr interviews 66.85% of the medial and final occurrences of *you know* come after stressed syllables, suggesting that rhythm plays a role in its occurrence, and Gumperz (1982: 167) points out the importance of "conversational rhythm" in

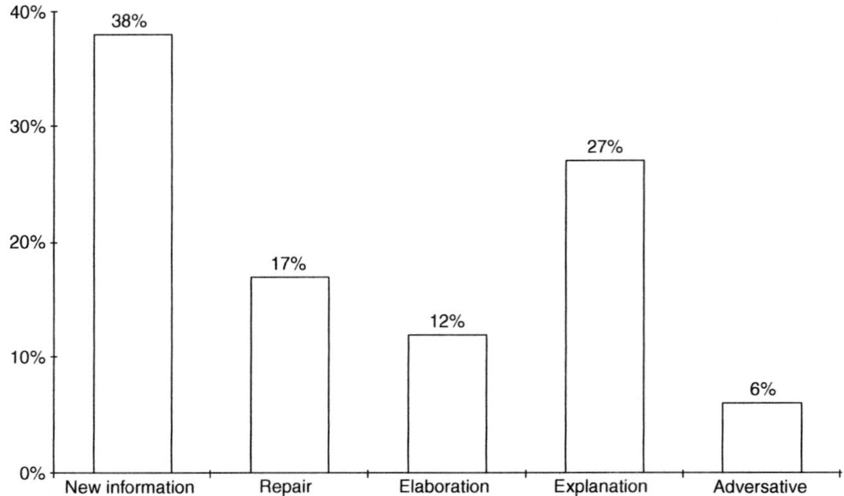

FIGURE 7.7. Use of *I mean* by Glasgow adults

establishing speaker-listener coordination. *You know* also has a simple CVCV structure with two sonorant consonants and two vowels that are high in sonority. In this it contrasts with its obvious competitor *you see* with its fricative /s/ and high front vowel. Erman (1992: 228) found *you see* to be less frequent than *you know*, and in Ayr the middle-class speakers (with one exception) show a preference for *you know* (Macaulay 1991b: 144). (There are very few examples of *you see* in the Glasgow conversations.)

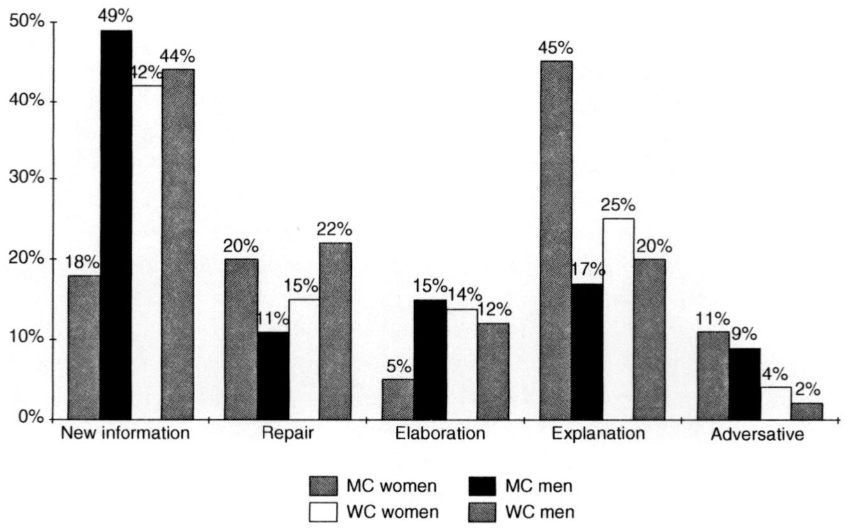

FIGURE 7.8. Gender and social class differences in the use of *I mean* in Glasgow (adults only)

Support for the view that *you know* is employed by speakers as an aid to speech production comes from the 34 sessions on the London-Lund Corpus. If *you know* were primarily addressee-oriented, one would expect it to be common in those sessions where the interaction consists of frequent changes of speaker with relatively short turns, as in (31). (I have simplified the transcription.)

(31)
    1. B: are you in touch with the St. Bee's crowd?
         A: well *you know* to a certain extent (Svartvik and Quirk 1980: 221)
    2. B: I don't suppose you need Old English and Anglo-Saxon
         A: well no but em *you know* I don't have any languages
         B: em well I hadn't done any English at all *you know* since O-level (Svartvik and Quirk 1980: 127)

However, it turns out that exchanges of this kind are exceedingly rare in the London-Lund Corpus. In the 15 sessions with more than 15 tokens of *you know*, only 42 examples of *you know* (7.8%) occur in turns consisting of fewer than 6 tone groups. The overwhelming majority (92.2%) occur in longer turns, many of them containing more than 30 tone groups. Even a casual scrutiny of the transcripts will reveal this pattern. It is reasonable to assume that longer turns require more complex processing and that the use of *you know* makes this easier.

Wennerstrom points out that midturn pauses are less likely to occur at points of possible syntactic completion: "Midturn pauses commonly occurred at points where neither a syntactic boundary nor a pitch boundary was present. It is 'safer' to pause in midphrase rather than at a phrase boundary if one wishes to avoid interruption" (2001: 173). The use of *you know* at phrase boundaries may be one way certain speakers, but not all, avoid pauses that might allow interruption.

There is considerable individual variation in the frequency with which the adult speakers use *you know* and *I mean* in both corpora. The range is shown in tables 7.3–6.

There are a number of observations to be made about the figures in tables 7.3 and 7.4. The first is that there is a wide range in the frequency with which speakers use *you know*, from zero to more than 15 instances per 1,000 words. The second point

TABLE 7.3. Range of frequency of *you know* by social class and gender in Ayr

		Lower-class				Middle-class	
		No.	*Freq.*			*No.*	*Freq.*
WR	(m)	2	0.39	DN	(m)	12	0.79
HG	(m)	4	0.41	WG	(m)	7	0.82
EL	(f)	11	0.83	JM	(m)	7	0.91
AS	(m)	48	2.27	AM	(m)	27	2.77
WL	(m)	59	3.63	NM	(f)	21	4.11
MR	(f)	30	6.86	IM	(m)	33	7.22
All		154	2.21	All	107		2.1

TABLE 7.4. Range of frequency of *you know* by social class and gender in Glasgow

		Working-class				Middle-class	
		No.	*Freq.*			*No.*	*Freq.*
17R	(m)	1	0.16	16R	(m)	0	0.0
17L	(m)	1	0.53	10L	(f)	8	1.75
14L	(f)	5	1.16	11L	(m)	13	2.5
13L	(f)	14	3.41	16L	(m)	18	3.84
18R	(m)	21	4.77	12L	(f)	18	4.1
14R	(f)	53	6.74	10R	(f)	93	12.8
13R	(f)	47	9.1	12R	(f)	32	12.84
15R	(f)	45	10.45	11R	(m)	42	15.67
15L	(f)	81	10.99				
18L	(m)	56	12.09				
All		324	6.44	All		224	6.53

is that this variation is not constrained by either social class or gender. Contrary to the general pattern, the most frequent users of *you know* in each social class are men.[10] The third point is that with the exception of two of the Glasgow conversations (17 and 15), the use of *you know* is not equally frequent by the two speakers. Usually one speaker uses this form much more often than the other. Note also that while generally the women use *you know* more frequently, for three of the groups the speaker with the highest frequency is a man. This is a warning not to generalize too quickly from group scores to predictions about individuals, particularly where gender is involved. Finally, one speaker was recorded in two sessions. The speakers identified as 13R and 14R are the same woman. The similarity in the frequency with which she uses *you know* (9.1 versus 6.74) with different interlocutors (her two scores are ranked consecutively in the order of frequency in table 7.4) suggests that this may be a consistent feature of her speech in such situations.

A somewhat similar picture appears for *I mean* in tables 7.5 and 7.6. Again there is great individual variation, from zero use in both corpora to 8.74 per 1,000 words

TABLE 7.5. Frequency of *I mean* by social class and gender in Ayr

		Lower-class				Middle-class	
		No.	*Freq.*			*No.*	*Freq.*
HG	(m)	0	0.0	DN	(m)	3	0.20
WR	(m)	4	0.80	JM	(m)	2	0.26
MR	(f)	9	2.06	WG	(m)	4	0.47
WL	(m)	34	2.09	AM	(m)	8	0.82
EL	(f)	40	3.03	NM	(f)	11	2.15
AS	(m)	185	8.74	IM	(m)	14	3.06
All		272	3.90			42	0.83

TABLE 7.6. Frequency of *I mean* by social class and gender in Glasgow

		Working-class				Middle-class	
		No.	*Freq.*			*No.*	*Freq.*
17L	(m)	0	0.0	12L	(f)	3	0.69
17R	(m)	0	0.0	16R	(m)	4	0.99
13R	(f)	1	0.19	12R	(f)	5	2.01
14L	(f)	2	0.46	10L	(f)	13	2.84
14R	(f)	5	0.64	16L	(m)	17	3.63
18R	(m)	16	3.63	11L	(m)	19	3.66
15L	(f)	29	3.93	10R	(f)	33	4.54
15R	(f)	19	4.41	11R	(m)	13	4.85
13L	(f)	26	6.33				
18L	(m)	32	6.91				
All		123	2.44			107	3.12

in the Ayr interviews and 6.91 per 1,000 words in the Glasgow conversations. Again there is a range of variation in both social classes. As with *you know*, although the women in Glasgow on average use *I mean* more frequently than the men, the speakers with the highest frequency in each social class are men. Once again the speaker indicated by 13R and 14R shows similar use of *I mean* in her two recordings. Even-Zohar observes that while the need for "void" particles (i.e., discourse lubricants) is universal, "certain individuals use them, even within the conventions of their particular culture, more intensely than others" (1982: 191). This is clearly demonstrated in the Ayr and Glasgow materials.

Like as an adolescent discourse feature

As we have seen, the Glasgow adolescents make significantly less use of the discourse lubricants *you know* and *I mean* than do the adults. There is, however, one feature used more by the adolescents that serves a similar function, namely, the word *like*. This item has been the focus of intensive study in recent years (Schourup 1985; Underhill 1988; Blyth, Recktenwald, and Wang 1990; Romaine and Lange 1991; Ferrara and Bell 1995; Miller and Weinert 1995; Andersen 1997, 1998, 2000; Jucker and Smith 1998; Tagliamonte and Hudson 1999; Dailey-O'Cain 2000; Macaulay 2001b). There also have been studies of similar items in other languages (e.g., Golato 2000; Maschler 2002; Fleischman and Yaguello, forthcoming). Many of these studies have made a point of trying to counter the negative image of this item. As a result, perhaps there has been a corresponding danger of exaggerating its value.

Like is a more difficult item to identify as a discourse feature than *you know* or *I mean* because it has so many uses—as a verb, as an adjective, and as a preposition—in addition to its recent nontraditional use by younger speakers. By nontraditional are meant uses such as those illustrated in (32).

(32)

    a. I *like* get three pounds a week (2R)

    b. why do people pure get *like* these professional photos and all this? (2L)

    c. I think someone *like* reported him (3R)

    d. I had *like* ten barracks in each (4R)

These examples come from the adolescent conversations, but there are some comparable examples in the adult conversations. The adolescents also use *like* as an introduction to quoted dialogue or sometimes to indicate unexpressed thoughts, as in the examples in (33).

(33)

    a. And I'*m like* "No that's sick"

    b. And I'*m like* "Woops"

    c. she'*s like* "Is your sister going out with a guy called Paul?"

    d. her ma'*s like* "Go on make me a coffee"

It is clear that in (33c) and (33d) the speaker is ostensibly reporting an example of speech (though there is no guarantee that these were the exact words used). In (33a) and (33b) the speaker may simply be reporting her reaction, which may or may not have been overtly expressed. It is not always easy to distinguish between these two uses.

There is a total of 301 examples of nontraditional *like* in the Glasgow adolescent conversations, a frequency of 7.0 per 1,000 words. Of these, 29% are examples of *be like*, as in (33). There is, however, a major social class difference in the use of *like*. The middle-class adolescents use nontraditional *like* with a frequency of 11.7 per 1,000 words, compared with a frequency of 2.1 in the working-class conversations. Even these figures are distorted by gender as there are no examples of nontraditional *like* in the conversations between working-class boys. The frequencies for the four groups are given in figure 7.9. The first column in figure 7.9 shows the frequency for all forms of nontraditional *like* in the adolescent conversations. The social class difference, with the middle-class adolescents using *like* more than five times as often as the working-class adolescents, is consistent with that found by Andersen (1997) in *The Bergen Corpus of London Teenage Language* (COLT), a 500,000-word corpus recorded in 1993. It is an unusual situation where forms that have been considered "nonstandard" are found to be more frequent among the middle-class speakers and suggests that *like* is an unusual type of discourse feature.

After *be like*, the most frequent use of *like* is before a noun phrase (24% of the tokens). One of the contexts in which *like* occurs before a noun phrase is shown in (34).

(34)

    a. I spent *like* twelve pounds trying to win a fish (2LR)

    b. when I was young I was *like* (0.2) six or something (2L)

    c. it's just *like* two minutes away from my dad's house (3L)

    d. he'd only a couple of thousand and I had *like* six hundred thousand (4R)

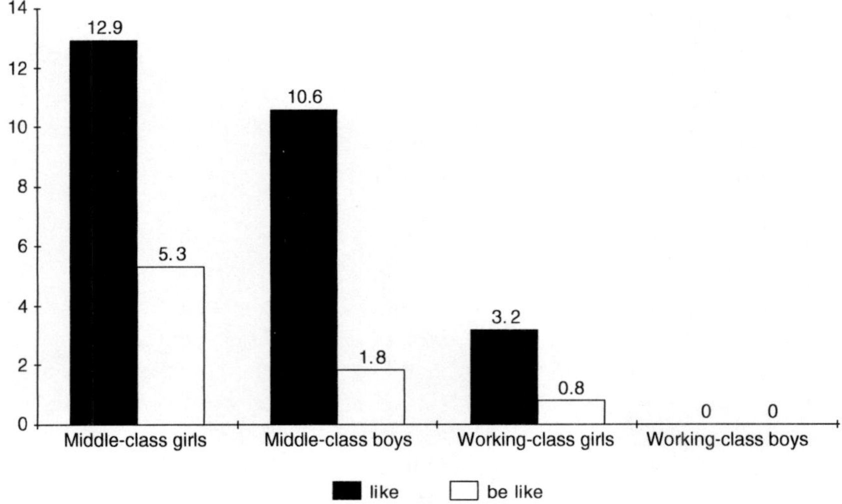

FIGURE 7.9. Frequency of *like* by Glasgow adolescents (frequency per 1,000 words)

In the examples in (34), *like* could be interpreted as signaling "approximately," and this sense is reinforced in (34b) by the terminal tag *or something*. However, only a third of the examples before noun phrases could possibly be interpreted in this way, and it is usually not clear whether the speaker intends to communicate any notion of approximation. The problem of interpretation can be seen more clearly in other examples of the use of *like* before noun phrases, as illustrated in (35).

(35)

    a. he's got *like* dead dark hair and all that (2R)
    b. and there was *like* a big Alsatian (2L)
    c. I thought it was going to be *like* a tape-recorder just sort of sitting on the desk (3R)
    d. the sixth one's *like* a water level (4R)

In the examples in (35) the speakers are making specific references to dark hair, to an Alsatian, to a tape recorder, and to a water level. They are not talking about things that are similar to these items, though that would be a more plausible interpretation if the speakers were adults who do not use *like* the way the adolescents do. There are also some examples where no notion of approximation or similarity could be intended, as illustrated in (36).

(36)

    a. he's at *like* University in Dundee (2L)
    b. her dad was *like* the referee for the football game (2L)
    c. why do people pure get *like* these professional photos and all this? (2L)
    d. The girls don't get *like* the gloves (3R)

The next most frequent use of *like* is before a clause (22% of the tokens), as illustrated in (37).

(37)
    a. and *like* the guy pure filmed him (3R)
    b. *like* I went to Steve's football game right (5L)
    c. and *like* he was pure talking about it (7R)
    d. *like* he was my best pal (7L)

This is the most common use of *like* by the working-class girls, as 45% of the tokens in their conversations are of this kind. Among the middle-class adolescents only 21% of the tokens are of this kind. Although clause-final *like* used to be common in Scottish speech (Miller and Weinert (1995) and occurs in the working-class adult conversations, there were only seven possible examples in the adolescent conversations. There were also few examples that could be considered cases of self-repair. This is consistent with Miller and Weinert's finding that *like* "is not typically associated with the hesitations, false starts and pauses that do signal organizational/processing problems" (1995: 372).

The working-class adults, mainly the women, also use *like* but much less frequently than the adolescents, 1.5 per 1,000 words. However, 15% of the examples are in final position, as shown in (38).

(38)
    a. so that she didnae need to use the phone *like* (14R)
    b. will she no even tell him off *like* (14L)
    c. at night-time it must cost them a packet you know *like* (13R)
    d. then we'd walk doon to the main street you know *like* (13R)

Examples (38c) and (38d) show how *like* can occur with *you know*. This happens in 16% of the cases in the working-class adult conversations, usually in final position. With one exception, the order is *you know* followed by *like*.

Gisle Andersen suggests that "*like* provides speakers whose dialect includes this linguistic resource with a means to dissociate themselves slightly from the expressions contained in the utterance" (2000: 17). However, he also somewhat paradoxically argues that *like* can both signal "the need for loosening or enrichment of concepts encoded by the material in its scope" (17–18). His motivation is partly to reject the view that *like* is "a mere filler or hesitation device" (19). This aim is consistent with the common belief that such fillers deserve to be viewed negatively. However, if *like* is seen like *you know* and *I mean* as a "discourse lubricant," then this negative characterization should not be implied.

The kind of difficulty Andersen runs into with trying to make a case for the positive value of *like* can be seen in his comment that "*like* usually precedes lexical material with a high information value" (2000: 31). However, it has been shown that hesitation phenomena tend to occur at points of high information value (Goldman Eisler 1968: 41) so that this observation does not support Andersen's view that *like* is not "a mere filler." Andersen goes on to suggest: "*Like* has a capacity to suggest the lack of full internalisation of expressions in the linguistic repertoire, and it is not unlikely that the reason why *like* is so frequent in teenage conversation is precisely its metalinguistic function" (2000: 31). There is little evidence to support this view in the Glasgow conversations. *Like* is used with a variety of common expressions that are fully integrated into the linguistic repertoire of the speakers. So it is unlikely that Andersen's suggestion will account for the frequency of nontraditional *like* in the adolescent conversations.

There remains the problem of why this feature should be much more common in the middle-class adolescent conversations, both male and female, but not in the middle-class adult conversations. On the one hand, it is tempting to see this as an influence from Hollywood films, such as *Valley Girl* and *Clueless*, or some other media influence from the United States. On the other hand, the working-class use of *like* is presumably a traditional one, particularly in final position.

Conclusion

Like *oh* and *well*, *you know* and *I mean* occur very frequently in the adult conversations, and *like* occurs fairly frequently in the adolescent conversations. These findings are consistent with Östman's characterization of impromptu speech and together with the data presented in the previous chapter can be taken as validation for the use of the conversations as legitimate specimens for analysis. In subsequent chapters no effort will be made to establish this point.

As discourse features, neither *you know* nor *I mean* seems to retain much of the basic semantic value of the verbs, nor does *like* retain much sense of similarity. The use of *you know* does not appear to be based on any assumptions of shared knowledge with the addressee, nor does the use of *I mean* indicate that the speaker is attempting to paraphrase what he or she has just said. Both *you know* and *I mean* as discourse features show many similarities in their use to items such as *oh* and *well*, and their semantic content is probably equally minimal. Fox Tree and Schrock (2002) argue for a distinction between *you know* and *I mean*, despite the many similarities in their functional use, because of their basic meanings, and it is possible that some of this basic meaning survives. Certainly, in the Glasgow recordings there is no correlation between the use of the two features (Pearson = .254).

The adolescent conversations in the Glasgow corpus show very little use of *you know* and *I mean*. This suggests that by the age of 14 these speakers, despite their obvious linguistic skills, have not yet developed the full range of styles in the adult community. The exception are the middle-class girls, who seem to be modeling their use of these discourse features on their mothers, since the middle-class women are the most distinctive users of *you know* and *I mean*, particularly in expressing intensity. The middle-class adolescents also use *like* as a discourse feature more frequently than do the working-class adolescents, suggesting in this case some influence from the American media.

The comparison between the two corpora shows a higher frequency for *you know* in the Glasgow adult conversations (6.48 per 1,000 words) than in the Ayr interviews (2.16 per 1,000 words). This could be a difference between the interview situation with a stranger and a conversation with a friend, though it could also be affected by the fact that the conversations were same-sex and some of the interviews were not.[11] (There were also fewer women than men in the Ayr sample.) There was no similar effect on the use of *I mean* (Glasgow adults 2.80 per 1,000 words, Ayr adults 2.60 per 1,000 words).

There are only minimal social class differences in the frequency of use of *you know*, but there are differences in how it is used. The middle-class speakers are more likely to use *you know* in a focusing function, as in examples (6) and (7). The lower-class speakers use *you know* more as a bracketing feature, particularly at the end of a clause. There is a similar difference of function in the case of *I mean,* which is more frequently used by the working-class speakers in Ayr and by the middle-class speakers in Glasgow. In Glasgow, the middle-class women use *I mean* more frequently than the other groups to provide explanations, whereas the other speakers are more likely to use *I mean* to introduce new information. The middle-class adolescents use *like* in a focusing function more than the working-class adolescents. These differences in the functional use of these discourse features are probably more important than the overall frequency of use.[12] It is clear from the individual figures given in tables 7.3–7.6 and other evidence cited from the London-Lund Corpus that the use of any one of these discourse features can be what Bernstein (1971: 98) called "an idiosyncratic speech habit."[13] For some speakers (but not for others) the use of a discourse lubricant helps to promote fluency. Yet the pattern of functional use that can be dimly perceived among the frequent users may be part of a more general discourse style. This point will be taken up later in chapter 14.

More salient than social class differences in the two corpora are gender differences linked to social class. In the Glasgow data *you know* is used twice as frequently by females as by males, and the most frequent users are middle-class women and girls. Similarly, in the Glasgow sessions females use *I mean* almost twice as frequently as males, with the middle-class women and girls again being the most frequent users. The middle-class females differ from the other groups in their use of *you know* and *I mean.* In the case of *you know,* the middle-class females are more likely to use it for purposes of emphasis or elaboration, and they are more likely to use *I mean* for explanations. This suggests that the use of these discourse lubricants is a distinctive part of the discourse style used by middle-class women and that their daughters are learning to follow their example.

8

Syntactic Variation

The previous two chapters have shown that the kind of discourse features that Bernstein included in the category of sympathetic circularity markers are not used significantly differently by middle-class and working-class speakers, contrary to his claims. The few significant differences are found in the categories of age and gender. It is reasonable to assume that in this respect Bernstein confused the characteristics of impromptu speech with those of the working class, and since features such as *you know* are frequently stigmatized, he may have thought that the middle-class speakers would generally avoid them. It has to be remembered that Bernstein did not have available to him such evidence as the London-Lund Corpus, which would have shown him how frequently these features are used by middle-class speakers. Bernstein also claimed that working-class speakers were more likely to use questions and short commands more often than middle-class speakers. As we have seen, there are significant age differences in the use of questions and imperatives in the Glasgow conversations, but no social class differences among the adults. Again, Bernstein may have been misled by his experience with adolescent boys.

Bernstein, however, also believed that there were important significant social class differences in the use of syntax. For example, he claimed that the speech of working-class speakers was characterized by "short, grammatically simple, often unfinished sentences, a poor syntactical construction with a verbal form stressing the active mood" (Bernstein 1971:42 [1959]). In this, Bernstein is probably guilty of confusing speech with writing. It has been pointed out often enough that the concept of sentence does not apply easily to spoken language (O'Connell 1988; Linell 1982; Miller and Weinert 1998). Short, syntactically simple clauses are characteristic of impromptu speech, and the passive voice is rare. However, the question of social class differences in syntax is worth exploring to find out whether there is any basis for the belief that there are such differences.

In the Ayr interviews I looked at all the syntactic constructions and found that the middle-class speakers on average used a wider variety of constructions and slightly more complex combinations of clauses (Macaulay 1991b: 91–95), showing some support for Bernstein's claim, but it is very weak since, with two exceptions, none of the differences is significant. The first exception is the use of nonrestrictive relative clauses, which are used five times more frequently by the middle-class speakers (p <.01).[1] The second is the use of dislocated syntax (see later text for examples), which is used significantly more frequently by the lower-class speakers. This aspect of syntax will be discussed more fully later in this chapter.

An examination of the Glasgow conversations shows similar patterns to those found in the Ayr interviews. Given the immense task of coding all the syntactic units in the Ayr interviews and the parsimony of reward, I did not attempt a similar coding of the Glasgow conversations but concentrated on a few major types of constructions. Most of the conversation is carried out in clauses with finite verbs, 85% in the case of the adults and 93% in the adolescent sessions. While there are no social class differences among the adults, the proportion increases to 99% among the working-class adolescents, in contrast to the 86% of the middle-class adolescent conversations. The average length of clauses is 6.7 words for the adolescents and 7.5 words for the adults. Both figures are slightly greater than the average of 6.2 words per finite clause that I found in Ayr (Macaulay 1991b: 97). The type and frequency of questions and the use of imperatives have already been discussed in chapter 6.

Coordinate clauses

Figure 8.1 shows the social class and age differences in the frequency of coordinate clauses (i.e., those introduced by *and, but,* or *so*).[2] Figure 8.1 shows that although the adults use coordinate clauses slightly more often than the adolescents and that for both age-groups the middle-class speakers use coordinate clauses slightly more frequently than the working-class speakers, there are no significant differences. Figure 8.2. shows the distribution by gender. It can be seen from figure 8.2 that with the exception of the middle-class adolescents, females use coordinate clauses more frequently than males, and the differences are greater than those in figure 8.1, but still not significant. The explanation for the unusually high proportion of coordinate clauses used by the middle-class boys lies in the descriptions of computer games in conversation 4, of which (1) gives a sample.

(1)   (Conversation 4—Middle-class boy)
      The thing is I was once playing this one where there were two bases
      and they both looked absolutely tiny
      and I was absolutely huge

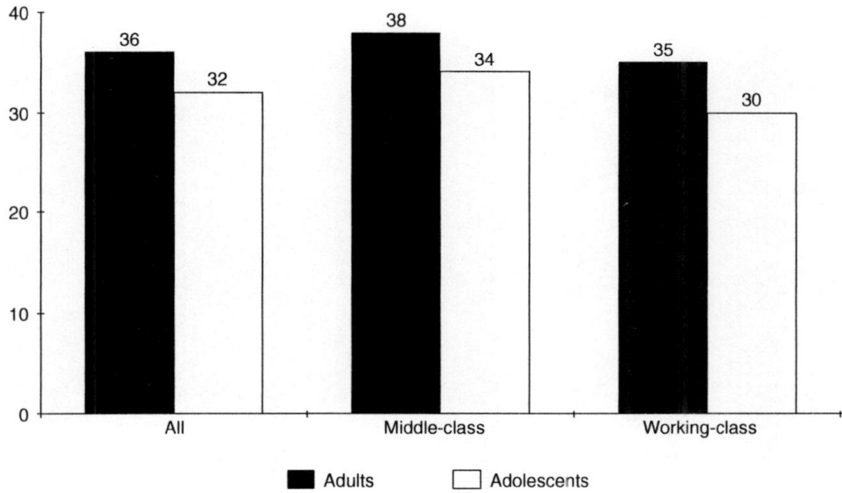

FIGURE 8.1. Frequency of coordinate clauses in Glasgow (frequency per 1,000 words)

and then I went
and then I—I went and attacked the first base
but got practically k—totally killed
and then by that time the other base had built itself up completely
but they couldn't find me because it was behind all these trees and rocks
so I had to blow away the trees and rocks for them

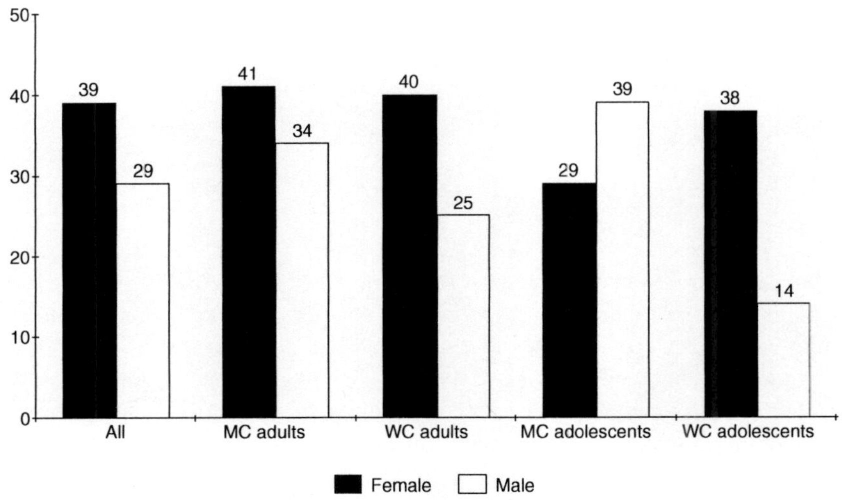

FIGURE 8.2. Age and gender differences in the use of coordinate clauses in Glasgow (frequency per 1,000 words)

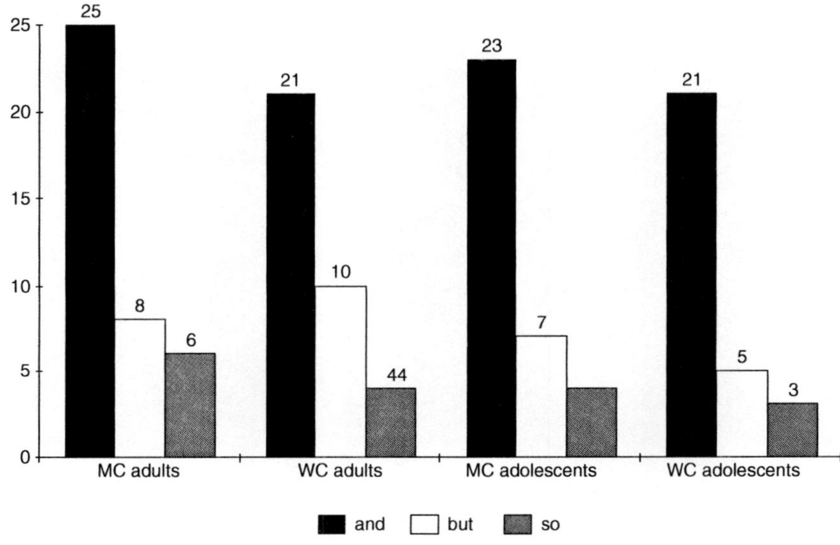

FIGURE 8.3. Comparative frequency of coordinate clauses in Glasgow (frequency per 1,000 words)

This kind of mixed narrative and explanation illustrates the high use of coordinate clauses.

Figure 8.3 shows that the distribution of coordinate clauses is similar for all groups. The general pattern is similar for all four groups, with only one significant difference: the adults use *but* more frequently than the adolescents ($p < .05$). Figure 8.4 shows the gender differences. In the case of *and* and *so*, the difference between the females and males is significant ($p < .05$), and in the case of *but* the difference approaches significance ($p = .059$)

Because clauses

One noticeable difference between the results obtained in Ayr and the Glasgow conversations is in the frequency with which the speakers use explanatory clauses beginning with (*be*)*cause*.[3] In Ayr the lower-class speakers used such clauses with a frequency of 1.9 and the middle-class speakers, 3.2. In Glasgow the adolescents used such clauses with a frequency of 5.7 and the adults, 5.6. The social class differences are shown in figure 8.5. It can be seen from figure 8.5 that the working-class speakers produced more clauses with *because*, except for the boys, where it is the middle-class boys who use these clauses more frequently than any of the other groups. The gender differences are shown more clearly in figure 8.6. It is the women and girls who use more explanatory clauses beginning with *because*, and this difference is significant ($p < .05$).

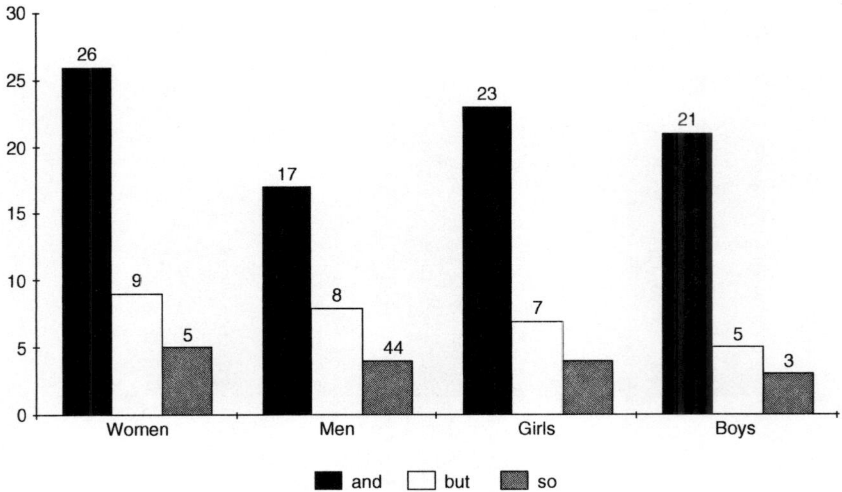

FIGURE 8.4. Age and gender differences in the types of coordinate clauses (frequency per 1,000 words)

Passive voice

In Ayr there is no great difference between the two social class groups in their use of the passive voice. The frequency of the passive in the lower-class interviews is 4.17 per 1,000 words and in the middle-class interviews, 3.56. However, the lower-class speakers had a higher frequency of *get*-passives: 21% compared with just over 4%

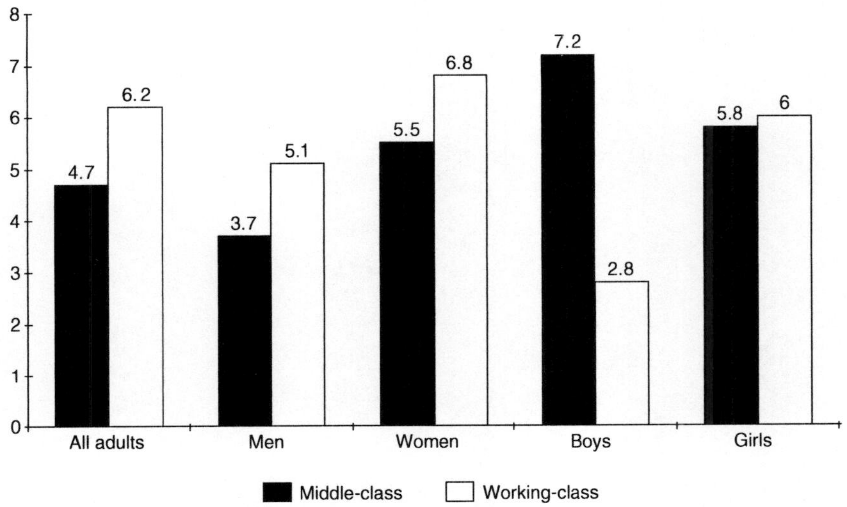

FIGURE 8.5. Frequency of *because* clauses in Glasgow (frequency per 1,000 words)

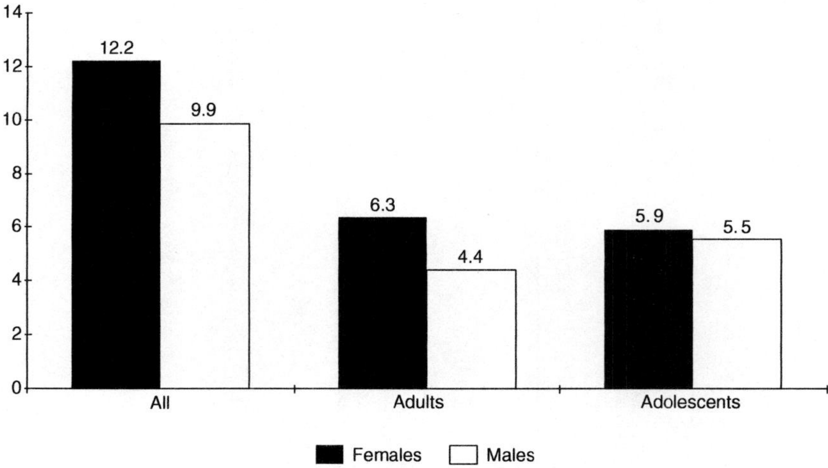

FIGURE 8.6. Gender differences in the frequency of *because* clauses in Glasgow (frequency per 1,000 words)

in the middle-class interviews.[4] The comparable figures for the Glasgow groups are shown in figure 8.7

It can be seen from figure 8.7 that the middle-class speakers, both adults and adolescents, use the passive voice more frequently than the working-class speakers ($p < .05$), and that the adolescents have a higher proportion of *get*-passives. The gender differences are shown in figure 8.8. This figure shows that the males use the passive

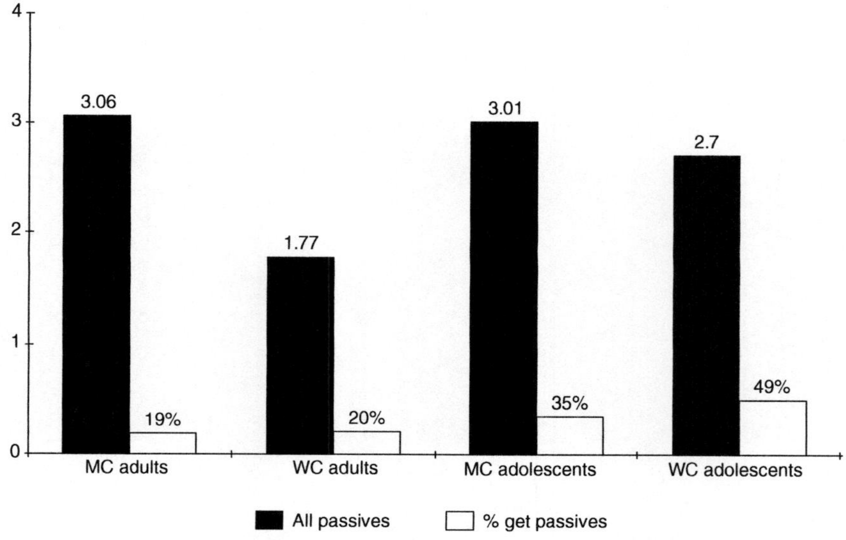

FIGURE 8.7. Frequency of the passive voice in Glasgow (frequency per 1,000 words)

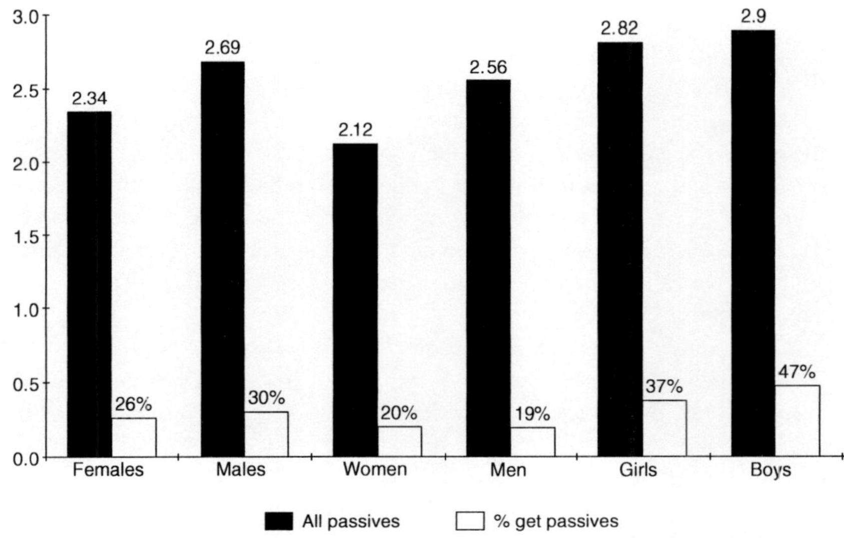

FIGURE 8.8. Age and gender differences in the use of the passive voice in Glasgow (frequency per 1,000 words)

slightly more frequently than the females and that it is the boys who use the highest proportion of *get*-passives, but none of these differences is statistically significant.

Dislocated syntax

In the Ayr interviews, the lower-class speakers made use of several syntactic constructions that have a highlighting or intensifying effect (Macaulay 1991b: 118–23). The five different constructions, demonstrative focusing, clefting, noun phrase preposing, left dislocation, and right dislocation are illustrated in (2).

(2) (Ayr, lower-class speakers)
    a. Demonstrative focusing
        i.   that's us going for another game (WL)
        ii. and that was you shut in the house for a week (EL)
    b. Clefting
        i.   it's a queer man and wife that doesnae have an argument (EL)
        ii. it's them that's running it now (MR
    c. Noun phrase preposing
        i.   an auld auld man he was you ken (WR)
        ii. and one of them he had been out with once or twice (AS)
    d. Left dislocation
        i.   Mr Patterson he was a gentleman (WL)
        ii. but my own family they've had a lot of leeway (EL)

e. Right dislocation
   i. she was a very quiet woman my mother (WR)
   ii. in fact he offered me a job Mr Cunningham (WL)

The lower-class speakers in Ayr used these constructions with a frequency of 2.91 per 1,000 words, in comparison with a frequency of 0.58 in the middle-class interviews ($p < .002$). A similar difference was found in the Glasgow adult conversations, with the working-class speakers using these constructions with a frequency of 2.4 per 1,000 words and the middle-class speakers, 0.23 ($p < .001$). The actual figures are shown in figure 8.9.

It can be seen from figure 8.9 and figure 8.10 that with the exception of demonstrative focusing, the middle-class speakers in both Ayr and Glasgow (columns 1 and 3) make some use of these constructions but very slight in comparison with the working-class speakers.

It is ironic that the primary syntactic difference between the two social classes should be the use of dislocated syntax. By any account of syntactic theory these constructions would be considered more complex than simple SVO sentences. Contrary to Bernstein, it is the working-class speakers who use the more complex syntax. This would come as no surprise to Halliday, who has argued that spoken language tends to favor greater "grammatical intricacy" in contrast to written language, which favors "lexical density" (1987: 71). In a comment on the situation in Ayr, I suggested: "It is hardly surprising that the lower-class speakers, with less education and probably less recourse to written materials in their daily lives, should employ discourse strategies that are characteristic of spoken language or that middle-class speakers should be more 'bookish' in their speech" (Macaulay 1991b:

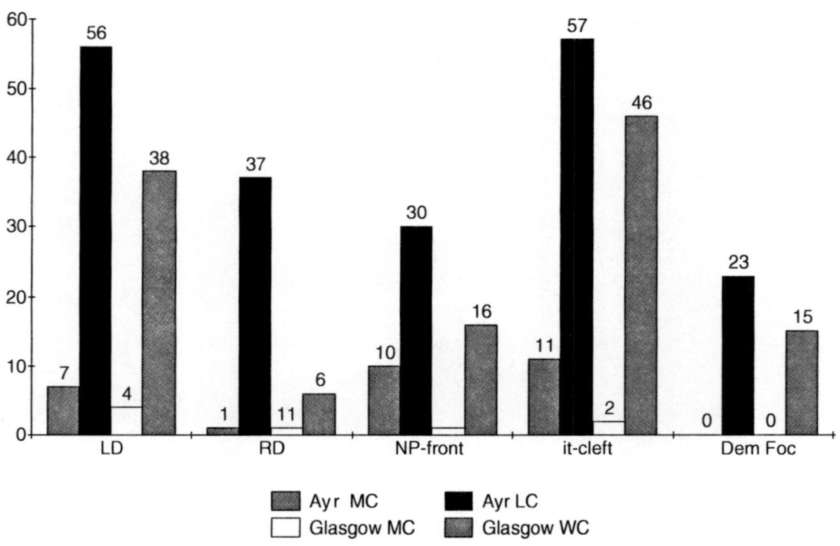

FIGURE 8.9. Numbers of examples of dislocated syntax in Ayr and Glasgow

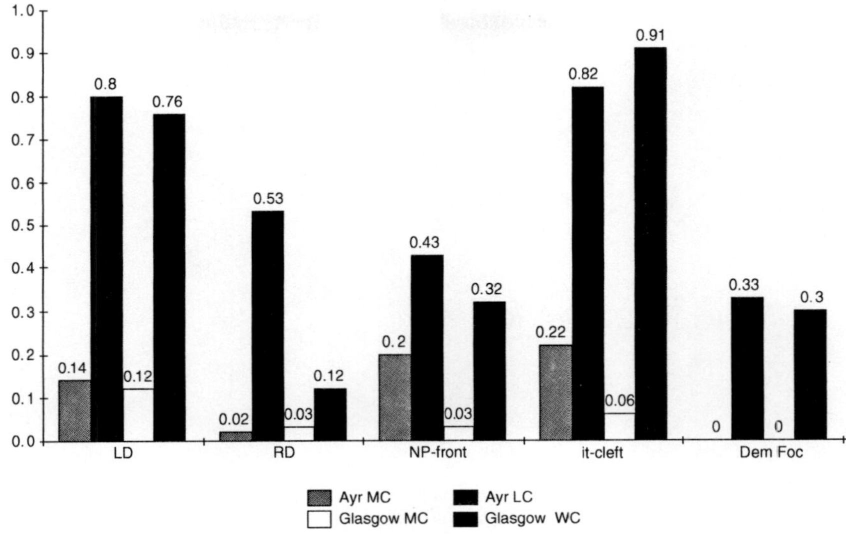

FIGURE 8.10. Frequency of dislocated syntax in Ayr and Glasgow (frequency per 1,000 words)

137). I am no longer sure that this is an adequate explanation. The question of discourse styles will be fully discussed in a later chapter when more examples of variation have been examined.

Conclusion

Several kinds of syntactic variation have been examined in this chapter. In several constructions there were age or gender differences but generally no social class differences. The two social class differences that are statistically significant are passive voice, which the middle-class speakers use more frequently than the working-class speakers ($p < .05$), and dislocated syntax, which the working-class speakers use much more frequently than the middle-class speakers ($p < .001$). On this evidence it is hard to see how Bernstein or anyone else could claim that there are important social class differences in the use of syntax.

9

Modals and Modality

Bernstein makes reference to "complex verbal groups" but does not explain what he includes in this category. One possibility is that he is referring to the verb phrases where there is more than one auxiliary verb. It is unlikely that he is simply considering cases where there is a progressive auxiliary (as in *it is raining*) or a perfect auxiliary (as in *it has rained*), or even a combination of the two (as in *it has been raining*). It is also unlikely that he is referring to verbs in the passive voice, since he makes separate reference to the use of the passive. Accordingly, it is reasonable to assume that he means verb phrases that contain a modal auxiliary, such as *can* or *must*. If so, his claim is that middle-class speakers use modal auxiliaries more frequently than working-class speakers. This is a question that can be explored in the Glasgow conversations.

Modal auxiliaries present a particular challenge for quantitative analysis. On the one hand, they are generally easy to identify and count. The exceptions are compound forms such as *going to* and *have (got) to*. On the other hand, the uses of modal auxiliaries are complex, and many subtle distinctions of meaning may be conveyed. Empirical approaches vary in the extent to which these uses are considered a unitary phenomenon. At one extreme is Ehrman (1966: 10), who treats each form as having a basic meaning, with subsidiary meanings that she calls "overtones." At the other extreme is Coates (1983: 108), who, for example, lists seven meanings for the modal *could*.

There is, however, one distinction that most scholars recognize, namely, that between the use of *must* in examples (1a) and (1b).

(1)

    a. I *must* look out for that (10R)

    b. I *must* be mad (10L)

In (1a) the speaker is referring to an obligation or compulsion to do something. In (1b) the speaker is drawing an inference from some situation. The first use has been termed either *root* (e.g., Coates 1983) or *deontic* (e.g., Palmer 1990). The second use is generally referred to as *epistemic*. Quirk et al. (1985: 219) refer to the first as *intrinsic modality* and the second as *extrinsic modality*. Palmer extends the notion of epistemic to include "any modal system that indicates the degree of commitment by the speaker to what he says" (1986: 51). This notion is difficult to apply operationally, particularly because, as Sweetser points out, "pragmatic factors will influence a hearer's interpretation of a particular uttered modal as operating in one domain or the other" (1990: 64). There is also general agreement (e.g., Coates 1983; Palmer 1990) that there are many cases where the meaning of a particular modal may be indeterminate. For this reason, relatively broad categories are to be preferred in tabulating instances of modal use in texts, and that is the policy I follow in this chapter. Even with broad categories, however, decisions on where to assign examples are not simple, and the results must be treated with caution.

One category about which there is likely to be little disagreement is the narrower sense of epistemic use that expresses an inference by the speaker. As the examples in (2) show, several modals can be used in this way.

(2)   (Examples from the Glasgow adult conversations)

    a. it *must* be awful for the people who work in the garage shop (12R)

    b. there *can't* be all that much in the way of industry (10R)

    c. Granny'*ll* be seventy-eight (10R)

    d. she said "Hello Sheena you *won't* remember me" (10R)

    e. she *would* be about seven months pregnant at that time (10L)

    f. they *wouldn't* be like these sheep that were standing there (16R)

As the examples in (2) show, inferential statements of this kind can be either positive or negative. *Mustn't* is used only in its deontic or root sense of obligation or compulsion; the negative form of epistemic *must* is *can't*, as in (2b). While epistemic uses of all four modals shown in (2) are found in the conversations, the most commonly used is *must*. Of the 103 examples of epistemic use found, 68% are *must*, 19% *will*, 10% *would*, and 3% *can't*. There are gender and social class differences, as can be seen in figure 9.1. The women have three times as many of the examples of epistemic use as the men, and the middle-class speakers slightly more than the working-class speakers. There are only 23 examples in the adolescent conversations; 70% are found in the girls' conversations, but it is the working-class adolescents who have more examples (70%) of epistemic use than the middle-class adolescents.

As for the frequency with which all the modals are used, figure 9.2 shows the distribution. Overall, the working-class speakers use modals significantly more frequently than the middle-class speakers ($p < .02$). As can be seen from figure 9.2, the

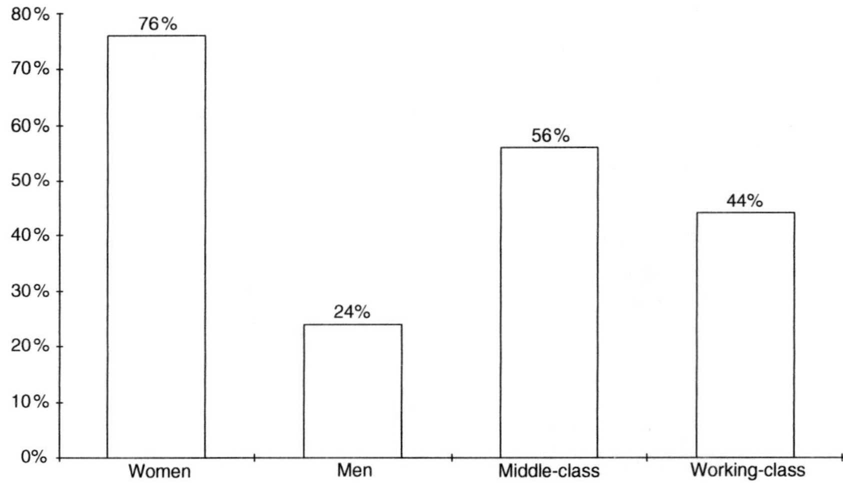

FIGURE 9.1. Epistemic use of modals by Glasgow adults

two most frequently used modals are *will/would* followed by *can/could*. In each case, the working-class speakers use the forms more frequently (*p* < .05). The figures for the Ayr interviews are given in figure 9.3. In Ayr there is no significant difference in the overall frequency with which the modals are used (LC 13.26 vs. MC 14.33). The figures for *could* and *will* are similar to those in the Glasgow conversations, but the others show differences. The most marked difference is that in Ayr the middle-

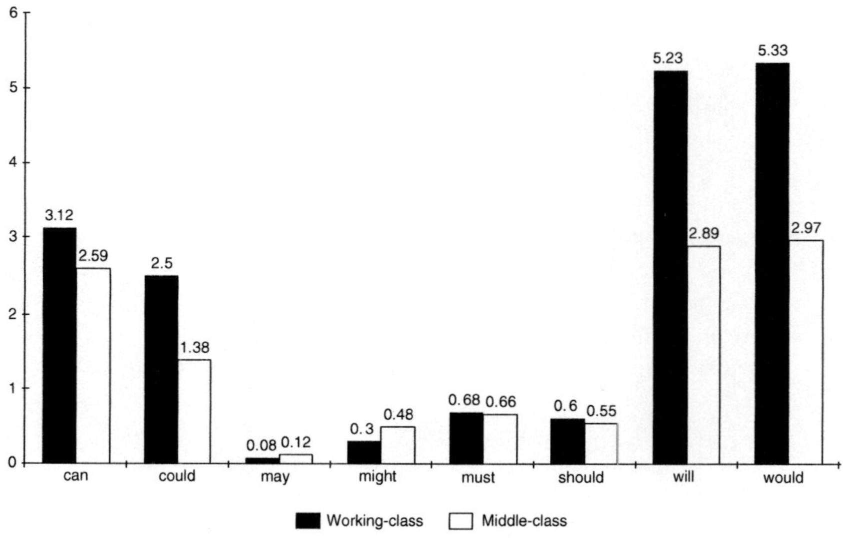

FIGURE 9.2. Frequency of modal use by Glasgow adults (frequency per 1,000 words)

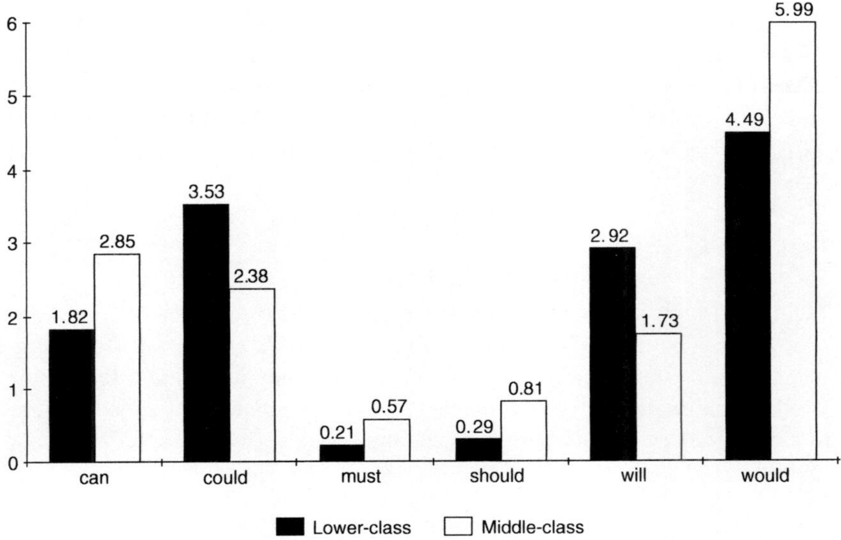

FIGURE 9.3. Frequency of modals in Ayr (frequency per 1,000 words)

class speakers use *would* more frequently than do the lower-class speakers. Figure 9.4 gives the frequencies for the most frequent modals in the Glasgow adolescent conversations. The overall frequency of modals is higher among the adolescents than among the adults ($p < .05$). The pattern, however, is very similar to that of the Glasgow adults (see figure 9.2) with the exception that the middle-class adolescents make more frequent use of *would*.

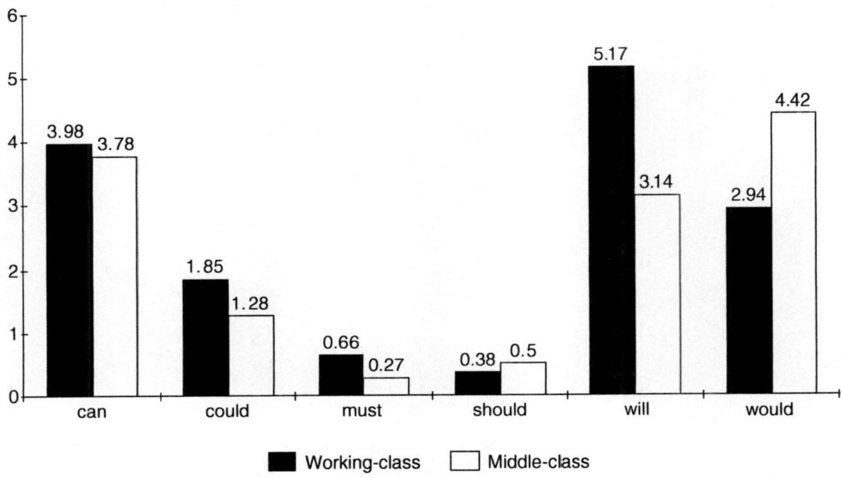

FIGURE 9.4. Frequency of use of modals by Glasgow adolescents (frequency per 1,000 words)

In Glasgow there are also gender differences, as can be seen in figure 9.5, which shows the four most common modals plus *going to*. Overall, women and girls use modals more frequently (20.17) than the males (14.5), a difference that fails to reach significance ($p = .102$). It can be seen in figure 9.5 that it is the males who are the most frequent users of *can/could*, while the females use *will/would* more frequently.

Can and could

Following Quirk et al. (1985), I have classified the tokens of *can/could* in three categories: permission, ability, and possibility. It usually is not difficult to assign examples to one of these three categories, but since they all contain the notion of "possibility," this category is the unmarked one, and items were assigned to either of the first two categories only where the meaning was clear from the context. Examples are given in (3).

(3)

    Permission
    a. first thing "*Can* I use the phone?" (10L)
    b. I'm going to ask the woman if I *can* hear it (7L)
    c. Louise's not even asked me if she *could* come (7R)
    Ability
    d. I *can* do it in about fifteen seconds you know (10L)
    e. she *can* now crawl (4R)
    f. so he *could* hit the ball a long way (11L)

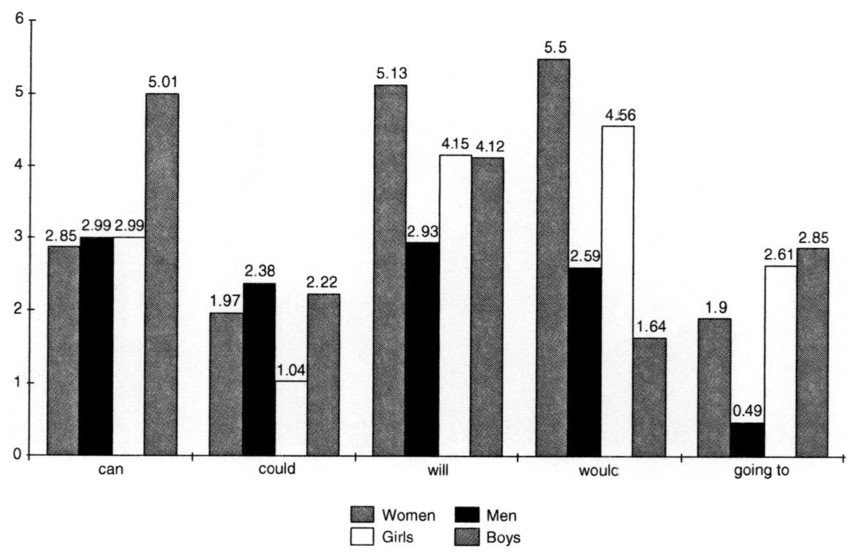

FIGURE 9.5. Gender and age differences in the use of modals in Glasgow (frequency per 1,000 words)

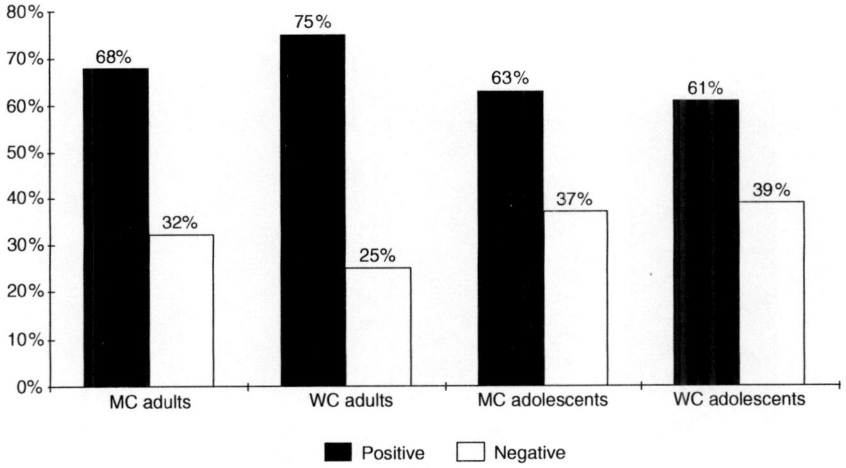

FIGURE 9.6. Positive and negative use of *can/could* in Glasgow

Possibility
g. that means I *can* go in on Sunday after creche (2R)
h. so the same word *can* mean different things (11L)
i. aye it *could* be good (13R)

The majority of instances are positive (*can* 64%, *could* 73%). The distribution of these forms can be seen in figure 9.6. For all groups, the affirmative is much more frequent than the negative. Also, for all groups, *can* is more frequent than *could*, as shown in figure 9.7. The age and gender differences in the use of *can/could* are shown in

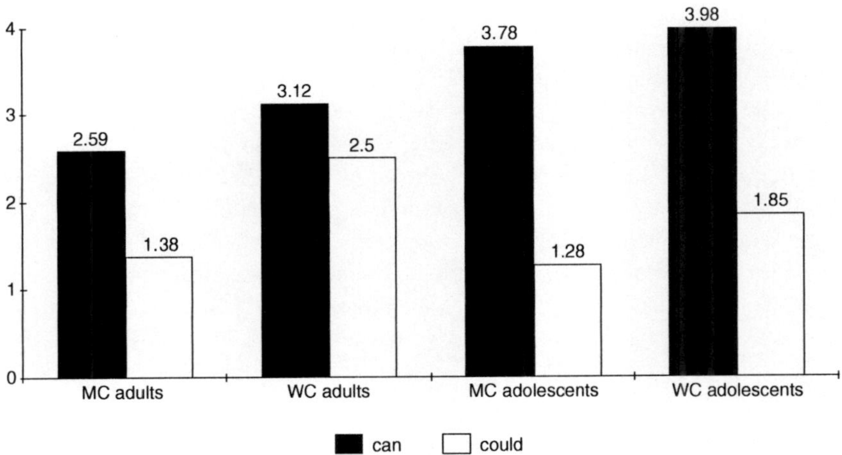

FIGURE 9.7. Age and social class differences in the use of *can* and *could* in Glasgow (frequency per 1,000 words)

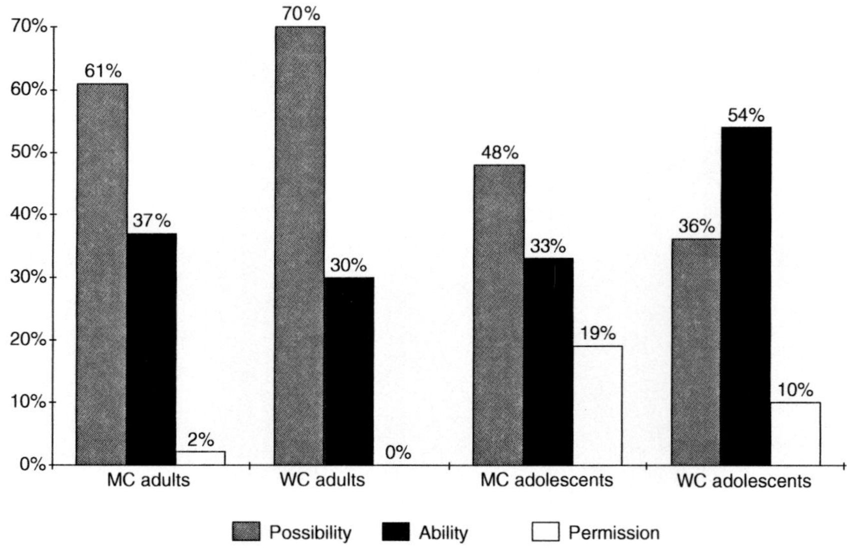

FIGURE 9.8. Uses of *can* and *could* in Glasgow

figure 9.8. It is perhaps not surprising that the adolescents should have more instances of the use of *can/could* with the meaning of permission, since they are more likely than the adults to need permission, but in fact few of the examples refer to permission granted to adolescents by adults.

Among the adolescents it is the boys who use *can/could* more frequently, as can be seen in figure 9.9. However, this does not explain the greater proportion in the sense of ability among the adolescents compared with the adults. The boys and girls use *can/could* in the sense of ability equally frequently (1.9 per 1,000 words). It is in the sense of possibility that the boys use *can/could* with a higher frequency (2.9 per 1,000 words) than the girls (0.9 per 1,000 words). Overall, there are no differences between the working-class adolescents and the middle-class adolescents in their use of these modals (WC *can* 3.98, *could* 1.85/MC *can* 3.78, *could* 1.28), but there are gender differences. The boys use *can* with a frequency of 5.01 compared with the girls' 2.99 and *could* with a frequency of 2.22 compared with the girls' 1.04. The boys thus use *can/could* twice as frequently as the girls. There are no comparable adult differences. The men use *can* with a frequency of 2.99 and *could* with a frequency of 2.38; the women's frequencies are 2.85 and 1.97, respectively. The social class differences are greater, with the working-class adults using *can* with a frequency of 3.46 and *could* with a frequency of 2.82. The figures for the middle-class adults are 2.59 and 1.46, respectively.

Will and *would*

These two modals are generally considered the modals of "volition" and "prediction" (Coates 1983; Quirk et al. 1985), but *would* is frequently used with "hypotheti-

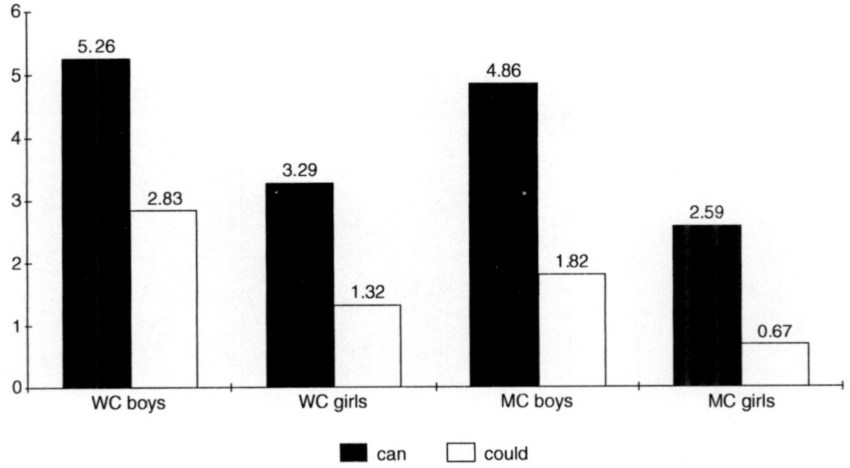

FIGURE 9.9. Gender differences in the use of *can* and *could* by Glasgow adolescents (frequency per 1,000 words)

cal" meaning. To these I have added the meaning "habitual" and, for *would*, "future in the past" (i.e., sequence of tenses, particularly in reported speech). These categories are illustrated in (4).

(4)

    Intention
    a. I'*ll* phone you back aboot it then (13R)
    b. I'*ll* just wear my joggies (7L)
    c. I *wouldnae* leave it on (15L)
    Prediction/hypothetical
    d. it'*ll* take a while for us even to think (14R)
    e. he'*ll* mature at his own stage (10R)
    f. you *wouldn't* compare him with the current back-row forwards (11R)
    Habitual
    g. sometimes she'*ll* go if we finish early enough (13L)
    h. and sometimes it'*ll* just suddenly go (4L)
    i. and they *would* produce a wad of filthy notes (12R)
    Future-in-the-past
    j. she said she *would* try and hoover it the next morning (15L)
    k. I thought she'*d* be pure sitting in here listening (2L)

The modals *will* and *would* often occur in contracted forms as '*ll* and '*d*, respectively. Figure 9.10 shows the proportions for both adults and adolescents.

    It can seen from Figure 9.10 that the contracted form of *will* occurs 87% of the time with adults and 75% of the time with adolescents, but the contracted form of

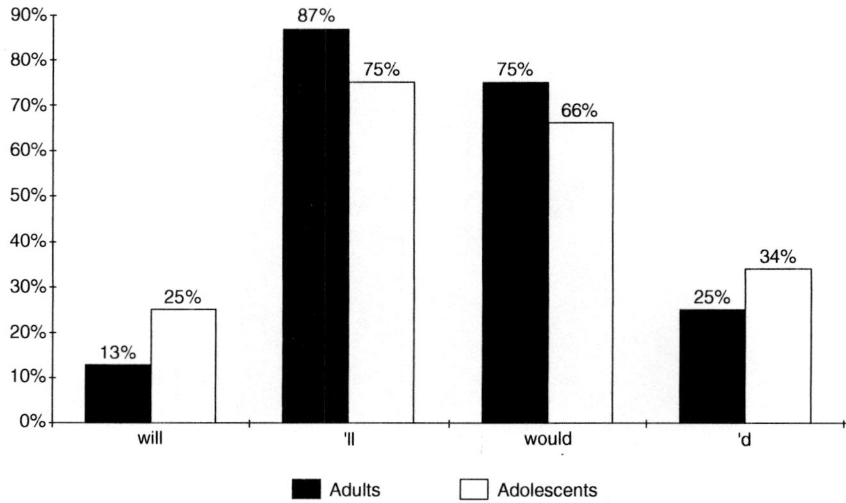

FIGURE 9.10. Proportion of contracted form of *will* and *would* in Glasgow

would occurs only 25% of the time with adults and 34% of the time with adolescents. The middle-class adults contract *will* 72% of the time, compared with 93% for the working-class adults. There is no social class difference between the adolescents, with both groups contracting *will* 75% of the time. The middle-class adults contract *would* 20% of the time, compared with 27% for the working-class adults. The middle-class adolescents, however, contract *would* twice as often (42%) as the working-class adolescents (21%). There are few gender differences in contraction, with the exception that the boys contract *would* 47% of the time, compared with the girls' 28%.

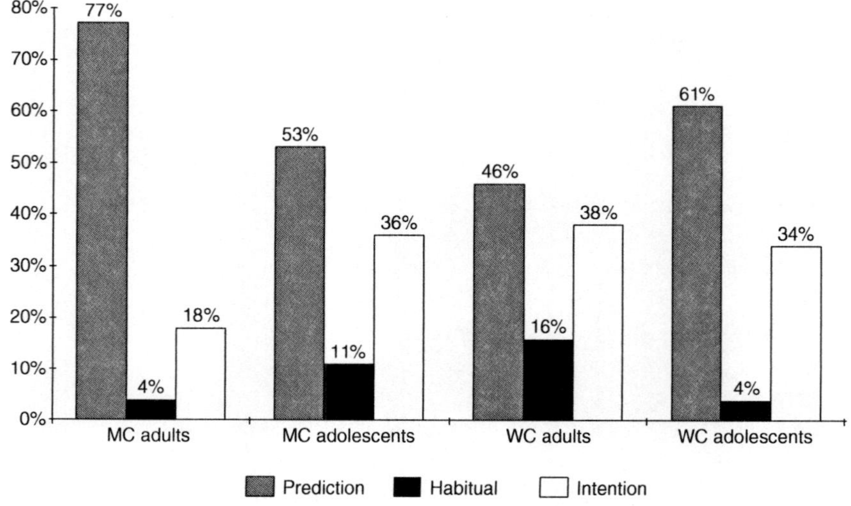

FIGURE 9.11. Uses of *will* in Glasgow

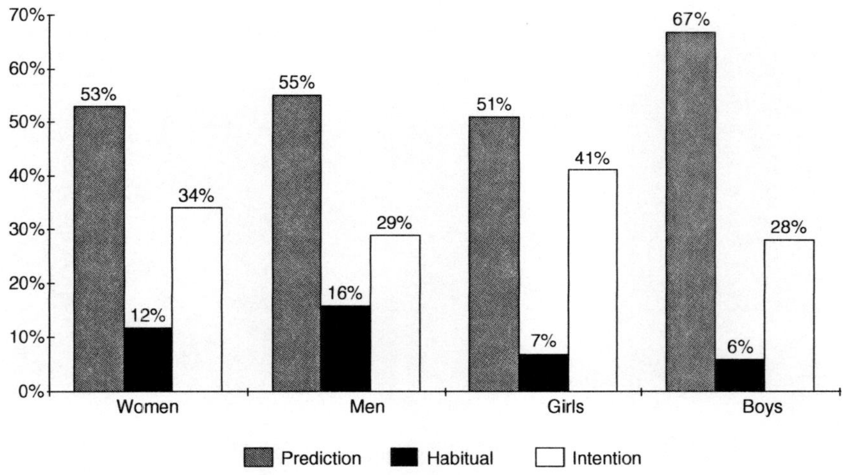

FIGURE 9.12. Gender differences in the use of *will* in Glasgow

As regards the uses of *will*, figure 9.11 shows the social class and age differences. It can be seen in figure 9.11 that for all four groups, prediction is the most frequent use, with intention next. Figure 9.12 shows that females use *will* to express intention slightly more frequently than the males. Overall, the females use *will* in the sense of intention 36% of the time, compared with 29% for the males, but the difference is not significant.

In the case of *would* the most common use is as a hypothetical, though this emphasis is less marked among the working-class adolescents, as can be seen in figure 9.13. There are few gender differences, as can be seen in figure 9.14. The main

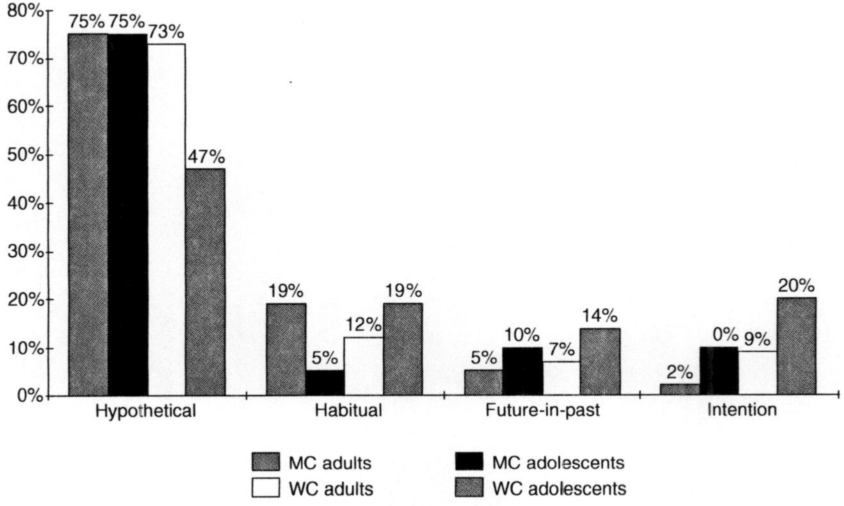

FIGURE 9.13. Uses of *would* in Glasgow

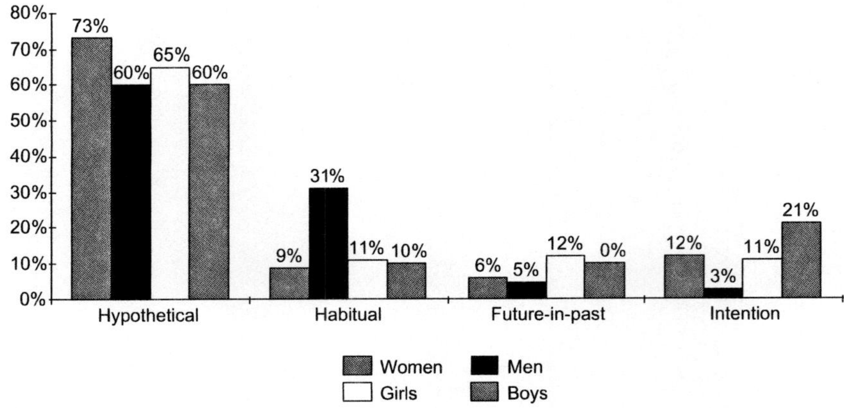

FIGURE 9.14. Gender differences in the use of *would* in Glasgow

differences are that the men use *would* more in its habitual function ($p < .05$) and the boys for intention (n.s).

With both *will* and *would*, the adolescents have more negated forms than the adults, as can be seen in figure 9.15. Overall, 16% of the instances of *will* in the adolescent conversations are negated, compared with only 5% in the adult conversations. In the case of *would* the proportion negated in the adolescent conversations is 23%, compared with 16% in the adult conversations.

Going to

In addition to *will* and *would*, the quasi modal *going to* is used to express both prediction and intention. These uses are illustrated in (5).

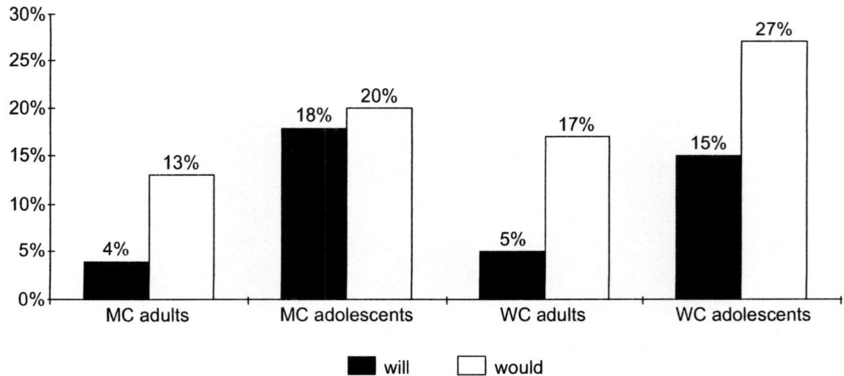

FIGURE 9.15. Age differences in the use of *will/would* with negation in Glasgow

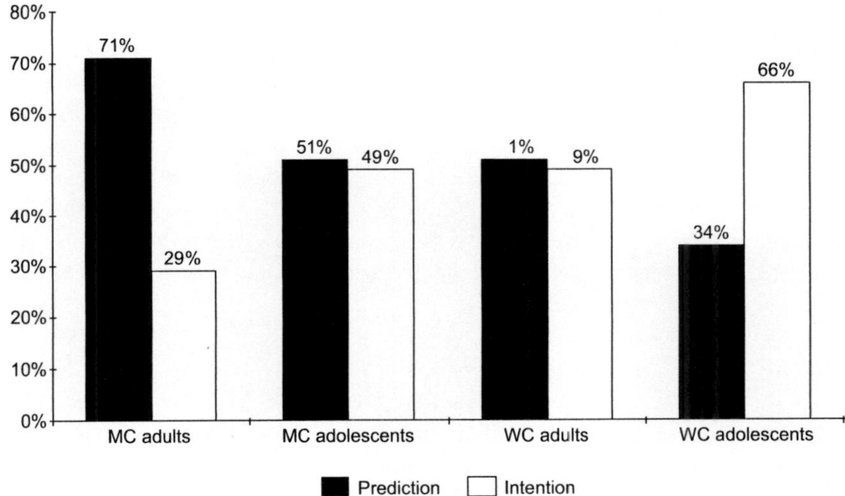

FIGURE 9.16. Social class and age difference in the use of *going to* in Glasgow

(5)

    Prediction
    a. oh that *is going to* be hard work (10L)
    b. there'*s going to* be a hamster show soon (2L)

    Intention
    c. I'*m going to* drink vodka tonight for a change (13L)
    d. and I'*m going to* wear joggies (7R)

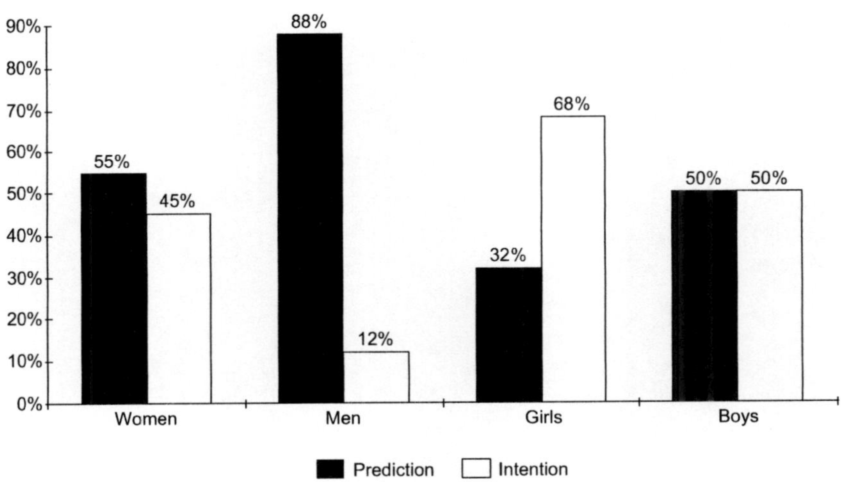

FIGURE 9.17. Gender differences in the use of *going to* in Glasgow

Figure 9.16 shows the social class and age differences in the use of *going to*. As with *will*, the middle-class adults use *going to* most frequently in its prediction function, whereas the working-class adolescents use it most often to indicate intention. There are also gender differences, as can be seen in figure 9.17, which shows that it is the females who use *going to* more often in the sense of intention (all females 55% vs. all males 42%). Females account for three-quarters of the instances of *going to* in the sense of intention. Since there are more female speakers than male, this difference is better expressed in frequencies; the females use *going to* in the sense of intention 1.25 times per 1,000 words, compared with a frequency of 0.58 by the males.

Other modals

There are only 14 examples of deontic *must* in the Glasgow conversations, 9 in the adult conversations and 5 in the adolescent conversations. The sense of obligation or necessity is expressed variously by *have (got) to, should, ought to, need to,*[1] and *be supposed to*. There are only 4 examples of *ought to*, which is not surprising (Miller 1993). The frequencies for the others are given in figure 9.18.

Since *must* rarely occurs in deontic use, *have (got) to* is the normal form of necessity, as in the examples in (6).

(6)

    a. "Listen John you *have to* get your finger out" (11L)
    b. there's problems but you*'ve got to* do what he tells you (18L)
    c. she says I'*ve to* phone her at six o'clock the night (7R)
    d. I've still *got to* persuade my mum and dad (2L)

Because there is no past form of *must* or nonfinite form, some form of *have to* must be used as in the examples in (7).

(7)

    a. I'*d to* laugh when I read the paper (10L)
    b. so she wouldn't *have to* come in (7L)

Three-quarters of the *have to* forms are not present tense (i.e., they could not be replaced with *must*). The distribution of forms is shown in figure 9.19. The main difference is that the middle-class adults have a lower proportion of *have got to* forms.

The one other form that occurs as a quasi modal is *used to* as in the examples in (8).

(8)

    a. she *used to* have to do two and a half days a week (10R)
    b. oor back windows *used to* be facing the railway (17R)

The frequency of this form is shown in figure 9.20. The figure shows that *used to* is not used very often by any of the groups but that the working-class speakers are

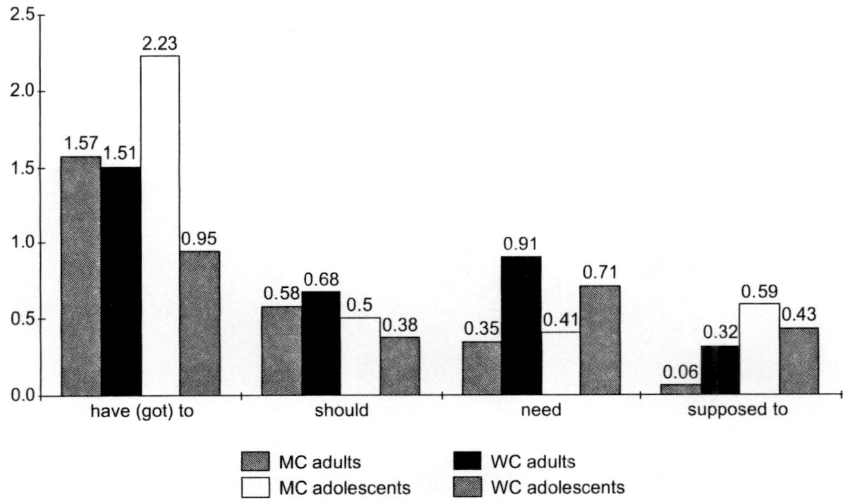

FIGURE 9.18. Frequency of *have (got) to*, *should*, *need to*, and *supposed to* in Glasgow (frequency per 1,000 words)

more likely to use it. As figure 9.9 indicated, it is the working-class adults who also use *would* most frequently in the "habitual" sense. This is, however, related to the amount of reminiscence in the working-class conversations, particularly the men's.

Not surprisingly, *shall* is almost totally absent from both the Ayr and the Glasgow materials (two examples in the Ayr interviews, one in the Glasgow adult conversations), but there is one amusing sequence in the session with two working-class boys, who have found a map of Glasgow in the office.

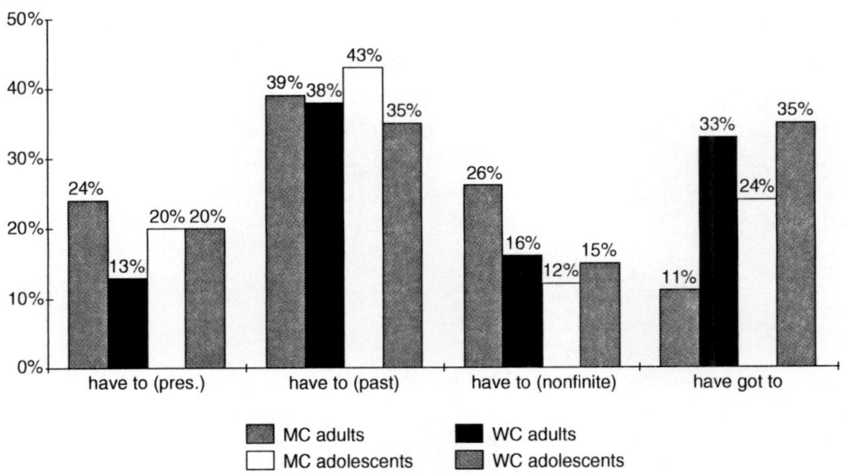

FIGURE 9.19. Uses of *have (got) to* in Glasgow

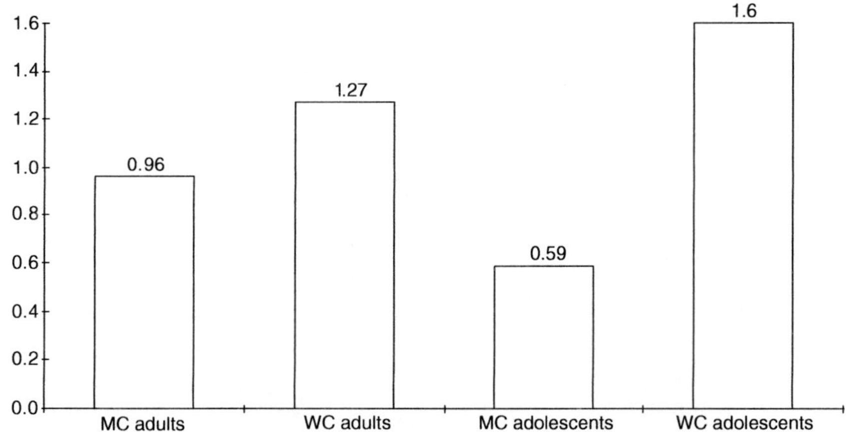

FIGURE 9.20. Frequency of *used to* in Glasgow (frequency per 1,000 words)

(10)   (Conversation 9—Working-class boys)
    R: shall we look at the city map?
    L: shall we look at the city of Glasgow?
    R: shall we put it up the right way first?
    L: shall we fuck
       did you know that Cowers Park is next to a bowling green?
    R: no really no

It is hard to believe that this use of *shall* is anything other than ironical, since the form is so rare in Scottish speech. It is possible that the boys are parodying a teacher's way of speaking, which they might identify with the standard variety spoken in England, where *shall* is more common than in Scotland.

Palmer (1990: 25–26) rejects *want* as a modal, though others (e.g., Strang 1962: 147) have considered it to be "marginal." Among the Glasgow adults there is a social class difference, with the middle-class speakers using *want* with a frequency of 0.67, compared with the working-class speakers' use at 1.61. This social class difference is not found in the adolescent conversations, where the middle-class speakers use *want* with a frequency of 2.69, compared with the working-class adolescents' 2.51. There is, however, a considerable age difference, with the adults using *want* with a frequency of 1.22, compared with the adolescents' 2.60.

Conclusion

Although there are minor differences, social class does not appear to be a major factor in variation in the use of modal auxiliaries, although the Glasgow working-class adults use them more frequently (17.84 per 1,000 words) than the middle-class adults (11.64) ($p < .02$). In Ayr and among the Glasgow adolescents there are no great differences in the frequency with which modal auxiliaries are used.

The gender differences in Glasgow are possibly more interesting. Females are responsible for three-quarters of the epistemic uses of modals, but this difference fails to reach significance ($p = .102$). Females also use *will/would* more frequently. Females use *will* and *going to* more frequently than males in the sense of "intention," whereas men use *would* more often with "habitual" reference. Boys use *can* and *could* almost twice as often as the girls, and they use these modals in the sense of "possibility" three times as frequently as the girls.

The adolescents use modal auxiliaries more frequently than the adults ($p < .05$). The most obvious differences are a greater use of *can/could* in the sense of "permission" and more negated forms of *will/would* than in the adult sessions. The adolescents use *want* twice as frequently as the adults.

The lack of many social class, gender, or age differences in the use of modal auxiliaries suggests that modals, unlike adverbs (see next chapter), are not a major contributor to differences in discourse style. Palmer explicitly contrasts the epistemic use of modals with adverbs: "MUST does not have the same kind of meaning as the adverbs *certainly*, *definitely*, etc., which are, indeed, indications simply of the speaker's confidence or commitment" (1986: 64). It appears that modality is a fundamental aspect of language use, and variation in its use depends on topic rather than any social factors. If the use of modal auxiliaries is what Bernstein meant by complex verbal groups, then the evidence from the Glasgow conversations contradicts rather than supports his claim.

10

Adverbs and Social Class

Among the characteristics of what Bernstein was then calling a *public language* (used by, among others, "the unskilled and semi-skilled strata") was "rigid and limited use of adjectives and adverbs" (1971: 42). Bernstein later investigated this notion empirically in his study based on the discussion groups with middle-class and working-class boys (Bernstein 1962).

Bernstein identified a category of "uncommon adverbs" by excluding adverbs of degree and place, *just*, and *really*, in addition to a number of items that normally would not be considered adverbs (e.g., *not, how*). Bernstein does not give the actual frequencies but only the results of the statistical analysis: "A greater proportion of the adverbs of the middle class are uncommon and the difference is significant beyond the 0.001 level of confidence" (1971: 101). It is difficult to know which items Bernstein included in his category of uncommon adverbs, but it is reasonable to assume that most of them would consist of adverbs derived from adjectives, such as *peculiarly*.

Derived adverbs in *-ly*

Adults

As reported in Macaulay (1991b, 1995, 2002b), I noticed a major difference in the concordances of the lower-class and middle-class speakers in Ayr in that the former had noticeably fewer examples of derived adverbs in *-ly*. The figures presented are in table 10.1, which shows that the middle-class speakers in Ayr used derivative adverbs in *-ly* three times more frequently than the lower-class speakers ($p < .001$).

TABLE 10.1. Relative frequency of derivative
adverbs in *-ly* in Ayr.

	Lower-class		Middle-class	
	No.	ªFreq.	No.	Freq.
Manner	28	0.40	82	1.61
Time/freq.	41	0.58	70	1.38
Degree	47	0.67	121	2.38
Sentence	76	1.08	174	3.42
really	55	0.79	106	2.08
Totals	247	3.52	553	10.87

ªper 1,000 words

This difference would have been even greater if it had not been for one exceptional lower-class speaker (Macaulay 1997: 125). At the time, I wondered whether this was an aberrant result somehow connected with the interview situation. I was therefore interested to see whether a similar distribution would be found in the Glasgow conversations. The comparable figures for the Glasgow adults are given in table 10.2.

Again, the middle-class speakers use these adverbs significantly more frequently than the working-class speakers ($p < .001$). It can be seen from tables 10.1 and 10.2 that while there are minor differences, the general pattern is remarkably similar in both, so the social class differences in the use of derivative adverbs found in the Ayr study cannot be simply an artifact of the interview situation. Nor is there any evidence in either corpus that uninflected adjectives (e.g., "I was firing that too *quick*") are used frequently by working-class speakers in place of derived adverbs.

What about gender differences? Figure 10.1 shows that there is a gender difference in the Glasgow middle-class speakers. It can be seen in figure 10.1 that it is the middle-class men who are the most frequent users of derived adverbs in *-ly* (n.s.).

In the Ayr interviews there are 133 different adverbs in *-ly*; 20 are found only in the lower-class interviews, 72 occur only in the middle-class interviews, and 41 are common to both sets of interviews (Macaulay 1991b: 123). In Glasgow there are 74

TABLE 10.2. Relative frequency of derivative adverbs
in *-ly* in Glasgow adult conversations

	Working-class		Middle-class	
	No.	ªFreq.	No.	Freq.
Manner	11	0.22	32	0.93
Time/Freq.	19	0.38	33	0.96
Degree	35	0.69	42	1.22
Sentence	92	1.82	197	5.74
really	93	1.85	104	3.03
Totals	250	4.97	408	11.89

ªper 1,000 words

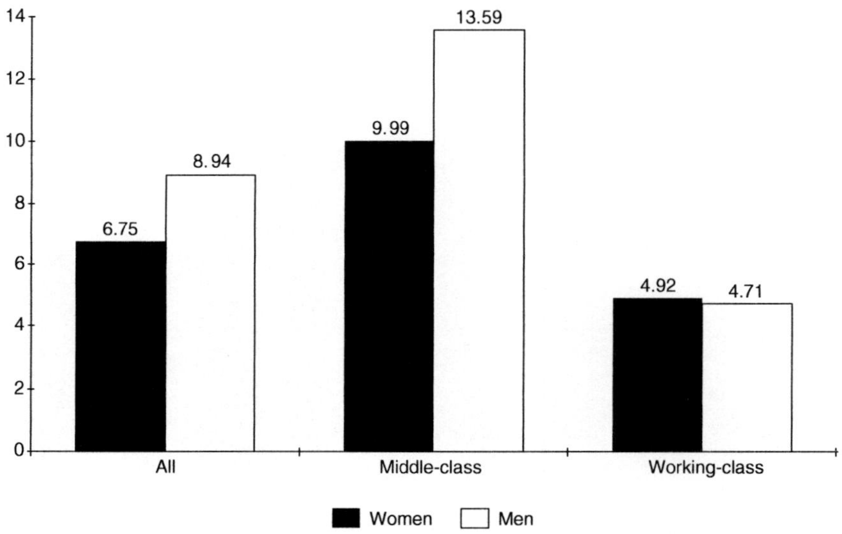

FIGURE 10.1. Frequency of derived adverbs in *-ly* in Glasgow (adults only)

different adverbs in *-ly* in the middle-class adult conversations and 37 different adverbs in the working-class adult conversations. Of these, 24 are common to both sets of conversations, as shown in table 10.3.

Of these adverbs, for both groups the most frequent is *really*, with a frequency of 3.03 per 1,000 words in the middle-class conversations[1] and 1.85 in the working-class conversations. (In Ayr *really* is used with a frequency of 2.08 in the middle-class interviews and 0.79 in the lower-class ones.) The next most frequent for both groups in Glasgow is *actually*, with a frequency of 2.8 for the middle-class speakers and 0.74 for the working-class speakers. (In Ayr *actually* is used with the frequency of 1.22 by the

TABLE 10.3. Derived adverbs in *-ly*
in both sets of Glasgow adult
conversations

absolutely	nearly
actually	normally
certainly	obviously
completely	possibly
constantly	probably
definitely	really
especially	roughly
eventually	thoroughly
exactly	totally
gradually	unfortunately
hardly	usually
mostly	wrongly

TABLE 10.4. Derived adverbs in *-ly*
found only in Glasgow middle-class
adult conversations

allegedly	necessarily
amazingly	occasionally
apparently	overly
awfully	particularly
badly	permanently
briefly	possibly
clearly	preferably
correctly	properly
deliberately	quickly
differently	rarely
distinctly	recently
drastically	regularly
easily	relatively
enormously	scholarly
evidently	significantly
fairly	slightly
fortunately	slowly
funnily	specifically
generally	strongly
happily	suddenly
immediately	supposedly
interestingly	technically
mathematically	terribly
mechanically	vaguely
monthly	virtually

middle-class speakers and 0.24 by the lower-class speakers.) Tables 10.4 and 10.5 give the adverbs that are found in only one set of conversations in Glasgow.

Whatever Bernstein meant by "uncommon adverbs," the evidence from the Ayr interviews and the Glasgow adult conversations supports his view that middle-class speakers are more likely to use certain kinds of adverbs. Tables 10.4 and 10.5, however, show quite clearly that the social class difference in the use of adverbs among the Glasgow adults is not simply a question of vocabulary or register. It would be as

TABLE 10.5. Derived adverbs in
-ly found only in Glasgow
working-class adult conversations

automatically	mainly
basically	officially
entirely	perfectly
honestly	politically
hopefully	seemingly
literally	specially
luckily	

TABLE 10.6. Frequency of adverbs in *-ly* in Glasgow adolescent conversations

	(*n*)	[a]*Freq.*
Middle-class girls	62	5.9
Middle-class boys	81	7.0
Working-class girls	41	3.0
Working-class boys	18	2.4
MC adolescents	143	6.5
WC adolescents	59	2.8

[a]per 1,000 words

absurd to say that the working-class speakers do not know words such as *slowly* or *quickly* as it would be to say that the middle-class speakers do not know words such as *basically* and *officially*. The words that turn up in a conversation will be highly dependent on topic, but topic alone cannot explain why the middle-class speakers in both Ayr and Glasgow use adverbs more frequently than the working-class speakers. The explanation for the difference must lie elsewhere.

Adolescents

What about the adolescents? The figures are given in table 10.6. Although the overall frequency of use is lower than in the adult sessions ($p < .05$), the pattern of social class differences is similar and the difference is still substantial.

Other adverbs

Adults

In the Ayr study I also tabulated numbers on the adverbs *very, quite,* and *just* (Macaulay 1991b:129–32). The Ayr figures are given in table 10.7, and the figures for the Glasgow adult sample in table 10.8. Once again the similarities are obvious. In both corpora, it is only *just* that is used by the working-class speakers with the same kind of frequency as by the middle-class speakers. The difference in the use of *very* in the Glasgow sample is even more striking than that in Ayr and is highly significant ($p < .001$).[2] Half of the working-class Glasgow adults do not use *very* even once. There is, as far as I know, no comparable study of variation in the use of adverbs in general, but Kroch (1995), in his study of upper-class Philadelphia speech, found that upper-class men were more likely than upper-class women or upper-middle-class men to use "intensifying adverbs" (e.g., *very, extremely*), though the results were not statistically significant. The high frequency of intensifiers among the upper-class and upper-middle-class speakers in Philadelphia is consistent with my findings.

The main gender difference in the use of *very* is in the middle class, as can be seen in figure 10.2. The middle-class women use *very* slightly more frequently than the middle-class men (n.s.).

TABLE 10.7. Relative frequency of *very*, *quite*, and *just* in Ayr

	Lower-class		Middle-class	
	No.	[a]*Freq.*	No.	*Freq.*
very	70	1.00	178	3.49
quite	70	1.00	127	2.49
just	338	4.84	255	5.01

[a]per 1,000 words

The social class difference among the Glasgow adults in the use of *quite* is also significant ($p < .002$). The use of *quite* can be either emphatic (what Quirk et al. 1985: 590 call "maximizers"), as in the examples in (1), or a hedge (what Quirk et al. 1985: 597–98 call "downtoners"), as in the examples in (2). All the examples in (1) and (2) are from middle-class conversations.

(1)

    a. but I think clothes-wise we're *quite* different

    b. and I was *quite* proud because I was still thirty nine

    c. I do it *quite* quickly
       I can do it in about fifteen seconds

    d. San Francisco's actually *quite* chilly so—

    e. it's *quite quite quite quite* different

(2)

    a. it is actually *quite* nice

    b. I mean Alison's still *quite* sort of young

    c. the actual wee beach is—is *quite* nice because it's sort of rough sand

    d. it's *quite* pleasant
       it's—it's sand-dunish and em

    e. but it's—it's er *quite* interesting to find how different people do speak

TABLE 10.8. Relative frequency of *very*, *quite* and *just* in Glasgow adults

	Working-class		Middle-class	
	No.	[a]*Freq.*	No.	*Freq.*
very	16	0.32	147	4.28
quite	60	1.19	125	3.64
just	311	6.18	179	5.22

[a]per 1,000 words

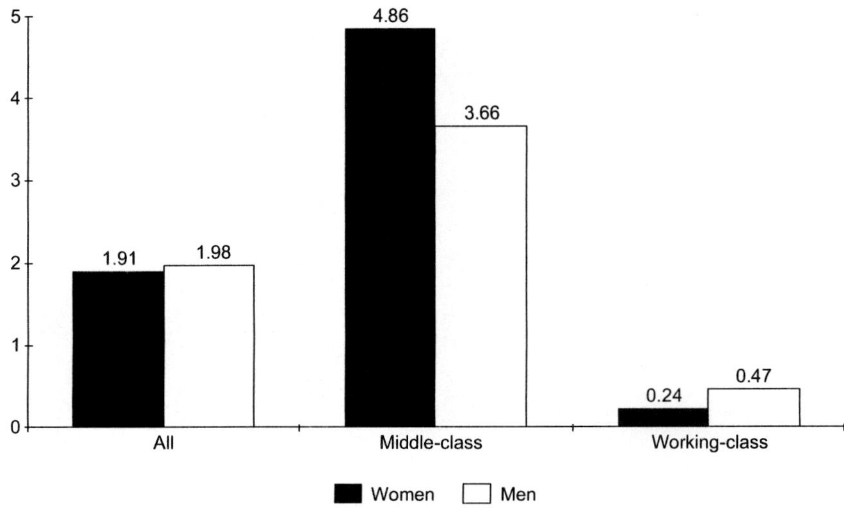

FIGURE 10.2. Frequency of *very* in Glasgow (adults only; frequency per 1,000 words)

Deciding between these two functions is sometimes difficult, so any figures reflect an interpretative decision. The middle-class speakers appear to use *quite* more frequently in its emphatic function (67%) than in its hedging function (33%). For the working-class speakers the difference is smaller: 56% emphatic, 44% hedging. However, the middle-class speakers use *quite* with an overall frequency of 3.64 per 1,000 words, compared with the working-class frequency of 1.19. The frequency with which the middle-class speakers use *quite* in its emphatic function is 2.42 per 1,000 words, compared with the working-class frequency of 0.66. In the hedging function the frequencies are middle-class 1.2 and working-class 0.52. The middle-class speakers thus use *quite* twice as often as the working-class speakers in a hedging function and almost four times as often in the emphatic function.

The final adverb to be examined is *just*. In the Ayr interviews the difference in the frequencies of *just* were minimal (MC 5.01/WC 4.84). The frequencies for the Glasgow speakers are shown in figure 10.3, which indicates that the social class differences are small and not significant. This is the only example of a very common adverb that the working-class adults use more frequently (6.72 per 1,000 words) than the middle-class adults (5.28). There are, however, also social class differences in the use of *just*. Although the working-class adults use *just* slightly more frequently (6.18 per 1,000 words) than the middle-class adults (5.22 per 1,000 words), they do not use it in exactly the same way.

In Ayr, following the analysis presented in Lee (1987), I separated the uses of *just* into four categories, as shown in (3). The first is with reference to time, usually the immediate past, as in examples (i.a, i.b). The second use is as an intensifier with the general sense of "exactly," as in examples (ii.a, ii.b). The third use is in the sense

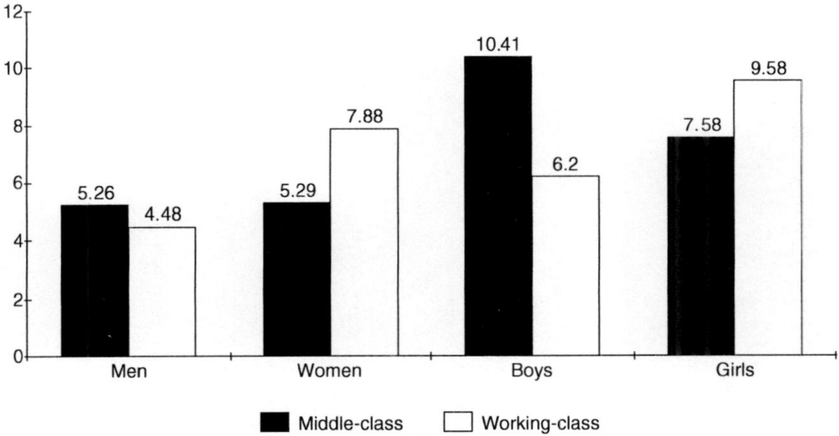

FIGURE 10.3. Frequency of *just* in Glasgow (frequency per 1,000 words)

of "only," as in examples (iii.a, iii.b). Finally, there is the sense of "simply," as shown in examples (iv.a, iv.b).

(3)   (the *a* examples are middle-class, *b* examples working-class)
       Immediate past.
             i.a.   I've *just* realized something (10R)
             i.b.   that it's *just* opened up again (13R)
       Exactly.
             ii.a. yes that's *just* what I was thinking (12L)
             ii.b. well *just* as it turns round the bend (15L)
       Only.
             iii.a. but it's *just* a baby (12L)
             iii.b. it was *just* the two of us (14L)
       Simply.
             iv.a. I'll *just* take everything out of the dining room (10R)
             iv.b. I'll *just* go alang (13R)

The examples in (3) show that both groups use *just* in all four senses, but they do not use them equally frequently, as shown in figure 10.4. The working-class adults use *just* more often in the "simply" sense, while the middle-class adults make more frequent use of the "recency" and "exactly" senses than do the working-class speakers. The latter middle-class use is most distinctive when employed emphatically with adjectives and verbs as in (4 a–c) and the second before the hedge *sort of* as in (4 d–e).

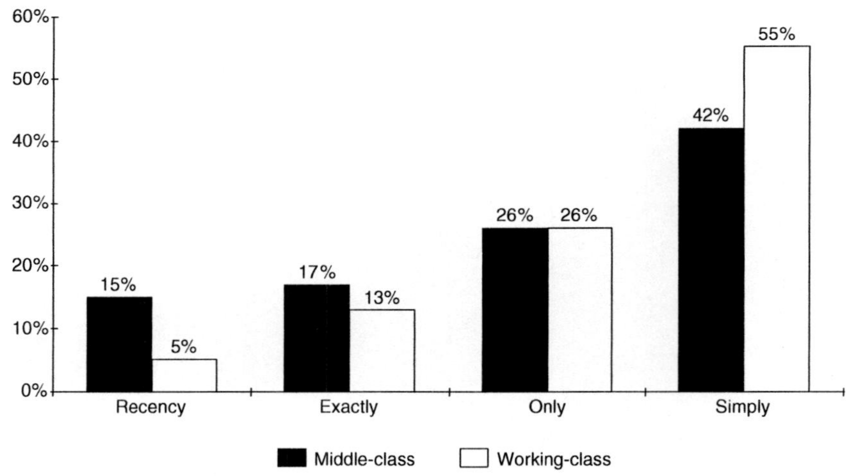

FIGURE 10.4. Uses of *just* by Glasgow adults

(4)

    a. It's *just* awful. I mean that's my lot plus another three—it's *just*
horrendous you know absolute madness (10R)

    b. and I mean she was *just* impeccable (16R)

    c. and it *just* poured (16L)

    d. oh it's *just* out of this world (12R)

There is nothing remarkable about this emphatic use but it does not occur in the working-class sessions.

The middle-class speakers also use *just* with hedges, as in (5).

(5)   (Hedges in bold)

    a. Truro's really *just* a **sort of** market town (10L)

    b. to stop and *just* **sort of** pitch their camp there for the day (16R)

    c. it's really *just* a **sort of** buffer (10R)

    d. it **kind of** had been programmed to really **sort of** *just* keep you in order (12R)

There are not many examples of these uses in the middle-class conversations, but there are none in the working-class conversations.

Adolescents

Table 10.9 shows the comparable figures for the Glasgow adolescents for *very*, *quite*, and *just*. The differences from the adult figures are quite striking. The adolescents use *very* ($p < .001$) and *quite* ($p < .05$) significantly less than the adults (both groups of adolescents barely use *very*), but they use *just* more frequently than the adults (n.s.).

TABLE 10.9. Relative frequency of *very*, *quite*, and *just* in Glasgow adolescent conversations.

	Working-class		Middle-class	
	No.	*[a]Freq.*	*No.*	*Freq.*
very	3	0.14	14	0.64
quite	2	0.09	54	2.46
just	177	8.39	199	9.06

[a]per 1,000 words

The middle-class adolescents use *quite* more than twice as often ($p < .01$) as do the working-class adolescents.

In the adolescent conversations there are no social class differences in the use of *just*, with the middle-class adolescents using *just* with a frequency of 9.06 per 1,000 words and the working-class adolescents with a frequency of 8.39 per 1,000 words. There are also few differences in the distribution of the senses, as shown in table 10.10.

The pattern and frequencies are remarkably similar to those in the adult conversations, showing that unlike *very* and *quite*, the adolescents are using the word in much the same way as the adults. There are even examples of the emphatic evaluative use (6a, b) and of the use of *just* with hedges (6c, d) that occur only in the conversations between middle-class adolescents.

(6)
    a. she's *just* dead annoying (5L)
    b. and I mean that's *just* stupid (5R)
    c. she's *just* sort of standing in for Mister Weir (3L)
    d. and eventually they *just* sort of ran out (4R)

As with the adults, there are few examples, but they occur only in the middle-class conversations.

The gender and social class differences among the adolescents are shown in figure 10.5. Overall the adolescents do not show a gender difference, with the boys using *just* with a frequency of 8.81 per 1,000 words and the girls 8.76. However, within the social class groups there is an inverted pattern. The middle-class boys use *just* with a frequency of 10.41 per 1,000 words, in contrast to the middle-class girls' fre-

TABLE 10.10. Uses of *just* by Glasgow adolescents

	Recency	*Exactly*	*Only*	*Simply*
Middle-class adolescents	11%	14%	29%	47%
Working-class adolescents	10%	13%	26%	51%
All adolescents	11%	13%	27%	49%

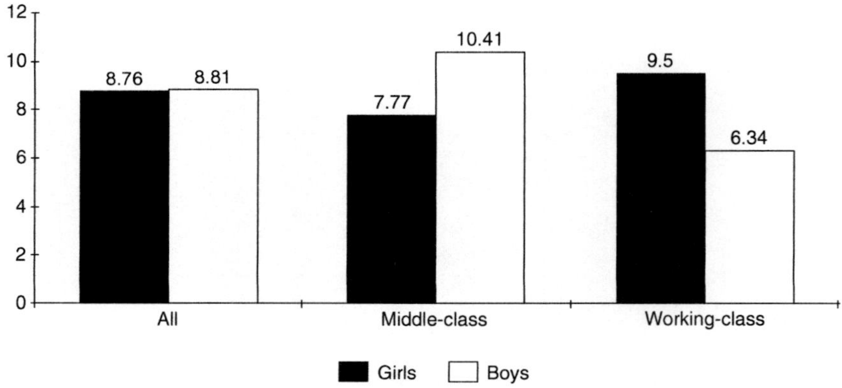

FIGURE 10.5. Frequency of *just* in Glasgow (adolescents only; frequency per 1,000 words)

quency of 7.77. In the working-class adolescent conversations, on the other hand, the boys use *just* with a frequency of only 6.34 per 1,000 words, while the girls use it with a frequency of 9.50 per 1,000 words.

However, the adolescents also use two uninflected intensifiers as shown in (7).

(7)

    a.   this is *pure* embarrassing

    b.   this is *dead* embarrassing

    c.   it's *pure* funny but

    d.   I'd look *dead* funny without a fringe wouldn't I?

    e.   and I was like *really* close to Chi

    f.   I was standing *pure* close to him

    g.   she *pure* does my head in

    h.   oh I *pure* hate these mics

    i.   I felt like *pure* greeting yesterday

    j.   cause like she knew she knew that she was *pure* making me *pure* sad and all that

    k.   she used to be *dead* fat

    l.   she's *dead* skinny now

    m.   they're *dead* healthy just now

    n.   see Stephanie she was *dead dead* quiet in primary

As can be seen from the examples in (7a–d), *pure* and *dead* can both occur as modifiers of adjectives, and the examples in (7e–f) show that *pure* is functionally and semantically similar to *really*.[3] It is possible, therefore, that the working-class adolescents use these uninflected intensifiers more frequently than the middle-class adolescents. That this is in fact the case can be seen in table 10.11.

Even if these totals are added to those in tables 10.6 and 10.9, the difference between the two groups is maintained. The total frequency of inflected and uninflected adverbs among the middle-class adolescents rises from 6.5 per 1,000 words to 24.06, while the corresponding increase among the working-class adolescents is from 2.8

TABLE 10.11. Use of *pure* and *dead* as intensifiers by
Glasgow adolescents

	Pure		Dead		Total	
	No.	Freq.	No.	Freq.	No.	Freq.
Middle-class	87	3.9	31	1.4	118	5.4
Working-class	106	5.0	28	1.3	134	6.4

per 1,000 words to 17.72. It is clear that the use of the uninflected intensifiers *pure* and *dead* has more impact on the speech of the working-class adolescents but does not radically change the picture. However, the social class figures mask an important gender difference, as is apparent in table 10.12. It can be seen from table 10.12 that while both boys and girls use these uninflected intensifiers, girls use them more than three times as frequently ($p < .05$), as can be seen more clearly in figure 10.6.

Adjectives

I also examined the use of adjectives by the two groups of speakers in Ayr and found that the middle-class speakers used adjectives with a frequency of 22.41 per 1,000 in contrast to the lower-class speakers, with a frequency of 11.74 ($p < .05$). The figures for the Glasgow sample show a similar distribution: the middle-class speakers use adjectives with a frequency of 34.16 and the working-class speakers with a frequency of 24.74 (n.s.). Once again, the pattern is repeated, as can be seen in figure 10.7, though the distance between the groups is not significant in Glasgow.

The pattern of social class difference found among the adults is repeated in the adolescent conversations. The middle-class adolescents use adjectives with a frequency of 29.79 per 1,000 words, and for the working-class adolescents the frequency is 21.86 (n.s). The social class differences that were found in the Ayr interviews have thus been repeated in the Glasgow conversations, among both adults and adolescents, though in neither case are the differences statistically significant.

It is not a difference in the frequency with which adjectives are used that distinguishes the social class groups in Glasgow. There are differences in the kinds of

TABLE 10.12. Gender differences in the use of *pure* and *dead* as
intensifiers by adolescents

	Pure		Dead		Total	
	No.	Freq.	No.	Freq.	No.	Freq.
Middle-class girls	58	5.6	23	2.2	81	7.8
Middle-class boys	29	2.5	8	0.7	37	3.2
Working-class girls	97	7.1	25	1.8	122	8.9
Working-class boys	9	1.2	3	0.4	12	1.6
All girls	155	6.9	48	2.0	203	8.4
All boys	38	2.0	11	0.6	49	2.6

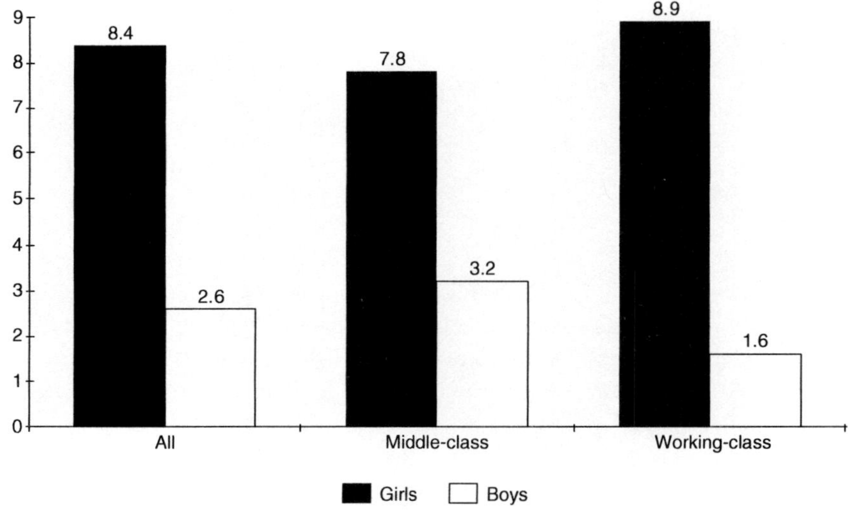

FIGURE 10.6. Combined frequencies of for *pure* and *just* in Glasgow (adolescents only; frequency per 1,000 words)

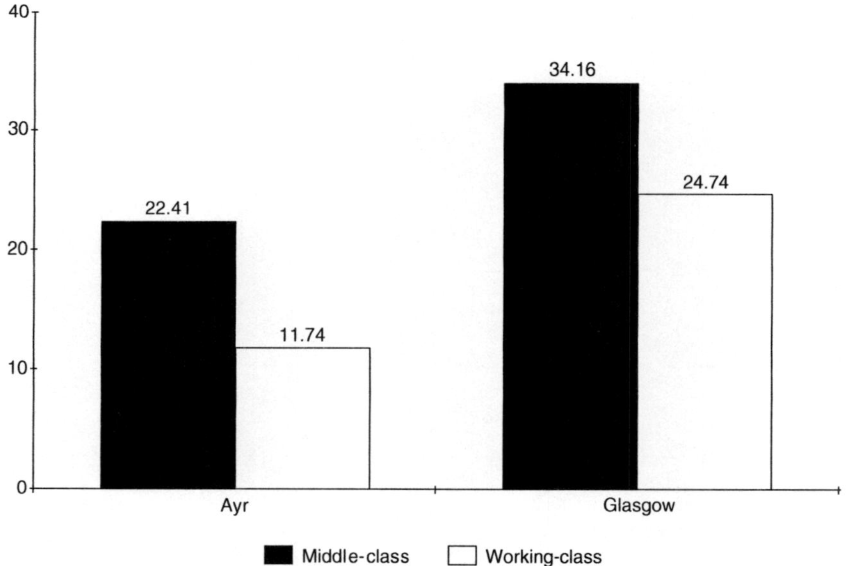

FIGURE 10.7. Frequency of adjectives in Ayr and Glasgow (adults only; frequency per 1,000 words)

adjectives used. Figure 10.8 shows the difference in frequency with which evaluative adjectives such as *brilliant, horrendous, impeccable* are used. Dixon (1982) has seven semantic subclasses of adjectives, of which only two are evaluative (value, e.g., *good, delicious*; and human propensity, e.g., *gracious, proud*). The others are dimension (e.g., *long*), physical property (e.g., *hard*), speed (e.g., *fast*), age (e.g., *young*), and color (e.g., *green*). In the following tables, evaluative adjectives include the types that Dixon classifies as value and human propensity. Adjectives of this type are more subjective than descriptive (Adamson 2000: 54).

Figure 10.8 shows that the middle-class speakers use evaluative adjectives twice as frequently as the working-class speakers ($p < .004$), and there are no gender differences.

Illustrations of the use of adverbs and adjectives

Some of the adverbs in table 10.4 suggest an attitude of confidence in making categorical judgments that is less apparent in the working-class conversations: *amazingly, awfully, badly, drastically, enormously, overly, properly*, and *terribly*. Even the other adverbs can have this effect when combined with adjectives as in (8).

(8)　(Conversation 10—Middle-class women)
　　　L10:　mhm her mother had me in stitches one day
　　　　　　when I bumped into them in town
　　　　　　and I think I'd had a *particularly* bad day with Kim
　　　　　　and she was telling me all about her Fiona
　　　　　　and what she was like at Kim's age
　　　　　　who—and she was *apparently absolutely* horrendous
　　　　　　and she said "It's all right
　　　　　　she grows out of it by the time she's eighteen"
　　　　　　and I'm going "Eighteen?
　　　　　　that's an *awful* long way away"

The speaker is a middle-class woman. Sequences of this kind with several adverbs in close succession do not occur in the working-class conversations. Similar sequences can be found in the middle-class male conversations. First an example from two middle-class men:

(9)　(Conversation 11—Middle-class men)
　　　11R:　and I'm *fairly* sure that if you don't speak well
　　　　　　and you don't speak *properly*
　　　　　　er it can mean that you're denied the—let's say a post or whatever
　　　11L:　hm
　　　　　　I think even in this place the number of promotions
　　　　　　there have been from the Language Department
　　　　　　is *clearly* out of proportion
　　　　　　significantly out of proportion to the number of promotions
　　　　　　that have been available to staff *generally*

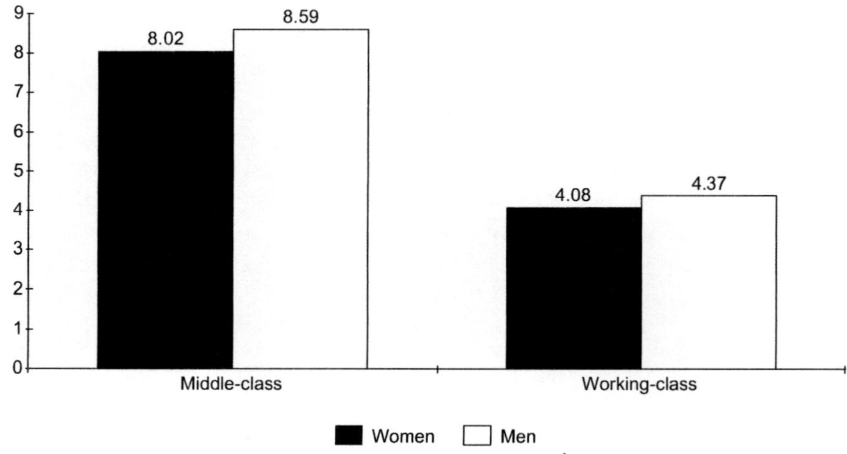

FIGURE 10.8. Frequency of evaluative adjectives in Glasgow (adults only; frequency per 1,000 words)

Here is another middle-class man:

(10)   (Conversation 16—Middle-class men)
        L16: and you come over a crest down a hill
              and there's a track on the left with a gate
              and you *probably* won't notice that
              but you would *immediately* notice
              there was very *suddenly* water on your left
              which rather looks like it might be a big inlet of Loch Lomond
              but it's not
              it's an *entirely* self-contained little lochan called the Dhu Lochan

Here is an example of the use of *very* from two middle-class men talking about the bay referred to in (10):

(11)   (Conversation 16—Middle-class men)
        16L: there's a *very* steep descent to it from the road . . .
              it's a *very* gradual descent to the bay . . .
              and it is actually a *very* nice walk
        16R: I—I was actually *very* favorably im—impressed
              with the way the—the parking areas had been sorted out
              em Shalachie Bay's *very* nice
              I was speaking to the little girl who's the warden there
              and she says that the—right up at Rowardennan it gets *very* busy

Sometimes *very* is repeated for emphasis:

(12)   (Conversation 16—Middle-class men)
    16L: unlike the Kenyan coast where there's you know
           there's no currents like that at all
           but *very very* strong currents at Durban
    16R: hmm
           yes I—
    16L: and—and red sand
           not the beautiful white Kenyan sand and Mozambique sand
           it's—it's like Clyde coast builders sand
           total total change um even compared to the Capetown sands
           which are all white
           very very red

There is nothing remarkable in the uses of *very* in examples (11) and (12) except that for some reason they do not occur in the working-class conversations.

Another use of adverbs by the Glasgow middle-class speakers is in close contact with hedges of various kinds,[4] as in example (13) from two middle-class women talking about a computer program:

(13)   (Conversation 12—Middle-class women; hedges in bold, adverbs in italics)
    L12: it was *quite* chatty
    R12: yes
    L12: you know it **kind of** had been programmed
           to *really* **sort of** *just* keep you in order
           and not—not work too hard
           which is *quite* good
           but it was *quite* an old-fashioned model
           I can't remember what it was
           but it was *certainly* different from
           all the pc's that we're using
           and the the Macs that are being used now
    R12: yes yes they're *quite* user-friendly
    L12: mm *very* user-friendly *really*
    R12: yes yeah
    L12: yes I'm not *really* computer-minded
           but I'm having to learn
    R12: Oh I'm sure you though—you—you are much more
           than you think *really*
    L12: well it's *quite* surprising the things I find myself doing
           or trying to do

Here is another example from a middle-class man:

(14)   (Conversation 16—Middle-class men)
    L16: but the—the—the—the actual wee beach is—is *quite* nice
           because it's **sort of** rough sand that you can sit on

> and then *just* at the water's end there are enough boulders
> to put people off from going in
> but if you *actually* go about six feet beyond the boulders
> it is all sand under water
> so it's *actually quite* nice for swimming

Conclusion

An examination of the Glasgow conversations suggests that Bernstein was correct when he drew attention to a difference between middle-class speakers and working-class speakers in the use of adverbs, though as we have seen the difference applies generally and not only to "uncommon adverbs." There are minor age and gender differences in the use of adverbs, but these are of little interest compared with the powerful social class difference. The implications of this finding will be discussed in the chapter on discourse style.

Articles and Pronouns

$\mathbf{A}$s was stated in chapter 1, the working assumption for comparative quantitative analysis is that all speakers have the same opportunity to use certain linguistic forms in what are similar recording conditions. Obviously, there is no reason to expect that every linguistic form has an equal chance of occurring in each recording. There are, however, some forms that are so frequent in any discourse that there is justification for starting out from the assumption that there will be no great difference in the frequency of their use. Two prime candidates are the indefinite article *a/an* and the definite article *the*. These two, along with *of*, *and*, and *to*, are the five most common items in any large corpus. It is therefore worth looking to see if there are group differences in their use.

There are two interesting aspects of figure 11.1. The first is that there are no social class differences. In fact, the frequency of the definite article is the same for the middle-class adults and the working-class adults. Since there are more than 3,500 tokens of *the* in the adult conversations, the similarity in the frequency of use by the two social classes is worth noting. The second point is that the adolescents use the articles with a frequency that is two-thirds that of the adults ($p < .001$).

There is one social class difference, but the numbers are too small to be more than suggestive. Complex noun phrases are rare in spontaneous spoken language (Miller and Weinert 1998: 135). The middle-class adults are more likely to use a noun phrase with several premodifiers, as in (1):

(1)   a. there used to be a *very short cropped blond* chap (10L)
        b. some of the men had *enormous great beer* bellies (10R)

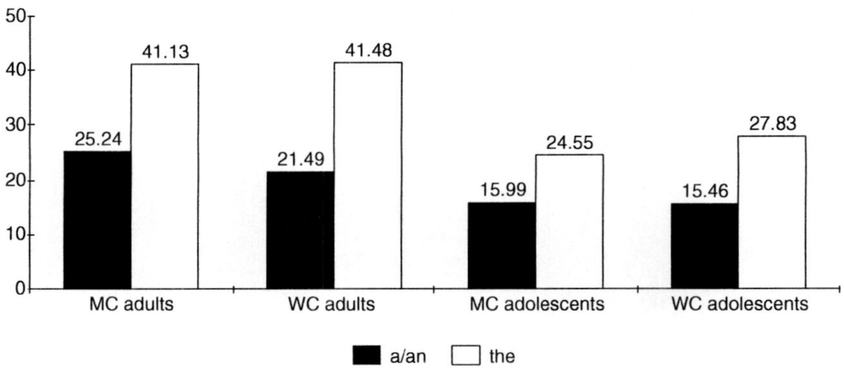

FIGURE 11.1. Frequencies of article use in Glasgow (frequency per 1,000 words)

   c. not the *beautiful white Kenyan* sand (16L)
   d. which is just a *warm wooly all-in-one* suit (16R)

All these examples come from the middle-class conversations and do not seem re-markable by the standards of written language, but they are very rare even in the middle-class conversations and almost absent in the working-class conversations. Consistent with the findings of Miller and Weinert (1988), none of these complex noun phrases occurs in subject position. The evidence suggests that complex noun phrases place a very heavy burden on the speaker because frequently the phrase is involved with hedges or repairs, as in (2):

(2)   a. and she's a *very **you know** neat em **kind of** gentle* person (10R)
      b. looks like em a ***sort of** Middle Eastern origin* lady (16L)

There is one striking example in the working-class conversations of what looks like an avoidance of a complex noun phrase:

(3)   because she's big in the mouth and a good orator and tough and forceful (17R)

The adolescent boys use complex noun phrases only for abuse:

(4)   a. *big hockhead slavery* cunt (6R)
      b. hello you *little stinky* bitch (9L)

In addition to age differences in the use of the articles, there are also gender differences, as can be seen in figure 11.2. This figure shows quite clearly that males use the articles more frequently than females, and that is true for adults and adolescents ($p < .05$). The gender differences are perhaps the more remarkable, given the lack of social class differences.

   Another linguistic category that is extremely frequent consists of the personal pronouns.[1] The age and social class differences are shown in figure 11.3. It can be

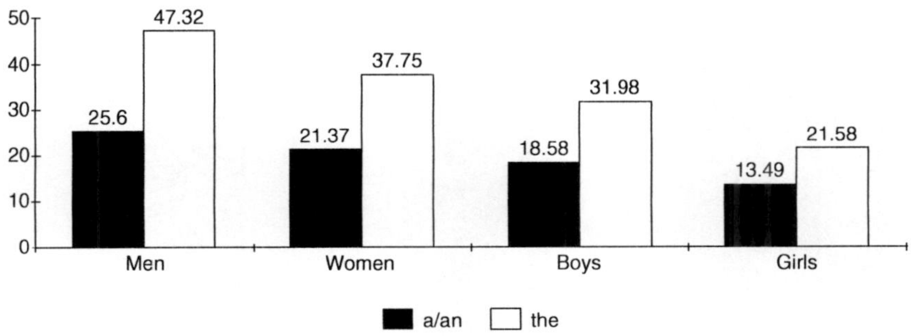

FIGURE 11.2. Gender differences in article use in Glasgow (frequency per 1,000 words)

seen in figure 11.3 that, in contrast to the articles, the adolescents use pronouns more frequently than the adults ($p < .01$). In fact, the combined frequency of pronouns and articles for the adolescents (213.97) is almost as high as that for the adults (224.02), which suggests that for the adolescents pronouns take over some of the functions for which the adults use full noun phrases. Figure 11.3 also shows that the working-class speakers use pronouns more frequently than the middle-class speakers, though this difference fails to reach significance ($p = .081$). The gender difference, however, is greater than the social class difference for both age-groups, as can be seen in figure 11.4. This figure shows that the women and girls use pronouns more frequently than the men and boys ($p < .001$). Figure 11.5 shows the frequency with which men and women use each pronoun.[2]

It can be seen from figure 11.5 that the women use the personal pronoun *he* (10.1 per 1,000 words) almost twice as often as do the men (6.9 per 1,000 words) and the pronoun *she* four times as frequently (20.2 versus 5.2).[3] The combined totals of the

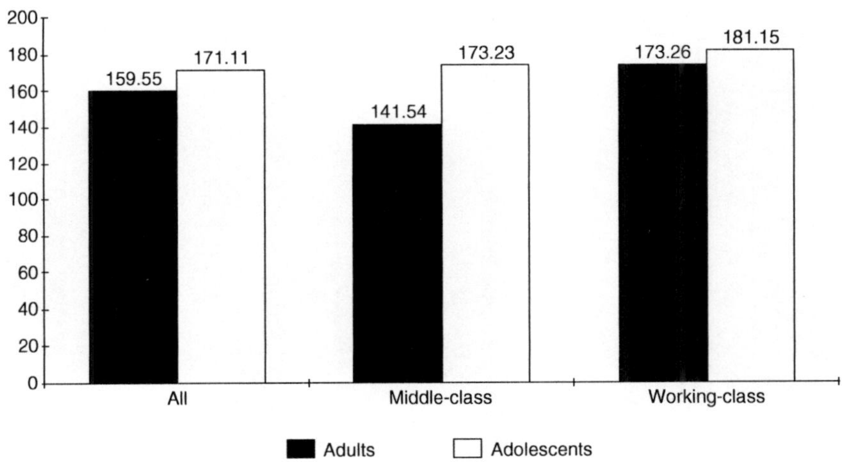

FIGURE 11.3. Frequency of pronoun use in Glasgow (frequency per 1,000 words)

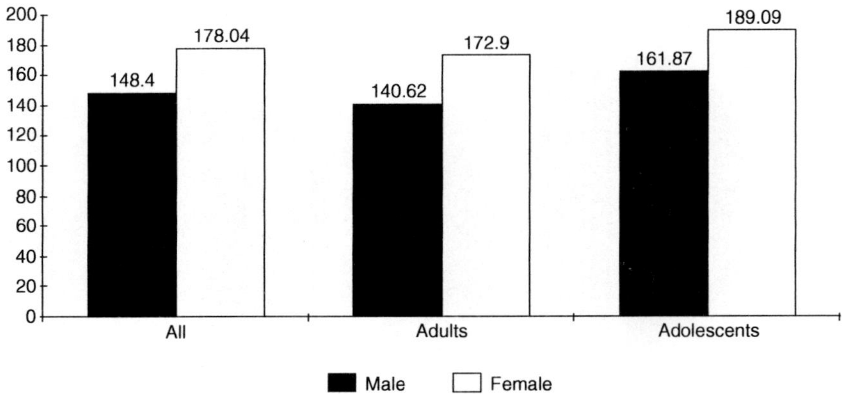

FIGURE 11.4. Age and gender differences in pronoun use in Glasgow (frequency per 1,000 words)

two pronouns are 30.3 for the women and 12.1 for the men ($p < .001$). These differences are all the more striking in that there are only minor differences in the use of the other pronouns, including the first-person pronoun *I*. Since the conversations were unstructured and open-ended, the similarity in the use of pronouns other than *he* and *she* between the two groups is almost more remarkable than their differences in the use of the gender-specific pronouns.

It can be seen from figure 11.6 that while both girls and boys use forms of the pronoun *he* equally frequently, the girls use forms of the pronoun *she* (30.6 per 1,000

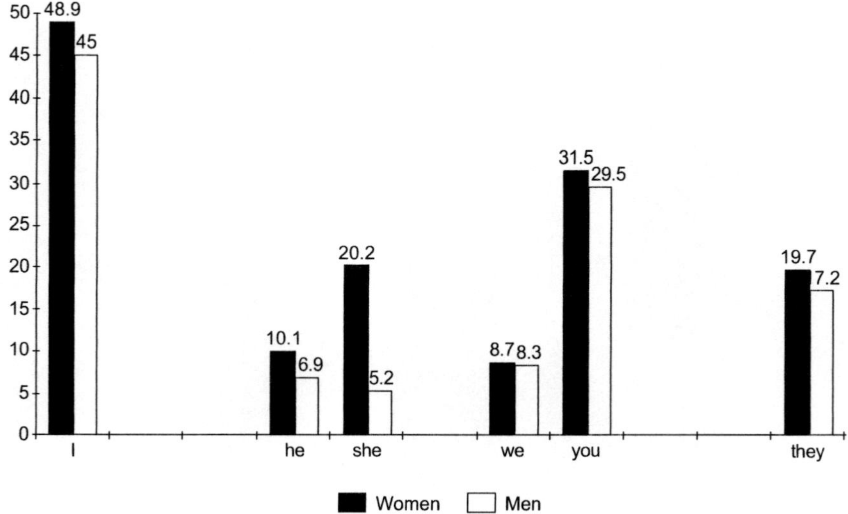

FIGURE 11.5. Gender differences in individual pronoun use in Glasgow (adults only; frequency per 1,000 words)

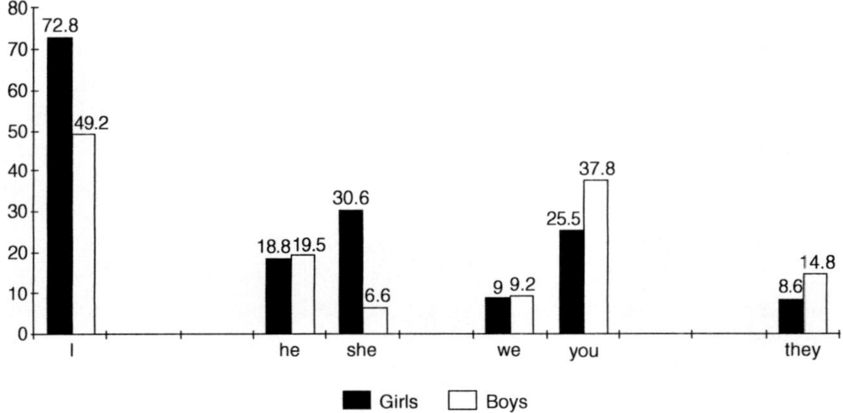

FIGURE 11.6. Gender differences in individual pronoun use in Glasgow (adolescents only; frequency per 1,000 words)

words) almost five times more frequently ($p < .001$) than the boys (6.6 per 1,000 words). Added to this is the more frequent use of the first-person pronoun *I* by girls ($p < .001$), so that it is clear that girls talk a lot more about girls than either boys or girls talk about boys.

There is another category of pronoun that shows social class and gender variation, namely, relative pronouns. In Ayr the middle-class speakers used WH-forms of the pronoun (*who, which*) more than five times as frequently (4.38 versus 0.79) as the lower-class speakers. Figure 11.7 shows that a similar social class difference exists in the Glasgow conversations. It can be seen that the middle-class speakers, both adults

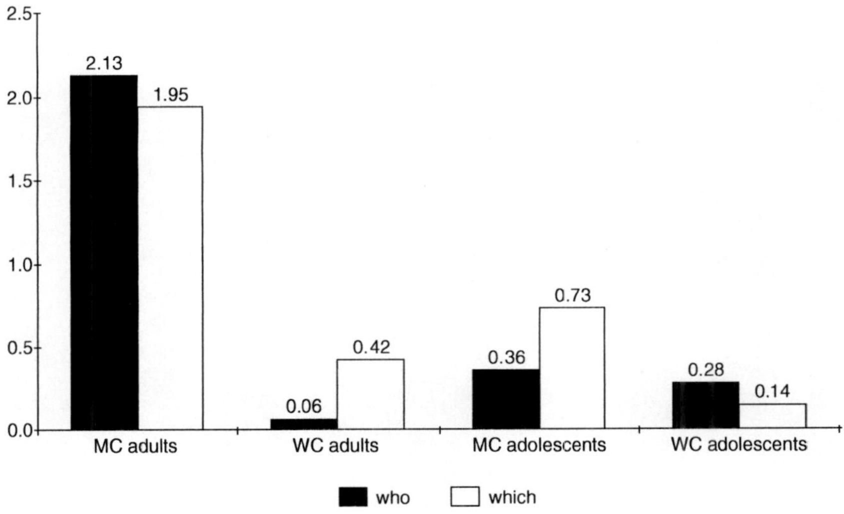

FIGURE 11.7. Frequency of WH-relative pronouns in Glasgow (frequency per 1,000 words)

and adolescents, use WH-forms more frequently than the working-class speakers ($p < .001$). There is also a gender difference, as can be seen in figure 11.8, which shows that the men and boys use *which* much more frequently than the women and girls ($p < .01$). Since *which* is more commonly used with inanimates, this difference suggests that the males are more likely to use relative pronouns with reference to things than to people. Also, the adults use *which* more often than the adolescents ($p < .005$)

The quantitative analysis of the articles and pronouns has shown that males are more likely to use full noun phrases with articles and *which* as a relative pronoun, and that females are more likely to use gender-specific pronouns with reference to males and females. Is there any other evidence that might be consistent with these findings?

One is the use of proper nouns. In the adult conversations there are various references to individuals by name. The frequency with which these occur is shown in table 11.1. It can be seen from this table that there are essentially no differences between the two social classes, but the gender differences are considerable, with the men making very few references to named people (2.6 per 1,000 words) compared with the women (9.7 per 1,000 words) ($p < .05$), and the women naming other women twice as frequently (6.6 per 1,000 words) as they name men (3.1 per 1,000 words) ($p < .001$).[4]

A similar picture can be found in the adolescent sessions, as is apparent in table 11.2, which shows both social class and gender differences. References to named people in the working-class adolescent conversations (24.6 per 1,000 words) are significantly more frequent than those in the middle-class adolescent conversations (17.9 per 1,000 words) ($p < .05$). More strikingly, the girls name people (29.0 per 1,000 words) almost three times as frequently as the boys (11.3 per 1,000 words) ($p < .001$). It is also clear that whereas both boys and girls name boys with about the same fre-

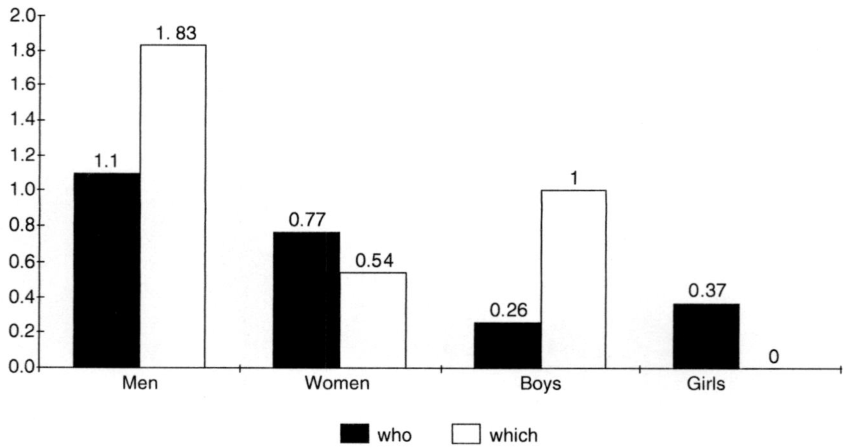

FIGURE 11.8. Gender differences in the use of WH-relative pronouns (frequency per 1,000 words)

TABLE 11.1. Named references to people in Glasgow adult conversations

	Refs. to men		Refs. to women		All	
	(n)	[a]Freq.	(n)	Freq.	(n)	Freq.
Middle-class adults	78	2.3	143	4.2	221	6.5
Working-class adults	134	2.7	232	4.6	366	7.3
Women	161	3.1	343	6.6	504	9.7
Men	51	1.6	32	1.0	83	2.6

[a]per 1,000 words

quency, girls name other girls much more frequently (20.6 per 1,000 words) than boys name girls (2.5 per 1,000 words) ($p < .001$).

The implication of figures 11.5 and 11.6 and tables 11.1 and 11.2 is that in the Glasgow sessions, with both adolescents and adults, the females talk about people more than the males do. This is consistent with the results obtained by Nordenstam (1992: 80) in a similar kind of study.[5] She found that in the same-sex dyads the women mentioned almost twice as many names (48) of intimate acquaintances and relations as the men did (26), but when the raw figures are converted to frequencies, 1.71 per 1,000 words for women and 1.28 for men, the difference is less striking, and the frequencies are much lower than in the Glasgow conversations.[6]

More evidence of this will be presented later. First, however, are there any similar simple counts in which the males score higher than the females? There is one complementary set of figures that does not depend upon any subjective judgment to identify: named references to places. Table 11.3 gives the figures for named references to physical locations in the adult conversations. It can be seen in table 11.3 that there are no social class differences, but the men name places (18.2 per 1,000 words) almost three times as often as the women (6.66 per 1,000 words) ($p < .05$).[7] Table 11.4 gives the figures for named references to physical locations in the adolescent conversations. It can be seen in table 11.4 that the working-class adolescents name places slightly more frequently than the middle-class adolescents, but the gender difference is greater, with the boys naming places (5.44 per 1,000 words) more than twice as frequently as the girls (2.45 per 1,000 words).

Looking at the conversations as a whole, it is possible to identify those parts where the participants are talking about other people. (There is an interpretative aspect here,

TABLE 11.2. Named references to people in Glasgow adolescent conversations

	Refs. to boys		Refs. to girls		All	
	(n)	[a]Freq.	(n)	Freq.	(n)	Freq.
Middle-class adolescents	154	7.0	240	10.9	394	17.9
Working-class adolescents	216	10.2	303	14.4	519	24.6
All girls	203	8.4	496	20.6	699	29.0
All boys	167	8.8	47	2.5	214	11.3

[a]per 1,000 words

TABLE 11.3. Named references to
places in adult conversations

	(n)	Freq.
Middle-class adults	385	11.22
Working-class adults	557	11.07
Women	345	6.66
Men	597	18.20

since it is not always easy to tell when one topic ends and another begins.) The figures in tables 11.5 and 11.6 are based upon word counts of the proportion of each
session devoted to the discussion of people known to the speakers. As with the numbers in tables 11.1 and 11.2, this excludes discussion of public figures such as
footballers or musicians

The range among the women is from 63% to 13% and among the men from 25%
to 5%. It is clear from these figures that in the Glasgow conversations the women
talk much more about people than the men do.

The figures for the adolescents are given in table 11.6. As with the adults, it is
the girls who spend more time discussing people. The gender differences are even
more marked by a comparison of the individual sessions. In one conversation between two middle-class girls, 88% is devoted to discussing their peers and teachers,
and in the two conversations by working-class girls the proportion is 76%. In contrast, among the boys the highest proportion is 38% in one of the conversations between middle-class boys, and in one of the working-class boys' conversation the
proportion is only 7%.

The pattern of gender differences in the Glasgow conversations is similar to that
found elsewhere. Johnstone, reporting on 68 stories collected by her students in Fort
Wayne, Indiana, found gender differences. Though she does not give figures, she
found that "women use more personal names in their stories than do men, even when
their audiences are unfamiliar with the names. Men provide more details about objects" (1990: 68). Similar results were found by Holmes in a New Zealand sample of
30 same-sex conversations. Holmes found that the stories reflected the different daily
preoccupations of men and women: "The women focus on relationships and people,

TABLE 11.4. Named references to places
in adolescent conversations

	(n)	[a]Freq.
Middle-class adolescents	68	3.1
Working-class adolescents	94	4.6
All girls	59	2.45
All boys	103	5.44

[a]per 1,000 words

TABLE 11.5. Proportion of talk
about people in Glasgow adult
conversations

	Proportion
Middle-class adults	35%
Working-class adults	25%
Women	38%
Men	15%

affirm the importance of their family roles, family connections and friendships. The men focus on work and sport, events, activities and things, and affirm the importance of being in control, even when they don't achieve it" (1997: 286).

Kipers (1987) recorded 470 conversations in the faculty room of a middle school in New Jersey. She found that in female-only conversations the most frequent topics were house and family (28%), social issues (21%), work (14%), and personal and family finance (12%). For male-only conversations the most frequent topics were work (39%), recreation (28%), and miscellaneous (11%). (The latter category consisted of "telling jokes," "the weather," "book read by the conversants," and "quitting smoking.") The greatest differences in individual topics are that their own children take up 9% of the women's conversations, 5% of the mixed-sex conversations, but less than 1% of the men's. In contrast, spectator sports occupy 13% of the men's conversations, 4% of the mixed-sex conversations, but none of the women's conversations. Nordenstam, although giving no proportions, found that in the same-sex dyads the men "talked about their jobs, sports, and cars, etc. . . . [the women] about children and personal relations, and jobs" (1992: 85).

Eggins and Slade (1997) examined three hours of casual conversation collected during coffee breaks in three different workplaces. They found that "the most frequently occurring stretch of talk in the all-male group was teasing or sending up (friendly ridicule)" (1997: 267). The men did not gossip and tended to talk about work or sports rather than personal details. In the all-female group there was a predominance of gossip ("broadly defined as talk which involves pejorative judgment of an absent other" [278]) and storytelling. There was no teasing. The women discussed "quite personal details including boyfriends, weddings, marriages, children,

TABLE 11.6. Proportion of talk about
people in Glasgow adolescent
conversations

	Proportion
Middle-class adolescents	37%
Working-class adolescents	56%
All girls	64%
All boys	24%

and relatives" (268). In the mixed group of men and women, "amusing or surprising stories dominated the conversation" (268), and there was some joke telling and teasing. In social psychology, a personality study of gender-related interests on a People-Things dimension found that "about four times as many men were on the Things side as were on the People side of the People-Things dimension, and about twice as many women were on the People side as were on the Things side, relationships that were highly significant" (Lippa 1998: 999).

Thus the Glasgow conversations are consistent with reports from other situations. Both the adolescent girls and the women talk much more about people than do the boys or the men. It has also been shown, however, that boys and men are more likely to talk about places. The quantitative analysis is consistent with the qualitative. In their use of articles and pronouns the males show themselves to be less interested in people than are the females.

12

The Use of Dialogue in Narratives

One of the commonest activities when people are sitting around talking in relaxed conditions is to tell stories (Labov 1972; Sacks 1974; Bauman 1986; Polanyi 1985; Johnstone 1990). It is one of the signs that an interview with an "intimate stranger" (Gregersen and Pedersen 1991: 54) is reaching a comfortable level when the speaker begins to tell stories without being prompted. The number of unsolicited narratives in the Ayr interviews was one of the factors that encouraged me to look more closely at the discourse structure of the interview transcripts. These stories are not told in response to a specific question, such as Labov's Danger-of-Death question (Labov 1972), but are told because the speaker thinks that the story would interest the listener. I was therefore interested to see whether the speakers in the Glasgow sample would tell each other stories in the context of the recording situation.

In the Ayr interviews, on average 29% of the lower-class transcripts contained narratives, as did 22% of the middle-class transcripts. Tables 12.1 and 12.2 are repeated from chapter 3 for convenience and show the proportion of narrative in the Glasgow conversations. Included in this category are only those sections where the speaker was describing an event or events that occurred at a specific time and place. Reminiscences referring to typical kinds of events that occurred in the past are not included.

It can be seen from tables 12.1 and 12.2 that the proportion of the sessions devoted to narrative is similar for the adolescents and the adults taken as groups, and is even higher than in the Ayr interviews. This is further evidence of the success of the methodology in obtaining good examples of impromptu speech. There was no instruction to these speakers to tell stories, and nobody was prompting them to do so.

TABLE 12.1. Proportion of narrative
in Glasgow adolescent conversations

Middle-class girls	28%
Middle-class boys	27%
Working-class girls	60%
Working-class boys	5%
All girls	46%
All boys	18%
Middle-class adolescents	27%
Working-class adolescents	40%
All adolescents	34%

They told stories because that is what people who know each other often do when they are "just chatting."

The overall figures, however, mask some significant differences. There is no overall social class difference, but the females have a significantly higher proportion of narratives ($p < .01$). The social class picture is confounded by a gender difference. The working-class women show a proportion of narrative that is three times higher than that of the working-class men ($p < .01$), and among the adolescents the working-class girls devote 12 times the amount that the working-class boys do to presenting narratives ($p < .001$). However, the social class difference among the females just fails to reach significance ($p = .055$), although the working-class women and girls have a higher proportion of narratives. Among the males the situation is reversed, with the middle-class men and boys producing more narratives ($p < .001$). A clearer picture can be seen by looking at the individual sessions, as shown in tables 12.3 and 12.4.

It can be seen from tables 12.3 and 12.4 that with two striking exceptions (conversations 7 and 14) the speakers tend to reciprocate; where one of the speakers tells many stories (e.g., conversation 8), the other speaker also does, and in conversation 6 neither of the boys tells any. This kind of reciprocity in telling stories is a common phenomenon (Sacks 1974).

Interest in the structure of oral narrative (e.g., Labov 1972; Johnstone 1990) has focused attention on situations where a speaker in telling a story reproduces the ac-

TABLE 12.2. Proportion of narrative
in Glasgow adult conversations

Middle-class women	32%
Middle-class men	35%
Working-class women	44%
Working-class men	13%
All women	39%
All men	23%
Middle-class adults	33%
Working-class adults	33%
All adults	33%

TABLE 12.3. Proportion of narrative in Glasgow adolescent conversations

	Left speaker	Right speaker	Total
Conversation 8—working-class girls	62%	77%	69%
Conversation 7—working-class girls	16%	68%	50%
Conversation 2—middle-class girls	36%	25%	29%
Conversation 4—middle-class boys	21%	31%	27%
Conversation 3—middle-class boys	22%	28%	26%
Conversation 5—middle-class girls	37%	10%	26%
Conversation 9—working-class boys	16%	5%	11%
Conversation 6—working-class boys	0%	0%	0%

tual words someone (including the speaker) allegedly said or thought at the time. Traditionally known as *oratio recta* (in contrast to *oratio obliqua*, or "reported speech"), this form of reporting "an utterance belonging to *someone else*" (Voloshinov 1986: 116, emphasis in original) has been examined as "direct speech" (Coulmas 1986), "quoted direct speech" (Macaulay 1987a), and "constructed dialogue" (Tannen 1989). Li claims that "direct speech is universal; indirect speech is not" (1986:39) and that "direct quote is the most common expression at the peak of oral narratives in many languages" (40). Tannen points that "many researchers (for example, Labov 1972, Chafe 1982, Ochs 1979, Tannen 1982, Schiffrin 1981) have observed that narration is more vivid when speech is presented as first-person dialogue ('direct quotation') rather than third-person report ('indirect quotation')" (Tannen 1986: 311). The use of dialogue is therefore a further indication of the quality of the interaction, since it shows the speaker "performing" the narrative (Wolfson 1976) for the benefit of the listener.

The percentage of the narrative in the Glasgow adult conversations that is conveyed in dialogue is shown in figure 12.1. It is the women who include the most dialogue in their stories ($p < .05$), at roughly a quarter of the narratives, while the men's stories only contain less than a tenth of dialogue. The figures for the Glasgow adolescents are shown in figure 12.2. Here it is the girls, particularly the working-class girls, who tell the most narratives, but the percentage of dialogue is fairly similar

TABLE 12.4. Proportion of narrative in Glasgow adult conversations

	Left speaker	Right speaker	Total
Conversation 14—working-class women	35%	71%	59%
Conversation 12—middle-class men	49%	38%	45%
Conversation 13—working-class women	36%	50%	44%
Conversation 10—middle-class women	33%	49%	42%
Conversation 16—middle-class men	30%	30%	30%
Conversation 15—working-class women	25%	33%	28%
Conversation 17—working-class men	9%	16%	15%
Conversation 18—working-class men	9%	14%	12%
Conversation 11—middle-class women	12%	9%	11%

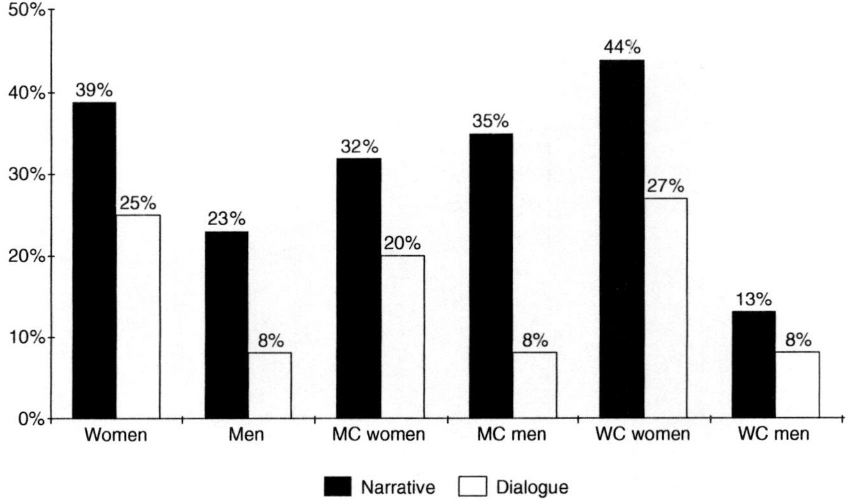

FIGURE 12.1. Percentage of conversation that is narrative and percentage of narrative that is dialogue in Glasgow (adults only)

for all groups, with the exception of the working-class boys. That exception is explained by the fact that the principal narrative in one working-class boys' conversation is a joke told mostly in dialogue, and thus is not equivalent to the use of dialogue in the other narratives.

One of the functions of quoted direct speech is to be able to convey information implicitly that it might be more awkward to express explicitly. As Goffman

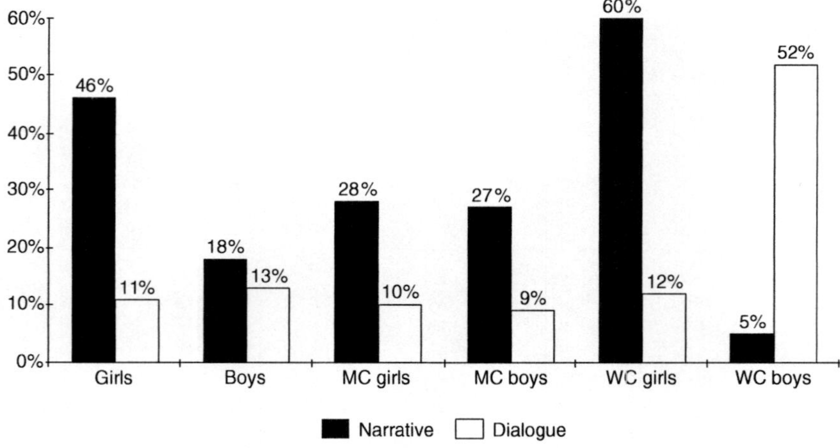

FIGURE 12.2. Percentage of conversation that is narrative and percentage of narrative that is dialogue in Glasgow (adolescents only)

observes, by repeating the words said by someone else, the speaker "means to stand in a relation of reduced responsibility for what he is saying" (1974: 512). This is particularly important in narratives that present the teller in a favorable light where the teller does not want to give the impression of boasting, because of what Pomerantz (1978: 88–92) has called the constraint on self-praise. It is not only in narratives with a dramatic impact that quoted direct speech can be used in this way. Here is an example from a Glasgow working-class woman talking about a conversation with her daughter.

(1)   (Conversation 13—Working-class women)
       1 That's what Diane was saying the other day
       2 we were talking about it
       3 she says to me "When er Susan's fifteen I'll only be thirty-two"
       4 thirty-four or something like that
       5 and I went "Aye and you'll be watching o'er her weans" [*children*]
       6 and I said "It's the granny that watches not the great-granny"
       7 she went "I'm not watching them
       8 I'm not watching the weans"
       9 I says "How not?
      10 I'm watching her"
      11 "Ah but that's different" she says
      12 "I'll be that and I'll be oot and I'll be enjoying myself"
      13 I says "Ah well she has a wean you'll be watching them"
      14 I says "I've done my bit as granny"

In line 10, "I'm watching her," the speaker is presumably using what would have been an exophoric pronoun referring to her daughter's child, present during the exchange. This exophoric use of pronouns is normally restricted to face-to-face communication because otherwise the referent of the pronoun could be obscure. Tannen has warned against taking for granted the accuracy of quoted dialogue: "What is commonly referred to as reported speech or direct quotation in conversation is constructed dialogue, just as surely as is the dialogue created by fiction writers and playwrights" (1986: 311). Tannen's point is that it is the narrator who has chosen to report the interaction in these words and thus is responsible for the impression that they give. The use of quoted dialogue shows that many speakers have a remarkable capacity for constructing dialogue and creating dramatic effects. In example (1), line 10, the speaker has used a form that is not probable outside of the kind of context in which the speaker reports it being used. It would be a very skillful playwright who could reproduce such a form. In line 13 the speaker produces another form that is more typical of spoken language: "Ah well she has a wean you'll be watching them." This is a paratactic construction, equivalent to a conditional clause *if/when she has a wean*. Again it would take a keen observer of spoken language to create such dialogue. There is, however, some evidence of a substantial memory for surface structure and not simply meaning in experiments testing recall of dialogue (Bates, Masling, and Kintsch 1978; Hjelmquist 1984). If this can happen in experimental situations where there is no emotional involvement, it is perhaps not surprising that speakers should be able to recall specific remarks that made an impression on them in a situation that they consider worth narrating.

There is no action in example (1). The speaker and her daughter are simply talking about baby-sitting. The speaker uses dialogue to reveal that her daughter does not appear to be sufficiently grateful for her mother's contribution. She could have reported this, but that might have been perceived as criticism of her daughter. By dramatizing the exchange to show the difference of attitude between her and her daughter, she allows the listener to draw her own conclusion. The speaker shows herself as having been helpful to her daughter, but there is a limit to her willingness to do it for her great-grandchildren: "I've done my bit as granny." By presenting it in dialogue form, 13R not only gives this information but also shows the way in which she and her daughter interact.

It is not only the working-class women who use dialogue in this way. The following example is from a conversation between two middle-class women.

(2)   (Conversation 10—Middle-class women)
        1 well I laughed last night
        2 Kate got in here at—
        3 what time did we get home from the concert?
        4 about ten to ten?
        5 first thing "Can I use the phone?"
        6 "Yes"
        7 so she phoned Norma
        8 and she phoned Sarah
        9 and then "Can I use the phone again?"
       10 I said "Yes
       11 who are you phoning this time?"
       12 "I'm just giving Peter a ring to let him know I'm home"
       13 so she missed Peter
       14 he was out so—
       15 he was apparently at his friend's Ricky's
       16 so she and Sarah set off to walk to Ricky's
       17 and then Peter phoned her
       18 and I said "I think she's away to meet you at Ronnie's."
       19 "Right"
       20 so at half ten I looked out the window
       21 and here they were in a clinch down there [*laughs*]
       22 so I daren't look out the window
       23 cause I did it once
       24 and got accused of being a perv [*both laugh*]
       25 so I said "Well you could at least be a bit more discreet about it"
10R: 26 that's right find a bush
10L: 27 I know
       28 "instead of standing out there
       29 and letting the whole of Ledi Road see you"

In (2) the speaker manages to convey what a tolerant mother of a teenage daughter she is while at the same time obviously maintaining certain standards. For example, her daughter asks permission to use the telephone, not only once but twice. In each case, the speaker grants it, although the second time there is an implied reproach ("who are you phoning this time?"). It is not clear whether the speaker uttered the remark about being discreet in lines 25 through 29 to her daughter or to herself. If it was made to her daughter, it would have been on the previous occasion referred to in lines 23 and 24, but more likely it was something the speaker "said" to herself (i.e., thought). The examples in (1) and (2) illustrate the power of quoted dialogue. It is not just, as Clark points out, that it can convey "all manner of speech characteristics" (1996: 175). The more important point is that the narrator can convey a great many subtleties in a complex situation that would be difficult, if not in practice impossible, to express otherwise. Through dialogue the speakers in (1) and (2) illustrate their relationship with their daughters. It would be a rather different kind of speech event if either of them had attempted to describe this relationship in abstract terms and could have been perceived as boasting. Instead, they are able to make their position clear without baldly asserting it.

The ambiguity of the word *said* in line 25 of (2) is not unusual. In many cases it is not clear whether the form of words has been uttered or simply thought. In some cases it is difficult to decided whether a sequence of words should be treated as an example of *oratio recta* or as a less direct form. Anyone who has transcribed a number of oral narratives knows that there are ambiguous utterances whose attribution to a speaker is problematic. In most cases, however, the direct speech is signaled not only by intonation but usually also by some "overt introducer" (Ferrara and Bell 1995: 265), "dialogue introducer" (Johnstone 1987), or "quotative" (Tagliamonte and Hudson 1999).

The most common introducer is one of the *verba dicendi*, such as *say*, though in some cases there is no introducer. For example, in example (2) there are several places where there is no indication of who the speaker is. The examples are repeated in (3):

(3)

    a.

        2 Kate got in here at—

        3 what time did we get home from the concert?

        4 about ten to ten?

⇒   5 first thing "Can I use the phone?"

⇒   6 "Yes"

    b.

        8 and she phoned Sarah

⇒   9 and then "Can I use the phone again?"

       10 I said "Yes

       11 who are you phoning this time?"

⇒   12 "I'm just giving Peter a ring to let him know I'm home"

    c.

       18 and I said "I think she's away to meet you at Ronnie's."

⇒   19 "Right"

In (3a), it is clear that it is Kate who says "Can I use the phone?" although this is not stated explicitly, and it is equally clear that "Yes" is the narrator's response. Similarly, in (3b), "I'm just giving Peter a ring to let him know I'm home" is Kate's reply to her mother's question, and in (3c) "Right" is Peter's response to the narrator. There is never any doubt in (2/3) about who is speaking and where the quoted speech begins and ends. The absence of an overt introducer has been termed a "zero quotative" (Mathis and Yule 1994). In example (2) there are three examples of zero quotatives (ll. 6, 12, 19). Each is an example of the second part of an "adjacency pair" (Sacks et al. 1974) in which the asking of a question assumes that an answer (or some response) will normally follow. When Kate says, "Can I use the phone?" it is natural to assume that the following "Yes" was uttered by the person to whom the question was asked. Quoted direct speech in this way (and many others) is consistent with what the conversation analysts have identified as normal behavior in conversation.

Tannen suggests that there is a continuum: "At one pole is no introducer at all, used in informal conversational narrative because of the great expressive power of the human voice. At the other pole is the use of graphic verbs as introducers—a form typical of literary narrative" [1986: 323]. Graphic verbs (Labov 1972) include *complain, mutter, whisper, groan*, and so forth (Tannen 1986: 322). Such overt characterizing of the speaker's tone and attitude is rare in oral narratives. Narrators more commonly use intonation and mimicry (Macaulay 1987a: 7–13) for these purposes.

The most common dialogue introducer or quotative is some form of the verb *say*. In the working-class narratives the form *says* is frequently used for all persons, including the first person singular. The quotative is also often repeated more often than is necessary for clarity, as can be seen in (4).

(4)   (Conversation 13—Working-class women)
      1 I mean she phoned me up
⇒   2 and I says "No"
⇒   3 I says "I canna dae it"
⇒   4 she says "How not?"
⇒   5 I says "I've already made arrangements to go oot with Ian" I says
⇒   6 and she went "Oh aye right"
⇒   7 and I says "But I'll not be going oot till ten"
⇒   8 I says "I'll I'll phone you back aboot it"
      9 so I come off the phone
     10 I was telling him
⇒   11 he says "If we're not going to go oot till ten o'clock
    12 you could go alang for a couple of hours
    13 cause it starts at eight"
⇒   14 I says "Aye that's what I'll dae then
    15 I'll just go alang"
⇒   16 then I says "I'll meet you at half ten"
    17 that was me gieing mysel another half hour
⇒   18 I thought "Oh"

The repetition of *I says* in passages like this one is rather like that of the discourse features *you know* and *I mean* for some speakers, in that it has a rhythmic effect rather than an informational purpose. *I says* in line 2 is even repeated in line 3, where one token would appear to have been clear enough; there is also a repetition at the beginning and end of her utterance in line 5.

Example (4) also illustrates two other quotatives, shown here as (5).

(5)

line 6	and she *went* "Oh aye right"
line 18	I *thought* "Oh"

Table 12.5 shows the variety of quotative verbs used by the Glasgow adults. The distribution of quotatives in the adult conversations is highly skewed. Of the total number of quotatives in the sample, the working-class women produce 71%, the middle-class women produce 19%, and the middle-class and working-class men between them have only 10% of the total, as can be seen in figure 12.3.

In addition, for all but three of the conversations (one between middle-class women and two between working-class women), quotatives are restricted to *say*, with a few examples of *think*. Consequently, 96% (55/57) of the examples of *go* are found in the three conversations between women, and 89% (49/55) are found in the two working-class sessions. In other words, there are only six examples of *go* in one of the conversations between middle-class women and a single one in one of the conversations between middle-class men. On this evidence *go* is primarily a working-class form, though it is impossible to tell whether it might be a feature of working-class men's speech, since there are so few quotatives in the sessions.

All eight examples of *be like that/went like that* are uttered by one working-class woman as in the examples in (6).

TABLE 12.5. Distribution of quotative verbs used by Glasgow adults

	%	N
say	72	(404)
go	11	(59)
be like	0.2	(1)
be like that	1	(7)
go like that	0.2	(1)
think	8	(46)
done that	0	(0)
other	1	(5)
zero	6	(35)
Total		(558)

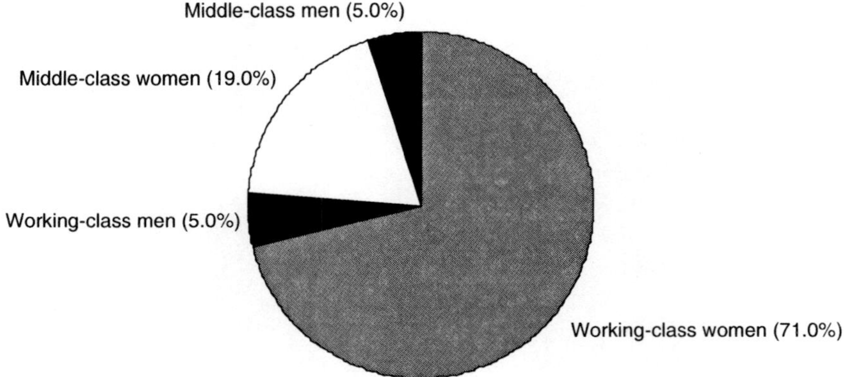

FIGURE 12.3. Distribution of quotatives in Glasgow adult conversations

(6)
- a. and she's like that "Oh I don't think he'll need them cos he'll no' be getting fags"
- b. and they were like that "How're you doing Mary?"
- c. we were like that "Sit doon sit doon"
- d. and he was like that "What's the answers?"
- e. she went like that er "Everything should just stay there"

This speaker also has a few examples where *be like that* is combined with *say* as in the examples in (7).

(7)
- a. I was like that I said "there's nae line"
- b. I was like that I says "No' really changed anything"

There are also examples where *be like that* occurs in the context of quoted dialogue but is not actually a quotative:

(8)

⇒   and I **was like that**
      I mean she phoned me up
      and I says "No"
      I says "I canna dae it"
      she says "How no'?"
      I says "I've a—a—already made arrangements to go oot wi' Ian" I says and she went
        "Oh aye right"

These forms appear to be a kind of hybrid quotative, and, as we shall see, they are also found in the adolescent conversations. Figure 12.4 shows the social class and gender distribution of the quotatives. Among the Glasgow adults the working-

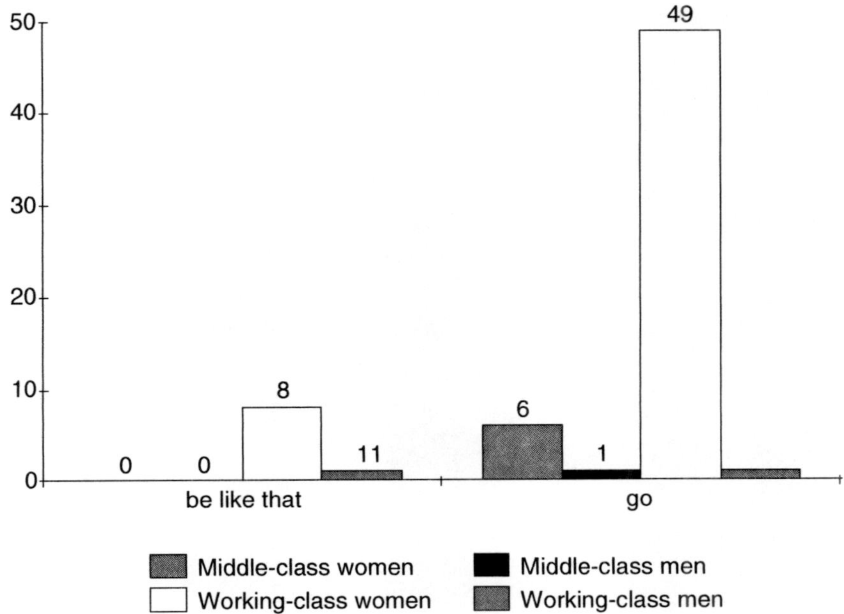

FIGURE 12.4. Numbers of examples of *be like that* and *go* (Glasgow adults)

class women lead in both categories. Although there was more speech recorded in the sessions with working-class women, the differences are too great to be explained that way. The evidence from the adult sessions suggests that *go* may have been used as a quotative in Glasgow for some time rather than being a very recent innovation.

The 246 instances of quoted dialogue in the adolescent conversations are unevenly distributed among the speakers, with 76% occurring in the sessions with girls, and two-thirds of those occurring in the two sessions with working-class girls, as can be seen in figure 12.5. The overall figures are therefore skewed by this distribution but the proportion of forms used by each group is revealing.

The kinds of quotatives used by the adolescents are shown in table 12.6. Unlike the adults, who use *say* 76% of the time, the Glasgow adolescents use *say* only 24% of the time.[1] Some form of *go* is the most frequent, accounting for about 26% of the examples. The next most frequent form is *be like*, with 14%. This form of quotative has received considerable attention recently.

In the United States the quotatives *go* and *be like* are considered to be relatively recent innovations, apparently starting among younger speakers, possibly in California. Butters (1980) comments on *go* as a fairly new phenomenon, and he similarly draws attention to *be like* (Butters 1982), indicating that such usages were probably unfamiliar at those dates to many of the readers of *American Speech*, the journal of the American Dialect Society. Blyth et al. found that older speakers in their sample were less likely to use *go* than were teenagers and college-age speakers, and no speaker older than 38 used *be like* (1990: 219). In Schiffrin's sample, only 10%

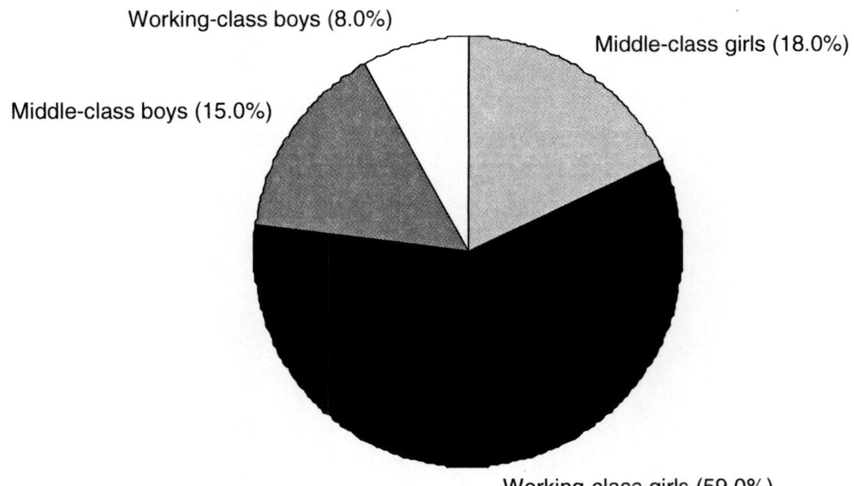

FIGURE 12.5. Distribution of quotatives in Glasgow adolescent conversations

of the 358 quotatives were *go* (1981: 58), and the overwhelming majority (97%) were in the historical present tense; she does not mention *be like*. In Tannen's study, of 84 quotatives, 13% were *go* and 8% were *be like* (1986: 315). Johnstone 1987, 1990, cites examples with *go* as well as *say* but does not give any figures on their frequency. Of *be like*, she says that it "is widely used by Americans in their teens and early twenties" (1987: 51) and wonders whether it is used elsewhere in the English-speaking world. Ferrara and Bell (1995), in a corpus of 115 speakers collected in Texas in 1990, found that there was a significant age difference in the use of quotatives. For both the younger speakers (18- to 25-year-olds) and older speakers (40+), the most

TABLE 12.6. Distribution of quotative verbs used by Glasgow adolescents

	%	N
say	24	(58)
go	26	(63)
be like	14	(33)
be like that	7	(17)
go like that	5	(13)
be	3	(8)
think	2	(6)
done that	2	(4)
zero	14	(33)
other	3	(7)
Total		(242)

common form of quotative was some form of *say* (42% and 91%, respectively). The younger speakers used a form of *go* 25% of the time and a form of *be like* 23% of the time. The older speakers used *went* 2% of the time and *be like* not at all (based on tables 2 and 3, Ferrara and Bell 1995: 274–75). Later samples in 1992 and 1994 apparently indicate increased use of *be like*, but Ferrara and Bell do not give percentages or age-grading details.

In 1995 Dailey-O'Cain recorded sociolinguistic interviews with 30 speakers who, like Dailey-O'Cain herself, "were all from a middle-class to upper-middle-class socioeconomic background, and had grown up in southeastern Michigan" (2000:7). She found 95 examples of quotative *like*, the majority in the 14–29 age-group and none from the speakers older than 50. Although the usage was higher among males, the difference was not statistically significant.

Dougherty and Strassel (1998), in a paper given at the New Ways of Analyzing Variation Conference NWAV-27, report on a study of 17 speakers aged 18 to 80, recorded in Philadelphia in sociolinguistic interviews by Dougherty in 1997. They found that the four 18- to 19-year-olds used *be like* with a frequency of about 70%, two speakers in their 20s with a frequency of 55%, two speakers in their 30s with a frequency of slightly more than 20%, and one woman aged 40 with a frequency of 15%. None of the speakers over 40 had any tokens of *be like*. Only the two 18-year-olds used *go* very often (12%); for the remaining 15 speakers the frequency of *go* was less than 5%. Dougherty and Strassel's results confirm the picture of the situation given by Ferrara and Bell.

Sanchez and Charity (1999), in a paper given at NWAV-28, report on the results of a set of 14 sociolinguistic interviews recorded in a predominantly African-American community. They found that of 1,550 quotatives, 44% were *be like* and only 1% were *go*. However, *be like* accounted for 62% of the quotatives used by speakers under 40 years of age and only 12% of those by speakers over 40. There was no age difference in the use of *go*. The pattern that emerges from these studies suggests that *go* became popular in the United States among younger speakers about 25 to 30 years ago but soon was replaced by *be like*, although older speakers continued to use *go*. Igoe, Lamb, Gilman, and Kim (1999), in another paper presented at NWAV-28, reported that out of a corpus of 311 quotatives collected by an introductory sociolinguistics class at the University of Pennsylvania, 54% were *be like*, but they also collected 18 examples (6%) of *be all* (e.g., "I'm all 'Whatever dude'"). All the latter examples were provided by Californians. There is no evidence so far that this form has been adopted farther east.

Tagliamonte and Hudson (1999) have shown that use of the quotatives *go* and *be like* has spread from the United States to British and Canadian university students aged between 18 and 28, in samples collected in 1996 and 1995, respectively. Their study shows, in answer to Johnstone's query, that *be like* and also *go* have spread to other parts of the English-speaking world,[2] though there would appear to be a time lag, with *go* still ahead in Canada and equal with *be like* in Britain. The most frequently used form of quotative in their sample, however, is still *say*.

Winter (2002) investigated the use of quotatives in a sample of 30 adolescents, aged 15 to 16, recorded in Melbourne in 1997–99. She found that *go* was the most frequent quotative (45%), followed by *say* (24%) and zero-quotatives (18%). However, she also obtained a small number of *be like* quotatives (8%).

The history of *be like* is important because of the way in which it seems to be entering the adolescent speech community in Glasgow. Some examples are given in (9).

(9)
    a. And I'*m like* "No that's sick"
    b. And *I'm like* "Woops"
    c. she'*s like* "Is your sister going out with a guy called Paul?"
    d. her ma'*s like* "Go on make me a coffee"
    e. I *was like* "What the fuck is that?"

Figure 12.6 shows the social class and gender distribution of *be like*. As with focuser *like* (chapter 6), it is the middle-class adolescents who use *be like* more frequently, whereas there is no overall social class difference in the use of *go*. However, there is a gender difference, with the girls using *be like* more frequently and the boys using *go*. The working-class girls show a preference for a hybrid form *be like that* or *go like that*, as illustrated in (10) and (11).

(10)
    a. I *was like that* "On you go"
    b. and I *was like that* "Shut up"
    c. you *were like that* "Aw shut up man"
    d. he *was like that* "Your maw came in by the way "
    e. I *was like that* "Shit"

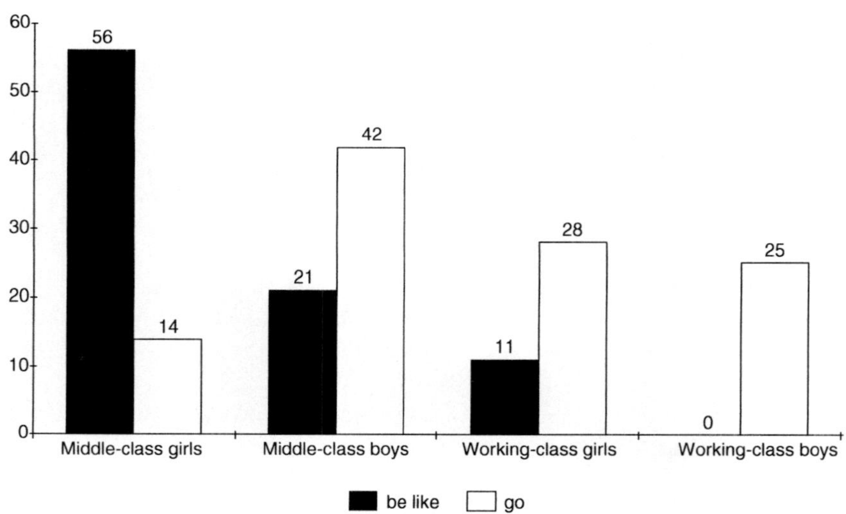

FIGURE 12.6. Percentage of *be like that* and *go* used as quotatives by Glasgow adolescents

(11)

    a. eh she *went like that* "Who else is going?"
    b. she just *went like that* "Fuck you you wanker"
    c. we all used to *go like that* "I wish I was like her like her"
    d. one of the boys *went like that* to him "You've lost your virginity"
    e. I *went like that* "A-a-ah my voice!"

It is unclear whether this is the result of some innovation or of some confusion in the transmission of the form. All the examples occur in the past tense, and both these forms seem to carry the suggestion of a gestural deictic ("like this"), but it cannot be a visual one. Later investigation suggests that *was like that/went like that* is becoming the preferred quotative among working-class adolescents. There is also a rare form *done that*, which again implies a kind of deictic reference. The examples are given in (12).

(12)

    a. and Stephanie *done that* "What are you talking about?"
    b. Kelly *done that* to David and me one day "You two should become best pals"
    c. I went up to Chantel and *done that* says "It's not me that hates you"

The last example, with the reinforcement of *says* to *done that*, suggests that this form had not become well established at the time of recording.[3] Later reports suggest that the form *I done* is used quite frequently as a quotative by working-class adolescents. Clearly, this is a very fluid area in which the popularity of forms may change rapidly.

    The use of so-called nontraditional quotatives (i.e., all those other than *say*, *think*, zero, and "other") is skewed. As has been observed earlier, quoted dialogue often contains discourse markers such as *well* and the turn-taking signal *oh*, particularly when there is no overt quotative. In the total set of nontraditional quotatives in the Glasgow transcripts, the most frequent form of quoted speech is a question, as in examples (13a–b). The next most frequent category is an answer or a statement beginning with a discourse marker, with more than half the examples beginning with *oh*, as in examples (13c–d). The next most frequent category is an answer to a question or a response to a statement, as in examples (13e–f). Two other categories are imperatives, as in examples (13g–h), and nonlexical items, as in examples (13i–j).

(13)

    a. And *I'm going* "Who's Bobby Lee?"
    b. and *she went* "Was that Heinz beans you gave me?"
    c. *She went* "Oh well that's good that's good Gran"
    d. And *I went* "Oh it's my mum"
    e. I says "Well will that mean that men get into the car-park?"
       She went "I would think so"
    f. I said "You'd better phone John
       she went "Aye"

  g. *we were like that* "Sit doon sit doon"
  h. *her ma's like* "Go on make me a coffee"
  i. *I was like* "La la la"
  j. and *he just went* "Eurgh"

The distribution is shown in Figure 12.7.

  It is clear from this that *go*, etc., are not simply alternatives to *say* and *think*. The nontraditional quotatives are rarely used to introduce simple statements or remarks but have a pragmatic and rhetorical force. Golato, in an article dealing with the new German quotative *und ich so/und er so* (and I'm like/and he's like), claims that this type of quotative "is sensitive to the context in which it is uttered" (2000: 32). The same would appear to be the case with the use of nontraditional quotatives by adolescents in Glasgow.

  Given the recent history of quotatives in the United States, it is likely that the use of *be like* and *be* as quotatives is a relatively new phenomenon in the speech of Glaswegians.[4] The figures from the recorded sessions are too slight to provide firm evidence of how these forms entered the community, but a plausible hypothesis is that *be like* began in the speech of middle-class adolescents (probably the girls) and was taken up by the working-class girls. (It is impossible to say anything about the usage of the working-class boys, since their sessions did not produce enough examples of quoted dialogue of the kind that would involve these quotatives.) Some support exists for the view that the working-class girls have not assimilated the *be like* form fully from the forms of *be like that* and *go like that*, which are rare in the conversations between the middle-class adolescents. These forms seem like an elaboration of the presumably more established quotative *go* in the direction of the new form *be like*. There are no examples of the combined *go like that* form in the conversations of

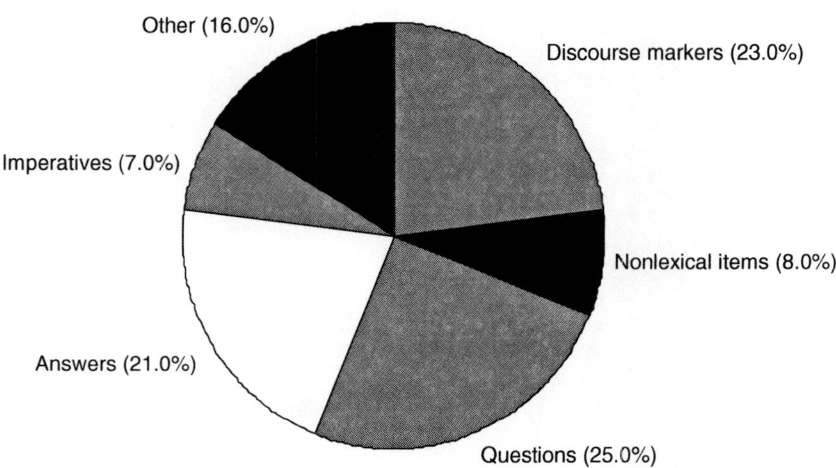

FIGURE 12.7. Types of quoted dialogue following nontraditional quotatives (all Glasgow speakers)

the middle-class adolescents, though there are three examples of *be like that* in one conversation between two middle-class boys.

Since the proportion of *be like* forms in the middle-class adolescent sessions is greater in the conversations between girls (56%) than between boys (21%), and since the middle-class boys have no examples of the newest form, *be*, by itself, it seems reasonable to hypothesize that the middle-class girls are the leaders in introducing new forms of quotatives. In several other features, as has been shown in earlier chapters, the middle-class girls seem to be following the example of their mothers, but that cannot be the case here, since there is no evidence of the adult speakers using *be like*.

The question remains of how *be like* has reached teenagers in Glasgow. It is unlikely to have been through direct contact with young Americans, though in these days of increased transatlantic traffic this cannot be ruled out. It is also possible that the middle-class girls heard it from their older siblings, who might be students of the kind studied by Tagliamonte and Hudson. Because undergraduates are more often from middle-class backgrounds, this would account for the social differences in the use of these forms. It is also possible that the transmission is through the medium of film and television.

Conclusion

The Glasgow conversations, like the Ayr interviews, give many examples of the speakers telling stories. In particular, the working-class women and girls take advantage of the situation to present information in a dramatic form, including the use of dialogue. Many speakers include dialogue as part of their narratives, thereby dramatizing the scene, allowing the listener to interpret what has happened rather than having an explanation imposed. Among the Glasgow adults, the women employ this device much more than the men. The middle-class women's narratives are 20% dialogue and the working-class women's 27%. In contrast, in men's narratives, both middle-class and working-class, dialogue makes up only 8% of the whole. It is perhaps not surprising that the working-class women should have such a high percentage of dialogue, since they have the highest proportion of narrative, but the middle-class men have a higher proportion of narrative than the middle-class women, though their percentage of dialogue is less than half that of the women.

The adolescents show the increased use of nontraditional quotatives, such as *go* and *be like*. There are enough examples of *go* in the adult conversations, mainly in the working-class women's conversations, to show that it is not a very recent form in Glasgow, but only the adolescents use *be like*. The predominance of the middle-class girls suggests that they are the leaders in using the new form. Analysis of the use of nontraditional quotatives shows that they are not simply a replacement for *say* but are used for heightened dramatic effect.

13

Results of Quantitative Measures

The previous six chapters have presented comparative figures on a variety of discourse features. As I warned earlier, there is a danger in being overimpressed by indications of statistical significance, with the risk of ignoring what may be more interesting results that fail to reach significance. Nevertheless, there are those who will insist that only those results that are statistically significant deserve to be taken seriously. Quite a few such results have been reported.

A total of 42 discourse features in the Glasgow conversations were analyzed using the Mann-Whitney nonparametric test. These tests produced 46 statistically significant differences. Of these 46 differences, 10 refer to social class differences, 16 to gender differences, and 20 to age differences. In other words, the statistically significant variation in the Glasgow conversations can be ranked as follows:

age > gender > social class

This underlines the necessity of looking at more than one extralinguistic dimension and the danger of taking one subset (e.g., adolescent boys) and making generalizations about social class, for example. Similarly, drawing conclusions about gender differences without taking age and social class into consideration may give a misleading picture. This might appear self-evident, but there are many studies of variation in discourse features that do not make this clear. For example, the London-Lund Corpus has provided scholars with a useful data set of transcribed speech, but the speakers are educated, middle-class adults with a predominance of males. As was shown in chapter 6, it is possible to look at gender differences in the LLC transcripts, but few have done so.

Social class differences

The first point to stress here is the large number of discourse features, 32, for which no significant social class differences were found. In 76% of the cases examined there were no statistically significant differences. This confirms the general finding from the Ayr interviews (Macaulay 1991b), where there were more similarities than differences between the two social classes. In Glasgow, there are no significant social class differences in the use of discourse features such as *oh, well, you know, I mean,* and *I think*. There are no significant differences in syntactic structures, except for the greater use of dislocated syntax by the working-class speakers ($p < .001$). The other measure where the working-class shows greater use is with modal auxiliaries ($p < .05$). The other significant differences show more frequent use by the middle-class speakers, including the use of the passive ($p < .05$) and the relative pronoun *who* ($p < .001$). However, the major social class differences cluster around adverbs and adjectives. The middle-class speakers use derived adverbs in *-ly* much more frequently than the working-class speakers ($p < .001$). The middle-class speakers also use *very* ($p < .001$) and *quite* ($p < .005$) more frequently. In addition, the middle-class speakers use evaluative adjectives more frequently than the working-class speakers ($p < .005$). Possibly related to this group of features is the fact that the middle-class speakers also use the hedge *sort of* more frequently than the working-class speakers ($p < .001$).

Of the many negative characteristics of working-class speech identified by Bernstein (1971: 42–43 [1959]; 1971: 96–97 [1962]; see chapters 5 and 6), only the difference in the use of passives and the reference to adverbs and adjectives have been supported. None of the other claims has been substantiated, and it is reasonable to believe that Bernstein did not have adequate evidence on which to base these claims. The evidence from the Glasgow conversations gives no support for the view that working-class speech is in any way impoverished. Despite important differences in education, income, and place of residence, the Glasgow speakers use language for the most part in very similar ways. The implications of their differences in the use of adverbs and adjectives will be discussed in the next chapter, which deals with discourse style.

Gender differences

Compared with the relatively small number of social class differences, there are 17 statistically significant gender differences. Of these, the overwhelming majority, 14, show more frequent use by females and only 3 more frequent use by males. This suggests that it is the females who demonstrate a more distinctive discourse style than the males. This point will be taken up in the next chapter.

The females show a higher use of *and* ($p < .05$), *but* ($p < .05$), and *so* ($p < .05$) as coordinating conjunctions. They also use more clauses of reason beginning with *because* ($p < .05$). The females show a much greater use of pronouns ($p < .001$), including the pronouns *I* ($p < .05$) and *she* ($p < .001$). This is presumably related to the greater frequency with which females refer to people ($p < .05$), particularly to other females ($p < .001$). The contrary differences are that males make more frequent reference to places ($p < 05$), use the definite article *the* more frequently ($p < .05$), and also the relative pronoun *which* ($p < .01$). The females also have more narratives ($p < .01$) and include more dialogue ($p < 0.5$). The females also use *oh* more frequently ($p < .005$). The women use modals more than the men ($p < .05$), and the girls use *pure* more than the boys ($p < .05$).

Age differences

There are 20 significant age differences. In 11 cases the adults show a higher frequency of use, and in the remaining 9 it is the adolescents. The first major difference is that the adolescents produce significantly fewer words ($p < .001$) given the same instructions as the adults. Five of the adults produce more than 5,000 words, but none of the adolescents uses as many as 5,000. On the other hand, four of the adolescents produce more than 3,000 words, whereas four of the adults use fewer. The adults use discourse features such as *well* ($p < .005$), *you know* ($p < .001$), and *I mean* ($p < .01$) more frequently than the adolescents. The adults also use the articles *a/an* ($p < .001$) and *the* ($p < .001$) more frequently. The adults use the adverbs *very* ($p < .05$) and *quite* ($p < .05$) more frequently, but the adolescents use *just* more frequently ($p < .01$). The adults also use *maybe* ($p < .001$) and *even* ($p < .001$) more frequently. The adults use more nonrestrictive relative clauses introduced by *which* ($p < .005$) and have more coordinate clauses introduced by *but* ($p < .05$).

The adolescents ask more Yes/No questions ($p < .01$) and more WH-questions ($p < .001$), adding up to more questions in total ($p < .001$). The adolescents also use more imperatives ($p < 001$). The adolescents make more frequent use of modal auxiliaries ($p < .05$). The adolescents also use more pronouns ($p < .01$) and in particular the first person pronoun *I* ($p < .005$).

Conclusion

It will be obvious from this summary that several of the statistical differences cluster together. For example, the use of the articles *a/an* and *the*, as might be expected, correlates strongly ($p < .01$, Pearson = .673), as does the use of the personal pronoun *she* with reference to females ($p < .01$, Pearson = .833). Other correlations include the use of *very* and *quite* ($p < .01$; Pearson = .519), which correlate negatively with the use of dislocated syntax ($p < .01$; Pearson –.590), as do derived adverbs in *-ly* ($p < .05$; Pearson = –.584). The use of *very* also correlates with the use of evaluative adjectives ($p < .01$; Pearson = .748).

In addition to the statistically significant differences, there are others that approach significance. They will be considered when we look at the implications of the differences for discourse style in the next chapter.

Discourse Styles

Although the question of stylistic variation has been important for quantitative studies of sociolinguistic variation since Labov's New York study (Labov 1966), there has been little agreement on what should be studied and how (Kiesling and Schilling-Estes 1998; Macaulay 1999; Eckert and Rickford 2001). For the most part, the examination of stylistic variation has been used as a way of identifying language change, with the assumption that style-shifting reveals the covert norms that govern whether speakers will or will not adopt new forms entering the community. The notion of discourse style examined in this chapter is a very different phenomenon.

As was stated in chapter 2, the working hypotheses for the quantitative analysis of discourse features in the present work are as follows:

1. All speakers have the same opportunity to use certain discourse features in the recording sessions.
2. Variation in the frequency of use of any of these features reflects a different discourse style.
3. Differences in using a discourse feature that correlate with membership of a social category such as age, gender, or social class show that such variation is not simply idiosyncratic.

We have seen in the preceding chapters that there is variation in a wide range of features and that this variation often correlates with membership in one of the categories of age, gender, or social class. In this chapter an attempt will be made to see whether the kind of variation that has been identified can be interpreted in terms of a difference in discourse style.

Adolescent discourse style

Nobody would expect adolescents to talk the same way as adults. Their knowledge, their experience, and their interests are very different. It is not surprising that some of the adolescents use expressions such as focuser *like* (chapter 6) or quotative *be like* (chapter 11) differently from the adults, since these features are used more widely by younger speakers in both the United States and the U.K. It is also hardly surprising that only the adolescents use taboo words such as *fuck* and *shite* in the recording situation. The frequency of the word *fuck* in the adolescent conversations can be seen in table 14.1:

There are also 10 instances of the word *shite* and 4 of *shit* in the sessions with working-class adolescents. There is one example of *shit* used by one of the middle-class girls. So, although the most frequent users of taboo expressions are the working-class boys, there are enough examples from working-class girls to show that they are comfortable with the use of such language even in the constraining presence of the tape recorder. Only two of the middle-class girls and none of the middle-class boys use any taboo expressions. None of the Glasgow adults uses such taboo language, even in quoted dialogue.

However, most of the differences between the adult and adolescent conversations are much less salient than these. The first significant difference is that the adolescents produce much less talk in the same amount of time. There are a number of possible explanations for this. It is clear, from many references to the slow passage of time and the difficulty sometimes in finding a topic, that the adolescents are generally less comfortable in the recording situation than the adults. This raises a question of whether hypothesis 1 holds for the adolescents. Although the basic instructions were the same for all groups, the recording situations may not have been strictly equivalent for the adults and the adolescents. Just as it is unwise to assume that all interviews are equivalent speech events (Macaulay 1999, 2001a), it is also possible that different responses to the recording situation affected the use of certain discourse features.

TABLE 14.1. Frequency of the word *fuck* in Glasgow adolescent conversations

	(*n*)	[a]*Freq.*
Middle-class girls	4	0.4
Middle-class boys	0	0.0
Working-class girls	18	1.3
Working-class boys	36	4.9
Middle-class	4	0.2
Working-class	54	2.6

[a]per 1,000 words

For example, it was found that the adolescents made significantly less use of the discourse features *well*, *you know*, and *I mean*, and their less frequent use of *oh* just fails to reach significance. On the one hand, if these features contribute to the fluency of impromptu speech (Östman 1982), then their relative absence from the adolescent conversations may be an indication that their speech is not as typical of their usual style as is the case for the adults. On the other hand, they may not make much use of these features under any circumstances. The use of taboo expressions suggests that those adolescents are not greatly inhibited by the recording situation. An examination of the kind of interaction in the adolescent sessions will help to dispel any doubts about the quality of the speech recorded.

The more frequent use of questions and imperatives reflects the nature of the interaction. Unlike the adults, who are for the most part content to let each other talk on whatever topic crops up in their conversation, the adolescents are constantly making demands of each other. Here is an excerpt from a conversation between two working-class girls.

(1)   (Conversation 7—Working-class girls)
       R: I know you—I know you don't like saying it—me saying this
           but I think Steve fancies you
       L: no he doesnae
           I don't know if he does
           but I always argue with him
       R: do you know that he nipped Jenny Baird?
       L: no
       R: don't say nothing but
           I wasnae supposed to say nothing
           but it was Liz—Liz that told me
       L: when?
       R: when she came doon for me in London and all that
           they were talking about it
       L: when was it?
       R: em
           I don't know
           it was only a few month ago
           two month ago
       L: two month ago
           oh wait till I see that Steve man
           I think I'll be just battering him

L's quick response to R's statement "I think Steve fancies you," "no he doesnae," shows that she is aware of the danger of this kind of statement. She does not want to get trapped into admitting that she has an interest in Steve, but her later remarks make it clear that she does. It is obvious from the way L says "no" (low steady tone, reduced volume) in response to R's question ("do you know that he nipped Jenny Baird?") that this is news to her, and not welcome news at that. What seemingly begins as a piece of flattery or reassurance "I think Steve fancies you" turns into a really bad news story. Exactly what constitutes *nipping* is not clear from the tapes, but it is clearly an activity that can be discussed openly and even observed, and it is clear that it is a minor but significant sexual activity, since L is upset by the news that Steve has been nipping Jenny. The best description came from the Glasgow poet Tom Leonard, whose wife, Sonya, had taught in a working-class school. She was told that nipping did not mean sex, and she thinks that it did not necessarily mean heavy petting either, since apparently "you might nip ten birds in a night." One girl, whom she described as "gallus" (i.e., bold), said: "Miss it's just like trying out something before you buy it." It seems to be a relatively recent usage. Girls can nip boys, and boys can nip girls, though the girls talk more about it.[1] L's concern is also shown in her desire to know exactly when this happened, presumably because of the timing of her relationship with Steve. L's question "When was it?" and her statement that she is going "to batter" Steve emphasizes her feelings. R had earlier expressed her anxiety that she should not be known to be the source of the information ("I wasnae supposed to say nothing ," "Don't say I says but"), which underlines the sense that this is something important. There are three coordinate clauses and eight subordinate clauses. Apart from being in the active voice, this sample does not confirm Bernstein's characterization of working-class syntax: "Short, grammatically simple, often unfinished sentences, a poor syntactical construction with a verbal form stressing the active mood" (Bernstein 1971: 42 [1959]).

Example (1) is not untypical of both conversations between the working-class girls. They are seemingly engaged in genuine exchange of information. Like Tannen's sixth-grade girls, "they settle upon the activity of exchanging stories with no visible discomfort" (1996: 104). They talk a lot about drinking and getting drunk in ways that do not seem just to be showing off for the tape. They know they are being recorded, but that doesn't stop them from using the time to talk to each other about the kind of things that they probably talk about under normal conditions. Tannen found in her study that "at all ages, the girls and women exhibit minimal or no difficulty finding something to talk about, and they talk about a small number of topics" (99).

So much for the working-class girls. What about the working-class boys? They find it very difficult to find a topic that they can sustain for more than a few turns. They begin by spilling the drink that had been left for them; like Tannen's males, they "frequently use the room as a topical resource" (1996: 99); they ransack the drawers of the desk in the office; they talk about their bodily functions and produce certain impolite sounds; they frequently comment on the time and how slowly it is passing; their most sustained topic is football (soccer), though even there they have a limited amount to say, perhaps because it is not a critical time in the football season; one session ends with one of them telling an extended joke about Protestants and Catholics, which he does not get to finish because the researcher comes in to say that time is (at last) up. But most of all they tease or abuse each other. Since we have already heard that Steve really likes one of the girls on the first tape, what does he have to say about it? It so happens that Steve was one of the boys recorded. Here he is being teased about one of the girls in the previous extract (7L). He is the speaker on the left channel.

(2)   (Conversation 6—Working-class boys)
   R: you do fancy Lynne Neilson?
   L: I don't fancy her
   R: aye you dae
   L: I don't
   R: you admitted it to Chuck
   L: aye that's what he said
      that's what he said.
   R: Jimmy
   L: do you believe what they say?
   R: Brown and all
   L: aye so I did
   R: that's three then against wan [*one*]
   L: I don't
      I said I like her and she's nice
      but I don't fancy her
   R: [*whistles*]
   L: don't need to believe me if you don't want to
      it's up to you
      I know I don't

There are two coordinate clauses and six subordinate clauses in this extract and no examples of "unfinished" structures. The excerpt in (2) is the third time the boys have talked about girls. R obviously feels that it is a good way to tease L and L's response suggests that he is not too comfortable denying the accusation. He tries to make an important semantic distinction between "liking" and "fancying." The working-class boys are constantly teasing each other. Here is another example.

(3)   (Conversation 6—Working-class boys)
   R: [*coughs*]
   L: smoker's cough
   R: I don't smoke
   L: aye you dae
   R: no I don't
   L: aye you dae
   R: no I don't
   L: you can spark up a fag here if you want
   R: I don't smoke
   L: there's nae ashtrays right enough
   R: I've not got any fags
      and I don't smoke
   L: aye

When 6R coughs, 6L sees his chance for a tease, and the repetitions are found elsewhere in exchanges of this kind (*I don't smoke/aye you dae/no I don't/aye you dae/no I don't*). Then 6L continues the tease by giving 6R permission and regretting the absence of ashtrays. This shows the boys interacting quite intensely, neither prepared to back down. In addition to the teasing, there is a great deal of name-calling. Some examples of abusive terms used by the working-class boys are listed in table 14.2.

Only the working-class boys produce this kind of behavior, though they also frequently address each other as *mate* and *man*. The terms of abuse, though apparently intended in one sense as insults, are also in some sense affectionate markers of solidarity. The working-class boys are also the only ones who get into arguments, and their arguments, like the teasing in (3), often take the form of repeated assertion and denial of a kind that has been found in younger children's arguments (Lein and Brenneis 1978) as in (4).

(4)　(Conversation 6—Working-class boys)
　　　L:　bet you you're in next week
　　　R:　bet you I'm no
　　　L:　bet you you are
　　　R:　bet you I'm no
　　　L:　bet you you are
　　　R:　bet you I'm no
　　　L:　we'll just need to wait and see then

Although the working-class boys, like Tannen's sixth-grade boys (1996: 104), find it difficult to sustain a topic, they are very much engaged with each other, quick to seize an opportunity to tease or provoke each other. They also frequently use imperatives, telling each other what to do and what not to do. In contrast to the working-

TABLE 14.2. Terms of abuse used by working-class boys in addressing each other

bass
bum
bully wee dick
dick
dirty wee wanker
fanny
fucking dick
fucking tit
knob
poof
prick
scumbag
shady sort of cunt
skunk
walloper [= 'prick']
wee dick
wee shite
you pish

class girls, however, they do not produce narratives in which they use quoted dialogue. Their main use of quoted dialogue is in telling jokes.

What about the middle-class adolescents? Two of the girls talk about pets, dogs, films, classes, and other girls. The other two middle-class girls talk only about other girls. An example is given in (5).

(5)   (Conversation 5—Middle-class girls)
      L: and—and—then—and then Donna wanted to get off with Mike Allen right?
      R: oh
      L: Mike Allen—Mike Allen in my class
      R: I think I know—quite tall?
      L: uh-huh
          [13 lines omitted]
      L: Donna wanted to get off with him
          [2 lines omitted]
          well this is what I've heard anyway
      R: mhm
      L: and then he was going to get off with Donna
          except em then em Liz and him were dancing
      R: mm
      L: and Liz was pure feeling his arse
          and like sort of licking his shirt
      R: [*laughs*]
      L: it's disgusting
          this is what em Mike told Robbie
          cos I sort of hang about with Robbie sometimes
          [2 lines omitted]
          so maybe that's why people want to batter Liz
      R: I know
          and it's a wee bit
          I mean she's a wee bitty big-headed I think

Here we are clearly in the realm of gossip ("this is what I've heard anyway," "this is what em Mike told Robbie"). It is a story of obvious interest to 5R and is not simply a topic raised to pass the time. Note how these middle-class girls use the discourse features *I mean*, *well*, *like*, and *sort of*, which are rare in the conversations between working-class adolescents. The judgmental comment about Liz ("she's a wee bitty big-headed I think") is similar to the evaluative comments of the middle-class adults and is quite typical of this conversation. Here is another example where the two girls are discussing a boy's unexpected choice of partner.

(6)   (Conversation 5—Middle-class girls)
      L: Do you like Sheila Black?
      R: I like them both
          but I mean who's prettier?
          I mean

L: Sheila [*whispered*]
R: aye I mean
L: let's not talk about looks
    that's a shame
    that's what it is really.
        [*Both laugh*]
R: wow this is the complete nice person here
L: no but I—I—I thought he'd go for Sheila as well
R: I know
    Sheila's pretty
    Sheila's nice
    and Lorna's not
        [*Both laugh*]
L: that's a shame
    that's a shame
R: Lorna
    that's not funny
    Lorna is Lorna's a nice person
    she's just a wee bitty tarty   [*the last word is whispered*]
L: yeah
    her blonde streaks and everything
R: oh
L: have you seen her boots?   [*high rising intonation*]
    her shoes?
    eurgh
R: and her jacket   [*practically a shriek*]

As the two of them go, on their voices get higher pitched and involved with laughter. They are aware that they are being bitchy and try to mitigate it by saying such things as "Let's not talk about looks," "That's a shame," and "That's not funny," perhaps because of the presence of the tape recorder, but they get carried away in their criticism of Lorna. Their comments on other girls' appearance are similar to the kind Eder (1995) recorded in her study of seventh- and eighth-grade girls in the United States.

Essentially the whole of this session is taken up with talking about other girls, particularly who each of the speakers likes or does not like, and also who would or would not "jump in" for Liz. These are the two adolescents who show the greatest variation in prosodic features, with frequent use of emphatic intonation and changes of tempo and loudness. As with the working-class girls, they are talking about situations and opinions that are important to them.

What about the middle-class boys? Two of them talk about football and other sports, classes, discos, films, other boys, and holidays. The second pair spend a brief time discussing holidays and then enter into a detailed discussion of computerized war games, which remains the topic for the remainder of the session. This is the most homogeneous of all the conversations, with essentially a single topic.

(7)   (Conversation 4—Middle-class boys)
    R: yeah
       have you seen and heard about Warcraft III?
    L: yeah
       I saw something about that on the internet
    R: it's meant to be an adventure game
       but what sort?
       like that—the sort you were talking about or?
    L: er probably
       I don't—I don't know
    R: have you seen a preview for Tomb Raider 2?
    L: no
       I've not seen that
       but I've got a demo for Tomb Raider 1
    R: I've completed Tomb Raider on the playstation
    L: uh-huh
    R: but Tomb Raider 2 she can now crawl climb
       she's got a harpoon gun
       she can do numerous other pointless things
    L: hm-m
    R: and I just think the graphics are quite a lot better

The conversation goes on like this for another half hour. The boys are clearly talking about a subject that keenly interests them both. The main point to note in the interaction is that the participants are mutually supportive and polite even when disagreeing with each other, and they sustain this throughout the session. They complete each other's remarks and give supportive feedback in the form of minimal responses. They are never competitive or abusive. This is in marked contrast to the aggressive interaction in the working-class boys' conversations.

In this and other ways, the Glasgow adolescent conversations underline the need to consider social class as well as gender. For example, Tannen notes in her sample that "there are occasional references to violence in the boys' talk, never in the girls'" (1996: 99). This is not true in the Glasgow recordings. It is true that there are references to violence in most of the boys' conversations, but there are also several references to violence in the conversations between the working-class girls and some in conversation 5 with middle-class girls. On the other hand, conversation 4 with middle-class boys, illustrated in (5), contains reference only to violence in computer games.

A close examination of the topics covered and the kind of interaction thus supports the claim that, despite the fewer number of words, the adolescent conversations meet hypothesis 1. The participants are actively involved in their exchanges and respond to the information, queries, and challenges that their interlocutors present. The repeated demands that the adolescents make of each other explain their greater use of pronouns and probably also their less frequent use of the definite and indefinite articles. They are less likely to talk about objects or people in general terms, and they do not qualify those references with nonrestrictive relative clauses. Their form of interaction also accounts for their greater use of modal auxiliaries, particularly the use of *can/could* and *will/would*, since these are often used in questions or requests. The content analysis is consistent with the quantitative results, showing that quantitative measures can provide an independent indication of discourse style.

Male and female discourse styles

One of the major gender differences is that the females tell more stories and include more dialogue in their narratives. Since many of their stories are about other females, this helps to explain their more frequent reference to people and in particular to other females, which is consistent throughout the women's and girls' conversations. This is also reflected in their more frequent use of pronouns, including the first-person pronoun *I*. The larger proportion of stories in the female conversations also probably accounts for females' greater use of coordinate clauses, since they are common in narratives, and possibly also why the females use more adverbial clauses with *because* and more modals. The more frequent use of *so* by females, however, is not totally related to the higher proportion of narrative. Example (8) gives an illustration from a middle-class women's conversation.

(8)　(Conversation 10—Middle-class women)
　　R:　well I still meet up with Sue Miller and Jean Simpson and two others
　　　　and it's worked very well up until the last time we went to meet at Sue's
　　　　and she'd forgotten that we were coming down
　　L:　oh her face would have been a picture
　　R:　the three of us traveling from this side—well the three of us traveling from this side
　　　　and Fiona McKenzie is on the South Side in Netherlee
　　　　and she said "Don't come for me eh just go on yourself
　　　　because if you go onto the new motorway it'll be quicker"
　　　　so we went down
　　　　and we got to Sue's
　　　　and Fiona was just standing beside the car
　　　　and we thought "Oh great she's arrived as well"
　　　　and she said "I don't like to disappoint you girls but there's no answer
　　　　and I've been round and eh"
　　　　she said, "I've looked in the kitchen
　　　　and there's nothing laid out on the table for us"
　　　　and I said "Well maybe it's in the fridge Fiona"
　　　　"No well it's not on and it doesn't look as though"
　　　　so we left a note and said "Hope everything's okay
　　　　we've gone to the pub
　　　　we'll phone you"
　　　　so Jean being Jean has her mobile phone
　　　　so we phoned from the pub—the pub it was the Royal Marine Hotel in Troon
　　　　and she was so embarrassed

Like many of the women's stories, this one is about people and in particular about other women. There are 28 personal pronouns (not including *it*) in this short extract of 226 words, and there are 9 named references to women and 4 to places. Half of the story is told in dialogue. There are 19 coordinate clauses, including 4 introduced by *so*, and 1 adverbial clause of reason introduced by *because*. There are two examples of *oh*. These are all features that have been shown to occur more frequently in the female conversations. The final line shows the use of *so* as an intensifier, which is found only in the middle-class women's conversations. The final line also provides an explicit description of Sue's state of mind. This is less common in the working-class narratives (see later text).

The males, on the other hand, have more frequent references to places, use the definite article *the* more frequently than the females, and also the relative pronoun *which*. This can be seen in example (9).

(9)   (Conversation 16—Middle-class men)
     L: I've put my foot in at Musenberg
        which is the beach immediately on the left of Cape Peninsula
        you know if you come over—
        Capetown itself straddles from the Atlantic side over to the other side
        but it's not Indian Ocean
        cos the—that's why there's False Bay
        and you know where Cape Aguilas is?
        Cape Point is not the southern end of Africa
        it's Cape Aguilas
        and they got it wrong
        so the next bay is called False Bay
        because it was—it was—it was
     R: oh I see
     L: a mistake that they thought that Cape Point was the southern tip
     R: it's a bit like the English that think that Land's End is the most westerly part of
        Britain
     L: exactly

In this short extract of 121 words, there are 14 named references to places and no named references to people. There are 6 personal pronouns (excluding *it*) and 1 use of the relative pronoun *which*. There are only 3 coordinate clauses and 1 adverbial clause of reason with *because*.

The examples in (8) and (9) have been deliberately chosen to highlight the gender differences, but they are representative of many others in the women's and men's conversations. The quantitative measures thus seem to be a reliable guide to a distinct difference in the discourse styles employed by females and males in the Glasgow conversations. There are also features that are not frequent enough to quantify but that become obvious in reading the transcripts. For example, in (8), 10L says "oh her face would have been a picture." This kind of cliché is more common in the middle-class women's conversations, though there also are examples in the middle-class men's conversations. Some more examples from conversation 10 are given in (10).

(10)
    a. it was six nights on the trot (10R)
    b. hop round in the morning (10L)
    c. we'd nipped into town to get this (10R)
    d. we're kind of piggy-in-the-middle of it all (10R)
    e. it was a dawdle [i.e., easy] (10L)

Here is an extended example from conversation 10 between these two middle-class women that shows two examples of this kind of language ("tootling along" and "chucked it down") in a vivid narrative. The speaker (10L) is describing driving from Scotland to Cornwall in bad weather.

(11)   (Conversation 10—Middle-class women)
    L: what I found the most frightening was that it being November
        and the roads were wet
        I've never seen so many lorries in my life
        and here's me tootling along in this wee Nova
        and you looked in your b—mirror
    R: uh huh
    L: and you just saw a line of lorries across all three carriageways behind you
    R: mhm uh huh
    L: bearing down on you with the light
    R: [laughs]
    L: and you thought [laughing] "Oh my God" you know
        you'd nowhere to go
    R: uh huh
    L: it was awful
    R: uh huh
    L: and then in Somerset it chucked it down
        and you couldn't see a foot in front of you

The speaker describes the trip in heightened language: "the *most* frightening," "*never* seen," "you *just* saw," "across *all three* carriageways," "*bearing* down," "*nowhere* to go," "*awful*," "it *chucked* it down," "*couldn't see* a foot in front." She describes the situation as an ordeal and presents herself as a helpless participant: "here's me . . . in this *wee* Nova" just "tootling along." The use of expressions such as *tootling along* and *chucked it down* is more common in this conversation, than in any other conversation, but some such forms are found in the other middle-class women's conversation and in the middle-class men's conversations. They, however, are not to be found in the working-class conversations.

The working-class women's conversations, like the middle-class women's, are filled with narratives, and the narratives contain much dialogue and frequent use of pronouns.

(12)   (Conversation 13—Working-class women)
        R: 1 and I was like that
              2 I mean she phoned me up
              3 and I says "No"
              4 I says "I canna dae it"
              5 she says "How no?"
              6 I says "I've already made arrangements to go oot wi Alec" I says
              7 and she went "Oh aye right"
              8 and I says "But I'll no be going oot till ten"
              9 I says "I'll phone you back aboot it"
             10 so I come off the phone
             11 I was telling him
             12 he says "If you're no going to go oot till ten o'clock
             13 you could go alang for a couple of hours
             14 cos it starts at eight"
             15 I says "Aye that's what I'll dae then
             16 I'll just go alang"
             17 then I says "I'll meet you at half ten"

In this excerpt of 120 words, more than half the story is told in dialogue. There are
25 personal pronouns (not counting *it*), and the listener has to be alert to track their
reference. The pronoun *she* in the second line refers to her sister-in-law, who had
been mentioned earlier. The pronouns *him* and *he* in lines 10 through 12 refer to her
husband, Alec, named in line 6. He is also the referent of the pronoun *you* in line 17.
In the Ayr interviews, I noticed a similar use of pronouns and commented: "The lower-
class speakers have apparently a different sense of the frame that can help identify
the referent of an anaphoric pronoun" (Macaulay 1991b: 82), but I also mentioned
that despite the burden placed on the listener, "there is usually little problem in identifying the referent" (85).

The working-class women's conversations resemble the middle-class women's
in being mostly taken up with narratives about people, whereas one of the working-
class men's conversations is even more taken up with naming places than the middle-
class men's.

Among the adolescents, it is the girls who have by far the greatest number of
narratives. Example (13) shows a typical narrative from one of the working-class
girls' conversations.

(13)   (Conversation 8—Working-class girls)
        L: I'll never forget the time Jeffrey collapsed my bed right
              the two of us were sitting in my room right
              and the phone went
              so I goes to answer the phone
              he was like that "Where are you going?"
              "I'm going to get the phone"
              he was like that "Right"
              I was standing

> it was Cathy I think on the phone right
> and I was sitting on the phone talking to Cathy
> you know what I'm like talking to her
> sit and talk to her for hours
> so I was sitting talking to Cathy
> and I heard this big crash
> I was like "What the fuck is that?"
> so I was "Aw right Cathy I'll phone you back
> I want to find out what that prick's done"
> she was "Aw right"
> so I went back into the room
> my fucking bed had collapsed

In this extract of 143 words, 20% is told in dialogue. There are 22 pronouns, and there are 7 coordinate clauses, 4 of which are introduced by *so*. There are 5 named references to people. Note that 8L uses *right* as a kind of bracketing feature. This style of narrative is very similar in many ways to the adult examples in (8) and (12) despite several important differences, such as the quotatives and the use of taboo language. The content of the conversations thus supports the implications of the quantitative analysis, showing the greater emphasis on people in the female conversations and the greater attention paid to places in the male conversations.

Social class differences in discourse style

The first point to emphasize is that out of 42 quantitative measures, there were only 10 statistically significant social class differences. In syntax there were only two significant differences, with the middle-class speakers using more passives and the working-class speakers more dislocated syntax. What this means is that basically the two social class groups use the same grammar in much the same way. The main stylistic difference is in the much more frequent use by the middle-class speakers of adverbs and evaluative adjectives. It was shown in chapter 10 that the middle-class speakers in Glasgow use derived adverbs in *-ly*, *very*, and *quite* significantly more frequently than the working-class speakers. This is consistent with the finding from the Ayr interviews. Is it possible to find an explanation for this difference? Adverbs have been a notoriously difficult category to define (Crystal 1966; Huang 1975; Ifantidou-Trouki 1993; McCawley 1979; McConnell-Ginet 1982; Quirk et al. 1985), so it may be helpful to take as a starting point three examples of empirical investigation.

As we have seen, Bernstein included adverb use in a list of features that he identified as characteristic of what he was then calling a *restricted code* rather than a *public language*: "The restriction on the use of adjectives, uncommon adjectives, uncommon adverbs, the relative simplicity of the verbal form and the low proportion of subordinations supports the thesis that the working-class subjects do not explicate intent verbally and inasmuch as this is so the speech is relatively non-individuated" (1971: 109 [1962]).

It is not immediately obvious what "explicate intent verbally" or "non-individuated" mean or what role adverbs might play in either. Bernstein went on to explain the different character of an *elaborated code*: "Individuated speech presupposes a history of a particular role relationship if it is to be prepared and delivered appropriately. Inasmuch as difference is part of the expectation, there is less reliance or dependency on the listener; or rather this dependency is reduced by the explication of meaning" (1971: 113). In other words, "uncommon adverbs" help to make utterances more explicit.

Labov, on the other hand, includes adverbs such as *really* as signals of intensity: "'Intensity' is defined here as the emotional expression of social orientation toward the linguistic proposition: the commitment of the self to the proposition" (1984: 43–44). Powell observes that certain adverbs can "act preemptively to inform and to persuade a hearer of the nature and importance of the speaker's evaluation" (1992: 76).

What evidence is there in the transcripts to support the hypothesis that the middle-class speakers use adverbs (1) to be more explicit, (2) to express intensity, or (3) to signal the speaker's evaluation? The *Oxford English Dictionary* gives as its definition for the word *explicit* in relation to knowledge: "Developed in detail; hence, clear, definite." In the Glasgow middle-class conversations there are examples of derived adverbs that might come under this heading, as in the examples in (14).

(14)

    a. they're *slightly* different but they're *exactly* the same colour (10R)
    b. and it's *immediately* at the roadside (16L)
    c. it just goes downhill *slowly* (16L)
    d. a wee bit ambiguous here and there but *generally* okay (11L)

In the examples in (14), the speakers appear to be trying to make the point clearly and thus can be considered illustrations of explicitness. There are, however, similar examples in the working-class sessions, as shown in (15).

(15)

    a. you would just go along until you get to *roughly* the first street (15L)
    b. there's *really* nothing to see in it but it's *really* quiet (18L)
    c. two *completely* different people (13R)
    d. he's aboot—he's *nearly* as tall as—taller than John
       must be aboot six two—six four or something. (14R)

There are not many examples in either set of conversations, and if this is what Bernstein meant by explicitness, then it does not appear to explain the social class difference in the frequency of adverbs. However, it is possible that a different notion of explicitness may be relevant.

As regards intensity, the examples in (16) are taken from the middle-class interviews in Ayr (Macaulay 1991b: 125).

(16)

    a. I found it *extraordinarily* boring (IM)
    b. I got *absolutely* sick of doing nothing (IM)
    c. but this zombie of a mother—*completely* apathetic (WG)
    d. a *terribly* crippled bent old woman (DN)

These examples support Labov's view of these adverbs as expressing intensity. There are 25 clear examples in the Ayr middle-class interviews but only 3 in the working-class interviews. Similar examples can be found in the Glasgow middle-class conversations.

(17)

    a. and she was apparently *absolutely* horrendous (10L)
    b. who's got *absolutely* no sense of golfing etiquette (11L)
    c. whereas the lady describing it thought it was *absolutely* perfect (11L)
    d. you're either running around going d—*absolutely* scatty chasing your tail or (10R)

However, there are some similar examples in the working-class sessions, though they are less common and most of the examples come from one man (18L).

(18)

    a. I was there it was—oh it was *absolutely* brilliant (18L)
    b. oh I mean it's amazing it's *absolutely* fantastic (18L)
    c. it seemed to me to be a *perfectly* good place (18L)
    d. everything's all just draining doon like that you know
       just *completely totally* unwinding (13R)

So, there is some support for the view that the use of adverbs to express intensity contributes to the difference in frequency between the two social classes. The use of adverbs to show intensity seems to be more characteristic of middle-class speech than working-class speech, as is also shown in the middle-class speakers' significantly greater use of *very* and emphatic *quite*. What about Powell's notion that adverbs are used to express the speaker's evaluation?

Evaluation is a complex notion. Hunston and Thompson, while admitting that the term is "slippery," give the following definition: "Evaluation is the broad cover term for the expression of the speaker or writer's attitude or stance towards, viewpoint on, or feelings about the entities or propositions that he or she is talking about" (2000: 5). What evidence is there that the middle-class speakers' use of adverbs reflects a greater concern with evaluation than is found in the working-class conversations, and what would be the significance of that greater emphasis on evaluation? Hunston and Thompson point out the ideological implications of evaluation: "Every act of evaluation expresses a communal value-system, and every act of evaluation goes towards building up that value-system. This value-system in turn is a component of the ideology which lies behind every text" (6).

Do the social class differences in the use of adverbs (and evaluative adjectives) reflect different ideologies? To explore that question it is necessary to look at some excerpts from the conversations in greater detail. Here is an example from one of the middle-class men's conversations.

(19)   (Conversation 16—Middle-class men)
       R: it was the last day actually
           and I was skiing in tandem with my instructress
           who was a very attractive lady
           [3 lines omitted]
           and she had long flowing brunette hair
           and she put on her dry-suit over the top of her swimsuit
           and I mean she was just impeccable
           the way these American ladies do get dressed up in their swimsuits
           and look really super
           as though they're going out for the night
           dry as a bone
           and this woman didn't get her sunglasses wet
           didn't get her hair wet

It is clear that 16R was quite impressed by his instructress, "who was a *very attractive* lady" and "had *long flowing* brunette hair" and "was *just impeccable.*" She "look(ed) *really super*" "*the way* these American ladies do." The use of adjectives and adverbs exemplifies the evaluative account of his experience. She remained "dry as a bone." There are no similar passages in the working-class conversations.

Here is an example from one of the working-class men's conversations.

(20)   (Conversation 17—Working-class men)
       17R: well we moved because we needed a bigger house
             but it was in a better—in a wee bit better area right
             and then your final move
             tae make you feel like you were at the creme de la creme sort of a style
             was the cottages where Ruchill school is right
             so you went up the hill
             you got up eh Mayfield Street
             over the the bridge where the old railway used to be
             and you had the golf course Ruchill school and the cottage type houses
             because it was Curzon Street Leyton Street and Brassie Street
             that was that
             but we never ever got tae that stage
             I was born in forty-five
             I moved tae Cromer Street in nineteen fifty-two
             I moved tae—we moved tae two houses in Cromer Street
             we were twenty-nine
             and then we went to number twelve
             which was a bigger house
             and then before I got married
             we moved to twenty-two Mayfield Street a corner house

> which was smaller
> because I had two sisters
> they were married
> and it was just my my ma and da and me left at home

This is an account of where 17R lived as a boy and a young man, and he clearly considers this information worth communicating, since he goes into considerable detail. Although the first ambition of his family was to move to a bigger house "in a wee bit better area," the ultimate goal was to move to the cottages to "make you feel like you were at the creme de la creme sort of a style," but 17R "never got tae that stage." Although this is something that the speaker feels is worth telling, he does not use emotive language to describe the various places in which he grew up. The adjectives are *bigger* and *smaller* and the reference to the cottages being *the creme de la creme* is ironical. There is none of the heightened language that 16R uses to describe his skiing instructress in (19) or 10L uses to describe her road trip in (11).

Here is another example, this time from a working-class woman. She is telling about how her son injured his fingers at work.

(21)   (Conversation 14—Working-class women)
>   14L: but he was raging that day he done that
>   he says that he was working
>   that there was like other men fae different stations
>   he says and there was like officers
>   he says "But you know when you're working away?"
>   he says "They were standing waiting
>   and they were right over you
>   and speaking to you aw the time you were working"
>   and he says he turned roond
>   there was five of them
>   he turned roond
>   and he slipped as well
>   and he fell on his backside
>   and he said "And that put me in a mood right away cos I felt as if to say"
>   he said "I felt like saying to them 'go on go away and let me work
>   and you know wait in the office or something'"
>   he says "I done that"
>   and he says "after that everything just seemed to go wrong"
>   and he says "and then I put this thing and it slipped"
>   and he went "My God"
>   he was cursing and swearing
>   he couldnae really say anything
>   cos they were like bosses
>   but the next day when he went back to work the fellow was saying to him
>   "What was up wi you that day?"
>   and he went "It's dead awkward when you're trying to work
>   and they're breathing doon your neck"

In this story it is obvious that the speaker's son felt that the cause of his injury was the distraction caused by the presence of "the bosses," but there are no adjectives or adverbs referring to this aspect of the situation. There is no explicit comment that it was inconsiderate or unfair of his superiors to put him under pressure. The most that he manages to say is that it was "dead awkward" to have them breathing down his neck. Neither the protagonist nor the narrator, his mother, makes any attempt to characterize the "officers"/"bosses" in evaluative terms. The event is presented in dramatic terms, with roughly half the story told in dialogue, and the listener is left to draw her own conclusions.

Example (22) comes from one of the conversations between working-class men.

(22)   (Conversation 18—Working-class men)
R: look at them nowadays
they're sticking pensioners up in the high flats within Gilshochill in Maryhill.
you get maybe an eighty-four-year-old pensioner
or someone that's bad legs
and she's up in maybe the fifteenth floor
and what happens if the lift breaks down?
you know what I mean
she's got to go up there
she's either got to wait if she's out for her messages
comes back
and the lift's out of order
she's either got to wait till the lift's fixed
which could be a couple of hours
standing down in the foyer with all the neds and the junkies
or she's got to walk up thae stairs
and give her poor feet more damage you know

The speaker's attitude is quite clear. He does not approve of putting older people in high-rise flats, but again there is no explicit comment on the situation using adjectives or adverbs. Unlike the middle-class examples given in (11) and (19), there is no expression of the speaker's "attitude or stance towards, viewpoint on, or feelings about the entities or propositions that he or she is talking about" (Hunston and Thompson 2000: 5). There are no judgments of the kind shown in (23), all taken from middle-class conversations.

(23)
a. it's actually a very interesting wee book (16L)
b. quite a strange experience (16R)
c. wasn't exactly posh (11L)
d. we were in quite a strange threesome (11L)
e. so it's been a real macho conversation so far (11R)
f. some of the men had enormous great beer bellies (10R)
g. and she was so embarrassed (10R)

None of these observations seem unusual by middle-class standards, but for some reason they do not occur in the Glasgow working-class conversations. Here is an extended example with two middle-class women talking about a computer program.

(24)   (Conversation 12—Middle-class women)
        (hedges in bold, adverbs in italics)
        L12: it was *quite* chatty
        R12: yes
        L12: you know it **kind of** had been programmed
              to *really* **sort of** *just* keep you in order
              and not—not work too hard
              which is *quite* good
              but it was *quite* an old-fashioned model
              I can't remember what it was
              but it was *certainly* different from
              all the pc's that we're using
              and the the Macs that are being used now
        R12: yes yes they're *quite* user-friendly
        L12: mm *very* user-friendly *really*
        R12: yes yeah
        L12: yes I'm not *really* computer-minded
              but I'm having to learn
        R12: Oh I'm sure you though—you—you are much more   than you think *really*
        L12: well it's *quite* surprising the things I find myself doing or trying to do

There are no passages even remotely resembling this in the Glasgow working-class conversations. There has to be some explanation.

Biber and Finegan, in their cluster analysis of styles of stance in the London-Lund Corpus of Spoken English (Svartvik and Quirk 1980), found that the cluster that corresponds to "involved, intense conversational style" (1989: 110) was characterized by "frequent use of emphatics, hedges, and other general evidential markers" (111). Since the LLC consists mainly of middle-class speakers, Biber and Finegan's findings support the kind of social class differences in the use of emphatic and other adverbs found in Glasgow. In example (24), of 115 words, there are 12 adverbs (5 *quite*, 4 *really*, *just*, *very*, *certainly*). There are also two hedges, and as we have seen, the middle-class Glasgow adults in general use more hedges than the working-class adults.

Biber and Finegan suggest that the certainty and emphatic forms in their conversational sample "seem to reflect a sense of heightened emphatic excitement about the interaction, while the hedges seem to reflect a lack of concern with precise details, indicating that the focus is on involved interaction rather than precise semantic expression" (1989: 110). This may be true of the middle-class speakers in Glasgow too but it would be hard to say that the working-class speakers are less involved in the interaction, and yet their conversations do not display these characteristics to the same extent. Biber and Finegan were interested in different styles employed in different genres, including written materials as well as spoken, so their emphasis is not on variation within conversational styles and cannot be expected to draw distinctions of this kind. Nevertheless, their conclusions are consistent with the middle-class Glasgow conversations. The question then becomes: What is it that characterizes the working-class speakers?

One clue may lie in the phrase "a lack of concern with precise details" (Biber and Finegan 1989: 110) with reference to hedges. It was apparent in the Ayr interviews that the working-class speakers were concerned about details. The most extreme example of this was Andrew Sinclair (Macaulay 1985; 1991b: 249–54).

(25)

> I mean as one of thirteen of a family—eh
> and I'm one of the oldest ones
> well there were four—two boys and two girls older than me

Not content with telling me that he was one of the oldest children, he goes on to explain exactly where he comes in the order of birth. He also told me a lot more about coal mining than I felt I needed to know.

(26)

> well the first job any boy starts in the pit is the craw-picking
> well that was up at the tables
> when the coal comes up the pit
> it goes down through tumblers and along these big moving tables you see with
> riddles on them
> and before it comes to you
> it goes through all these different sizes of riddles you see
> and it goes on to different conveyors
> which takes it to the washer
> you know how you get singles trebles doubles dross et cetera and that
> and the desk went right round the table
> and our job as craw-pickers was
> you'd to pick the stones out of the coal
> as it passed down from the table and into the wagons you see

These are only two examples of the many details that Sinclair included in his long interview.

The Glasgow working-class speakers also include many details.

(27)   (Conversation 13—Working-class women)

> R13: and eh that's what happened there
> everybody was aw watching their bottles going doon you know
> doon and doon and doon
> the next thing oor table—
> it was like a half bottle of vodka and a half bottle of whisky and six cans of Pils
> and th—there was near enough another carry-oot was getting ordered

> L13: do you know you know that's what I would have ha—had with me
>   I wouldn't have had the vodka
>   I'd have had like that my Pils maybe
> R13: aye
> L13: but I thought "Oh to hell
>   I'm going—I'm going to drink vodka tonight for a change"
> R13: aye but see that last one?
>   the *Times* were gieing a can of Pils oot free in the Coop at the time
>   can you mind o that?
> L13: oh right
> R13: so everybody was aw on Pils
>   everybody that came in aw had aw these Pils
>   they must have all been buying the *Times*
>   and g—giving—giving aw these Pi—cans of Pils
> L13: you were get—you were getting—you—
> R13: cause their tables were full of them
>   everybody
>   you could guarantee there was aboot six at each table aw drinking Pils
>   and aw these cans were up
>   and a big black bag at the—the bottom of the hall
>   aw the cans were getting put into
>   cause that's what I was on an aw
>   and then as I say we ended up going on to Haddows and getting mair

This is a narrative about a night's drinking, but nothing much happens in the story. Yet the details are important: the vodka, the whisky, the cans of Pils (beer). The evaluation comes in the line "there was near enough another carry-oot was getting ordered." This means that despite the amount of drink on the table, they were thinking of getting more from the off-license (liquor store), and in the end they did: "we ended up going on to Haddows and getting mair." It was clearly a night of prodigious drinking, but it is never described in summary form; instead, it is communicated through the details.

Here is another example, this time from a conversation between two working-class men.

(28)   (Conversation 17—Working-class men)
> R17: I told you Galbraiths was my first job
> L17: uh huh
> R17: right
>   I only—I was only in Galbraiths aboot a year
>   an then I went to work in the matchwork
>   because everyone worked in
> L17: Bryant Mays
> R17: Bryant Mays
> L17: that's right
>   uh huh

R17: in Tuna street which—we still called it Ruchill
      but it was really under the Maryhill banner
L17: aye
R17: well you walk down Ruchill street to come to the ma—
      you'd the three factories
      McLellans the rubberworks
L17: that's right aye
R17: Fergusons the paintworks
L17: that's a—
      uh huh
R17: and Bryant Mays
L17: uh huh

To many people it might not seem that it was an important part of the story of R17's second job that there were two other factories on the same street, but R17, like males generally, as we have seen, likes to mention places.

Here is another example from the other conversation by working-class men.

(29)   (Conversation 18—Working-class men)
        L18: because I used to remember em trying to copy them
              because we had Beatle suits
        R18: mhm
        L18: there were four of us
        R18: this is Ruchill
              when you were a boy
        L18: this is in Ruch—
        R18: in the sixties aye
        L18: oh this was in oh well my goodness
              well aye
              they had all em black with no collar
              remember thae suits right
        R18: aye aye
        L18: the Beatles when they first started the—the no collar
        R18: the collarless suits aye
        L18: I could only get—
              I couldnae get a black one
              I had a grey one
        R18: mhm mhm
        L18: you know all my pals had a black one
              and I had a grey one
        R18: aye

Once again the details do not play any role in the subsequent story, but they are clearly important for the speaker. Johnstone, in her study of Fort Wayne narratives, points out the importance of details in storytelling: "Many Fort Wayne personal experience stories include far more detail than should, from the point of view of strict relevance, be necessary, detail which turns out to have no bearing on the narrative core at all" (1990: 91). Johnstone refers to this as "extrathematic detail" and explains its prevalence in Fort Wayne stories: "Since audiences do not break into stories with requests for clarification, tellers cannot expect to be told when settings are unclear. It is thus to a teller's advantage to err on the side of too much orientation, at the risk of including some irrelevant material, rather than on the side of too little, at the greater risk of not being understood at all" (107).

How does this relate to the difference in the use of adverbs? In an earlier paper (Macaulay 1995: 51–53), I argued that the working-class use of quoted dialogue allowed the hearer more freedom to interpret the situation than the use of evaluative adverbs and adjectives, which impose the speaker's interpretation. In the same way, the kind of details provided in examples such as (19–21) provide the hearer with the information necessary to understand the situation, rather than summarizing it in any way by an explicit comment. In contrast, middle-class examples such as those in (30) and (31) give an interpretation rather than details.

(30)

    R12: yes yes they're *quite* user-friendly
    L12: mm *very* user-friendly *really*

(31) L16: but the—the—the—the actual wee beach is—is *quite* nice

    . . . .

    so it's *actually quite* nice for swimming

Thus, similar to the findings from the Ayr interviews, the working-class speakers in the Glasgow conversations appear not to want to impose their views on their hearers but rather to let the hearers make up their own minds. One of the ways in which they do this is by rarely employing the adverbs and evaluative adjectives that the middle-class speakers use more frequently. The evidence of the Ayr and Glasgow studies suggests that the working-class speakers are much less anxious than the middle-class speakers to inform the hearer directly how they feel about the situation. This is not an idiosyncratic difference, since it is consistent across a wide range of speakers from both social classes. Nor is it a matter of register that might be related to level of education, since it extends to the use of words that are part of everybody's vocabulary, such as *very, just,* and *quite.* We are, in fact, confronted with the question that Bernstein wished to investigate. How does the evidence from the Ayr interviews and the Glasgow conversations relate to Bernstein's claims? Here is the description of the codes in Bernstein (1962):

> Two general types of codes can be distinguished: *elaborated* and *restricted.* They can be defined, on a linguistic level, in terms of the probability of predicting for any one speaker which syntactic elements will be used to organize meaning. In the case of an elaborated code, the speaker will select from a relatively extensive range of alternatives and therefore the probability of predicting the pattern of organizing elements is considerably reduced. In the case of a restricted code the number of these alternatives is often severely limited and the probability of predicting the pattern is greatly increased. (1971: 77 [1962])

At this time Bernstein clearly identified his *elaborated code* with middle-class speech and his *restricted code* with working-class speech. Does the examination of the Ayr interviews and the Glasgow conversations support or refute Bernstein's descriptions? As is the case so often with Bernstein, it is not quite clear what aspects of language he is referring to by the term *syntactic elements*. If he means syntactic structures, then there is no evidence that the middle-class speakers use "a relatively extensive range of alternatives," in contrast to the working-class speakers. Although the middle-class speakers do make more use of the passive voice, they make much less use of dislocated syntax. In this sense, though it is not one that Bernstein would have wanted to hear, the working-class speakers choose from a more extensive range of alternatives. However, neither the use of the passive nor the use of dislocated syntax plays a major role in either set of conversations.

If, however, by *syntactic elements* Bernstein means such word classes as adverbs and adjectives, then it is true that in the Ayr interviews and the Glasgow conversations the middle-class speakers not only use them more frequently but also choose from a greater range of alternatives. However, it is not correct to infer from this that in the case of the working-class speakers "the probability of predicting the pattern is greatly increased." What is predictable in "the pattern of organizing elements" is that the middle-class speakers will use adverbs more frequently and the working-class less frequently ($p < .001$). It is not the case that the working-class speakers use a smaller set of adverbs and adjectives more predictably; instead, they use them much less frequently.

Bernstein goes on to state the psychological implications of the two codes:

> On a psychological level the codes may be distinguished by the extent to which each facilitates (elaborated code) or inhibits (restricted code) the orientation to symbolize intent in a verbally explicit form. Behavior processed by these codes will, it is suggested, develop different modes of self-regulation and so different forms of orientation. The codes themselves are functions of a particular form of social relationship or, more generally, qualities of social structure. (1971: 78 [1962])

I find it almost uncanny that Bernstein here puts his finger on what seems to be the implication of the stylistic differences between the middle-class speakers and the working-class speakers, though he would almost certainly not agree with my interpretation of his statement. For Bernstein, the use of an elaborated code "implies sets of advanced logical operations," whereas in the restricted code "the emphasis is on the emotive rather than the logical implications" (1971: 28 [1958]). In fact, the more frequent use of adverbs and adjectives by the middle-class speakers has nothing to do with "advanced logical operations" but instead reflects the attitude and evaluation of the speaker to the topic. It might even be right to interpret this as an emphasis on "the emotive," exactly the reverse of the conclusion Bernstein draws. Bernstein may be right to claim that this discourse style helps to "develop different modes of self-regulation and so different forms of orientation," though I am less comfortable with the notion of causation than Bernstein was.

The middle-class speakers certainly seem very comfortable using evaluative language in describing events in their everyday life. In this sense the middle-class speech style may quite well be a function "of a particular form of social relationship or, more generally, qualities of social structure." In their conversations, the middle-class speakers show no hesitation in making their attitude clear, and one of the ways in which they do this is through the use of adverbs and evaluative adjectives. This is the sense in which they are more explicit. In whatever way it came about, they have been socialized to feel confident in expressing their opinions and even their prejudices. This has become part of their *habitus,* to use Bourdieu's term: "The objective homogenizing of group or class habitus which results from the homogeneity of the conditions of existence is what enables practices to be collectively harmonized without any intentional calculation or conscious reference to a norm" (1977: 80).

The middle-class use of adverbs is an example of Bourdieu's "different *ways of saying,* distinctive manners of speaking" (1991: 38). For Bourdieu, "what circulates on the linguistic market is not 'language' as such, but rather discourses that are stylistically marked" (39). However, it is hard to see the use of adverbs in terms of the kind of symbolic capital that Bourdieu describes. Working-class speakers in Scotland are not criticized for their inability to use adverbs. There is no stigma associated with the lack of adverbs, nor any prestige associated with their use. Nor can the use of adverbs be considered part of Giddens's "expert knowledge" (Giddens 1991: 30). It is not necessary to attend university to learn the words *very* and *quite.* However, the difference in adverb use may be a manifestation of power in Foucault's (1980) sense.

There may also be a parallel in Brown and Levinson's (1987) politeness theory. The use of evaluative language, such as adverbs and adjectives, could be interpreted as a face-threatening act, since the speaker is making his or her attitude quite clear, thus putting the hearer into a situation of (actively or passively) accepting or rejecting that position. The working-class speakers do not put their interlocutors in this face-threatening situation in the same way.

It is not that these middle-class speakers are aggressive or dogmatic; in fact, some are quite timid in many ways. But when they use words such as *amazingly, awfully, badly, drastically, enormously, overly, properly,* and *terribly,* they take it for granted that their middle-class interlocutors will share their view that something is amazing or awful, and so forth. It seems likely that they do this "without any intentional calculation or conscious reference to norms," but with an assumption of a mutual assessment of the situation. This can be seen in the immediate signals of agreement that often follow an evaluative statement in the middle-class conversations, as in (32).

(32)

    a. 16R: it looks awfully like that
          16L: good good good good good
          16R: yes it looks awfully like that
    b. 12R: unfortunately if you're using a computerized system
                   you can't do that
          12L: no it's very left brain isn't it?
    c. 12R: oh they're—they're really excellent
          12L: wonderful
    d. 16R: it didn't seem a terribly good idea
          16L: no

The working-class speakers do not manifest the same *habitus* as the middle-class speakers. Here is one of the working-class women explaining how when she was at work she heard that her mother had died. (I have simplified the transcription slightly but not changed anything essential.)

(33)   (Conversation 14—Working-class women)
    R: they didnae know that I called her "mother"
       and when they phoned me to tell me
       they says that Mrs Baird had died
       that's the way I got the message ower fae Lewis's
    L: oh right but they wouldnae've known it was like—
    R: but they didnae know that was like my mum sort of thing you know
       and I went "Oh it's my mum"
       and they went "Oh we didnae know that"
       or they wouldnae've told me
       there would've been a nurse or somebody wi' me to tell me
       but they just gave me a phone call doon to the department
       and then that's when they took me up to the staff office
       and gave me a cup of tea and aw that
       and then I just got sent hame

It is reasonable to assume that the news came as a shock to 14R, although it was not a complete surprise, but she makes no mention of her feelings or her reaction. The story focuses on the fact that her employers did not know that Mrs Baird was her mother (or at least the person she called "mother"), and so they were less considerate in breaking the news than they would have been if they had known. When they found out, they treated her gently, giving her a cup of tea and sending her home. It is hard to believe that one of the middle-class speakers would have told a story of this kind without describing his or her feelings on hearing the news. The only reaction 14R reports is her response, "Oh it's my mum," and the listener is left to interpret her attitude from that. We do not know whether this news was, unexpected or not, a relief or a shock. There is also no explicit evaluative comment from the listener, such as *that's terrible* or *how awful*, as might have been expected. Examples such as this suggest that Bernstein may have been right when he suggested that this kind of discourse style reflects "a particular form of social relationship or, more generally, qualities of social structure."

Without going as far as Bernstein later did in his claims about socialization, is it possible that there is a difference in the way in which middle-class and working-class children are brought up that affects their discourse style? There is one study in the United States that focuses on this kind of question. Heath (1982, 1983) carried out a nine-year ethnographic study in three communities in the Piedmont Carolinas. She labels the three communities Maintown (a white middle-class area), Roadville (a white working-class district), and Trackton (a poor African-American community). For the present purposes it is the contrast between Maintown and Roadville that is the significant one. Heath describes how Maintown parents often talk with their preschool children when engaged on a task or waiting in a doctor's office: "For example, adults point to items, and ask children to name, describe and compare them to familiar objects in their environment. Adults often ask children *to state their likes, or dislikes, their view of events*, and so forth" (1982: 53, emphasis added). In contrast, in Roadville, "Adults at tasks do not provide a running commentary on what they are doing. They do not draw the attention of the child to specific features of the sequences of skills or the attributes of items. They do not ask questions of the child, except questions that are directive or scolding in nature" (62). Taken out of context, these quotations may appear more judgmental than they do in context, but they are based on a very sympathetic understanding of all three communities, and Heath is concerned to show how the strengths children from each community bring to their early schooling can be used to help them adjust to the educational process. However, she does comment on the working-class children: "Roadville children need to have articulated for them *distinctions in discourse strategies and structures*" (72).

Heath is writing about a very different situation from Scotland, and I am not suggesting that her description would apply to social class differences in socialization in Glasgow or Ayr, since there many fundamental differences. But her observation on the differences in upbringing that have an effect on discourse strategies in her communities might point toward a similar kind of difference in Scotland. This was also the question that interested Bernstein, though I find his view of family structure less congenial.

However, it is necessary to emphasize that there is no implication that the working-class speakers are lacking in some ability. The difference in discourse styles is exactly that, only a difference in style. There is no reason to argue that there is something virtuous or beneficial in using more evaluative language. I have presented evidence elsewhere (Macaulay 1997: 139–62; to appear) that working-class speakers in Scotland are capable of remarkable eloquence, and some of those were among the individuals I interviewed in Ayr. None of the Glasgow conversations achieves aesthetic quality of that kind. The conversations are more mundane; the working-class speakers are no less articulate than the middle-class speakers, but there is clearly a difference in style.

The middle-class speakers in the Glasgow conversations are more willing to talk about what they think and feel, and even to admit weaknesses. One woman says that she would not consider going back to teaching because she finds the idea frightening. A mathematician admits that he makes mistakes in counting and writing checks. One man reports that he thought his voice "sounded dreadful" when he first heard it on a recording. Another states that he hates to go shopping. One woman confesses that she should "make a bigger effort" to go to concerts and so on. Another talks about the feeling of guilt when "you kind of chuck your children around." Personal details of this kind are much rarer, though not totally absent, in the working-class conversations. The speakers talk about their lives, their families, and their houses, but they are rather reticent about themselves, as illustrated in example (30), where the speaker did not mention her reaction to her mother's death. It is as if it is not appropriate to speak too personally. This attitude would be consistent with a reluctance to use evaluative language that shows the feelings or attitude of the speaker to what is being spoken about.

It is obviously impossible from the evidence of the Ayr interviews and the Glasgow conversations to have a clear understanding of why this social class difference in discourse styles should exist. For that, an in-depth ethnographic study such as Rampton (1995) or Eckert (2000) would be necessary. The unfortunate political fallout from Bernstein's categorization of restricted and elaborated codes has led to an avoidance of such questions in sociolinguistic research, but perhaps someone will be interested enough in the situation to undertake some empirical research. Until then, we are left with some intriguing data.

Given the different ways in which the data for the two studies were collected, the difference in discourse styles cannot simply be the effect of the methodology. The consistency of the social class differences is remarkable, since there is nothing obvious in the choice of topics that might affect the use of adverbs (or adjectives). Nor can the patterns of use be the result of interviewer bias, since there were no interviewers in the Glasgow sessions. Since quantitative studies of discourse variation are not yet common, it would be unwise to place too much significance on the results of two small-scale studies, but the fact that the social class differences show up so strongly in two quite different kinds of sample suggests that there is something fundamental that affects speech style in the two social class groups in western Scotland. There may be similar differences elsewhere, waiting to be discovered.

Discourse Sociolinguistics

The previous chapters have illustrated the use of quantitative measures to investigate variation in the use of certain discourse features. The method employed included the following procedures:

- Complete transcription of the recorded speech in normal orthography
- Separation of the contribution of each speaker
- Calculation of the total number of word forms for each speaker
- Creation of a concordance for each speaker
- Identification of discourse features for quantitative analysis
- Calculation of the frequency of each feature for every speaker
- Calculation of the mean frequency for categories of speakers
- Statistical analysis of the variation in the use of a feature by different groups

Calculation of the frequency of each feature for every speaker is essential for the purposes of comparison because it is highly unlikely that all the speakers will produce an identical amount of speech. It is not the number of tokens of a feature that matters but the number in relation to the total amount of speech recorded. In the present work, the frequencies have been calculated on the number of instances per 1,000 words. This method has some advantages over frequencies per turn, sentence, clause, or line of the transcript, since the latter units vary in length and depend upon the investigator's interpretation. The calculation of the total number of word forms, however, is not without its problems either. In the present work, minimal responses such as *mhm* and *uhuh* have been treated as equal to full lexical items, but hesitation forms such as *em* and *uh* have not been included in the word count. A different decision about these items would have affected the totals for each speaker, though probably not to a significant extent. Possibly more problematic is any decision about contracted forms such as *I'm*, *couldn't*. In the present work, these are treated as single words. It would be possible to count these as examples of two words, which would require additional scrutiny of the concordances. If, however, all speakers contract these forms, there would probably be little effect of separating them on the comparative totals. Decisions on what to include and what to exclude in the word count are relatively simple to make and need to be made only at the start of the analysis, in contrast to decisions about turn boundaries, sentence or clause structure, or lines in the transcript, which must be made at a local level. The calculation of frequencies based on word totals thus illustrates the first principle that I would like to propose for the quantitative analysis of discourse variation.

Principle I
To the extent possible, decisions about what to count should not depend upon local interpretations of function or meaning.

It will have been obvious in many places in earlier chapters that it is frequently impossible to follow principle I, but to the extent that it can be followed, the better chance there is that the results can be used for comparison with those in other studies. Since studies of discourse variation are time-consuming, it is unfortunate if their results cannot be compared directly because of interpretative judgments that are difficult to replicate. This concern underlies the second principle.

Principle II
The raw scores of word counts should be provided so that other researchers can compare them with their results.

For a researcher wishing to compare results with an earlier study, there is nothing more frustrating than to be told only that a result was or was not statistically significant, with no indication of the actual scores. (Bernstein's 1962 study is a classic example of what not to do.) Principle II does not affect the results or the methodology but provides valuable information for other researchers.

Principle III
Where possible, treat discourse features first as unitary phenomena before considering subfunctions.

Most discourse features are multifunctional, but decisions about different functions have to be made at a local level and thus violate principle I. Counting all instances of a feature before subdividing it into categories allows for maximum comparability. This principle is closely linked to the next.

Principle IV
Discourse features are units of form.

As was shown in chapter 7, there have been different interpretations of the meaning of features such as *you know* or focuser *like*. While notions of shared knowledge or similarity may not have affected the approach taken by investigators to these two items, such assumptions may make it more difficult for other investigators who do not share them. An ascetic approach in which discourse features are first of all treated as units of form avoids introducing controversial interpretations at an early stage.

Principle V
Discourse features do not belong to a closed class.

There have been various attempts to list the number of discourse markers or pragmatic particles, but this goal is premature. The use of adverbs examined in chapter 10 is an example of a discourse feature that is not generally included in the list. There may be others that would repay investigation.

The five principles listed here are intended as a heuristic guide for the investigation of discourse variation in the hope that some consistency of approach can be achieved. Because investigation of discourse variation must examine samples of talk in action, the use of a specific feature is locally determined, and thus any conclusion from a specific data set may not generalize to other situations. For this reason, any conclusions drawn from a single study may give an unreliable indication of a more widespread difference. Consequently, one of the ways in which the reliability of the results can be tested is the extent to which similar results are found elsewhere. It is only through convergence of results from replications of earlier studies or evidence from studies using different samples or different methodology that we can have any confidence in the results (Campbell and Fiske 1959).

Munroe and Munroe have emphasized the need for replication in anthropology: "Replicative undertakings, which are not prized in anthropology, nevertheless must occupy a central place in comparative investigations, just as they do in other scientific activities" (1991: 164). However, confirmation (or refutation) will be convincing only if the results are obtained by methods that allow meaningful comparison.

The examples that have been examined in the present work come from two very different kinds of speech event: unstructured interviews with a stranger and dyadic conversations between friends. There are many other kinds of speech event that present different challenges for transcription and analysis, but if the approach set out in the preceding five principles is adopted, there will be a basis for comparison. The use of quantitative methods to investigate discourse variation is still at a very elementary stage, but I am sure that ultimately this will prove a fruitful source of valuable information about linguistic diversity.

Appendix

			Total words	Narrative/ words	% Narrative	Dialogue/ words	% Dialogue
Adolescents							
2-L	female	middle-class	2,313	833	36	48	6
2-R	female	middle-class	3,681	920	25	89	10
3-L	male	middle-class	1,978	435	22	53	12
3-R	male	middle-class	2,985	836	28	53	6
4-L	male	middle-class	2,420	508	21	69	14
4-R	male	middle-class	4,149	1,286	31	92	7
5-L	female	middle-class	2,703	1,000	37	115	12
5-R	female	middle-class	1,724	172	10	112	65
6-L	male	working-class	1,827	0	0	0	0
6-R	male	working-class	2,528	0	0	0	0
7-L	female	working-class	2,356	377	16	17	4
7-R	female	working-class	4,608	3,133	68	453	15
8-L	female	working-class	3,430	2,127	62	201	9
8-R	female	working-class	3,284	2,529	77	299	12
9-L	male	working-class	1,754	281	16	165	59
9-R	male	working-class	1,306	65	5	16	16
			43,046	14,502	34	1,782	12
Adults							
10-L	female	middle-class	4,582	1,490	33	334	22
10-R	female	middle-class	7,265	3,543	49	835	24
11-L	male	middle-class	5,195	2,122	49	189	9
11-R	male	middle-class	2,681	953	38	102	11
12-L	female	middle-class	4,375	644	12	29	5
12-R	female	middle-class	2,492	240	9	0	0
13-L	female	working-class	4,109	1,476	36	451	31
13-R	female	working-class	5,164	2,597	50	652	25
14-L	female	working-class	4,314	1,526	35	507	33
14-R	female	working-class	7,860	5,604	71	1,780	32
15-L	female	working-class	7,372	1,818	25	193	11
15-R	female	working-class	4,306	1,438	33	363	25
16-L	male	middle-class	4,686	1,427	30	118	8
16-R	male	middle-class	3,033	903	30	29	3
17-L	male	working-class	1,870	163	9	0	0
17-R	male	working-class	6,276	1,024	16	190	19
18-L	male	working-class	4,633	439	9	0	0
18-R	male	working-class	4,403	623	14	0	0
			84,616	28,030	33	5,772	21

	Words 000s	Well	Freq.	oh	Freq.	you know	Freq.	I mean	Freq.
Adols.									
2-L	2.313	13	5.62	19	8.21	6	2.59	1	0.43
2-R	3.681	16	4.35	41	11.14	8	2.17	3	0.81
3-L	1.978	2	1.01	6	3.03	3	1.52	0	0
3-R	2.985	3	1.01	12	4.02	1	0.34	0	0
4-L	2.42	5	2.07	7	2.89	0	0	2	0.83
4-R	4.149	6	1.45	7	1.69	0	0	1	0.24
5-L	2.703	7	2.59	20	7.4	2	0.74	0	0
5-R	1.724	5	2.92	33	19.14	2	1.16	36	20.88
6-L	1.827	6	3.28	3	1.64	1	0.55	1	0.55
6-R	2.528	3	1.19	5	1.98	1	0.39	2	0.79
7-L	2.356	6	2.55	12	5.09	0	0	1	0.42
7-R	4.608	1	0.22	16	3.47	2	0.43	0	0
8-L	3.43	3	0.87	3	0.87	1	0.29	7	2.04
8-R	3.284	4	1.22	16	4.87	6	1.83	2	0.61
9-L	1.754	2	1.14	6	3.42	2	1.14	0	0
9-R	1.306	1	0.77	6	4.59	2	1.53	0	0
Total	43.046	83		212		37		56	
Adults									
10-L	4.582	12	2.62	56	12.22	8	1.75	13	2.84
10-R	7.265	53	7.3	48	6.61	93	12.8	33	4.54
11-L	5.195	28	5.39	9	1.73	13	2.5	19	3.66
11-R	2.681	4	1.49	9	3.36	42	15.67	13	4.85
12-L	4.375	9	2.06	23	5.26	18	4.11	3	0.69
12-R	2.492	19	7.62	54	21.67	32	12.84	5	2.01
13-L	4.109	19	4.62	28	6.81	14	3.41	26	6.33
13-R	5.164	14	2.71	26	5.03	47	9.1	1	0.19
14-L	4.314	4	0.93	45	10.43	5	1.16	2	0.46
14-R	7.86	16	2.04	46	5.85	53	6.74	5	0.64
15-L	7.372	76	10.31	19	2.8	81	10.99	29	3.93
15-R	4.306	19	4.41	50	11.61	45	10.45	19	4.41
16-L	4.686	11	2.35	26	5.55	18	3.84	17	3.63
16-R	3.033	17	5.61	23	7.58	0	0	4	0.99
17-L	1.87	10	5.35	16	8.56	1	0.53	0	0
17-R	6.276	68	10.83	6	0.96	1	0.16	0	0
18-L	4.633	19	4.1	31	6.69	56	12.09	32	6.91
18-R	4.403	16	3.63	15	3.41	21	4.77	16	3.63
Total	84.616	414		530		579		237	

	Words 000s	and	Freq.	but	Freq.	so	Freq.	(be-)cause	Freq.
Adols.									
2-L	2.313	49	21.2	20	8.6	10	4.3	21	9.1
2-R	3.681	55	14.9	24	6.5	16	4.3	24	6.5
3-L	1.978	44	22.2	7	3.5	12	6.1	8	4
3-R	2.985	58	19.4	9	3	8	2.7	9	3
4-L	2.42	71	29.3	15	6.2	6	2.5	12	4.9
4-R	4.149	160	38.6	41	9.9	21	5.1	54	13
5-L	2.703	60	22.2	22	8.1	10	3.7	12	4.4
5-R	1.724	12	6.9	15	8.7	5	2.9	4	2.3
6-L	1.827	5	2.7	6	3.3	2	1.1	4	2.2
6-R	2.528	20	7.9	5	1.9	6	2.4	9	3.6
7-L	2.356	32	13.6	9	3.8	8	3.4	2	0.8
7-R	4.608	145	31.5	57	12.4	15	3.3	43	9.3
8-L	3.43	81	23.6	11	3.2	24	7	21	6.1
8-R	3.284	116	35.3	13	3.9	12	3.7	16	4.9
9-L	1.754	35	19.9	6	3.4	4	2.3	5	2.9
9-R	1.306	8	6.1	2	1.5	1	0.8	3	2.3
Total	43.046	951		262		160		247	
Adults									
10-L	4.582	90	19.6	44	9.6	35	7.6	35	7.6
10-R	7.265	276	37.9	48	6.6	48	6.6	17	2.3
11-L	5.195	111	21.4	35	6.7	26	5	15	2.9
11-R	2.681	41	15.3	24	8.9	8	3	7	1.3
12-L	4.375	107	24.5	28	6.4	28	6.4	11	2.5
12-R	2.492	47	18.9	15	6	3	1.2	39	15.7
13-L	4.109	78	18.9	29	7.1	23	5.6	30	7.3
13-R	5.164	139	26.9	54	10.5	21	4.1	37	7.2
14-L	4.314	95	22	25	5.8	13	3	32	7.4
14-R	7.86	240	30.5	72	9.2	24	3.1	62	7.9
15-L	7.372	171	23.2	117	15.9	48	6.5	41	5.6
15-R	4.306	104	24.2	40	9.3	36	8.4	23	5.3
16-L	4.686	114	24.3	47	10	30	6.4	28	5.9
16-R	3.033	64	21.1	16	5.3	13	4.3	8	2.6
17-L	1.87	8	4.3	2	1.1	0	0	1	0.5
17-R	6.276	99	15.8	86	13.7	27	4.3	48	7.6
18-L	4.633	69	14.9	33	7.1	5	1.1	23	4.9
18-R	4.403	54	12.3	26	5.9	12	2.7	15	3.4
Total	84.616	1907		741		400		472	

	Words	Imp	Freq.	Passives	Freq.	Y/N Q's	Freq.	WH Q's	Freq.	All Q's
Adols.										
2-L	2.313	7	3	5	2.16	42	18	35	15	77
2-R	3.681	8	2.2	11	2.99	97	26	56	15	153
3-L	1.978	5	2.5	11	5.56	86	43	21	11	107
3-R	2.985	4	1.3	13	4.36	76	25	41	14	117
4-L	2.42	0	0	4	1.65	7	3	5	2	12
4-R	4.149	1	0.2	8	1.93	21	5	7	2	28
5-L	2.703	0	0	12	4.44	72	27	29	11	101
5-R	1.724	3	1.7	2	1.16	46	27	48	28	94
6-L	1.827	2	1.1	4	2.19	41	22	45	25	86
6-R	2.528	22	8.7	8	3.16	36	14	28	11	64
7-L	2.356	14	5.9	1	0.42	36	15	26	11	62
7-R	4.608	4	0.9	7	1.52	36	8	11	2	47
8-L	3.43	2	0.6	18	5.25	21	6	17	5	38
8-R	3.284	4	1.4	12	3.65	8	2	22	7	30
9-L	1.754	31	17.7	5	2.85	18	10	17	10	35
9-R	1.306	34	26	2	1.53	12	9	29	22	41
	43.046	141		123		655		437	40	1092
Mean		8.8		7.9		40.9		27.3		68.3
Adults										
10-L	4.582	0	0	10	2.18	25	5	8	2	33
10-R	7.265	0	0	24	3.3	17	2	12	2	29
11-L	5.195	1	0.2	18	3.46	1	0	3	1	4
11-R	2.681	0	0	7	2.6	6	2	7	3	13
12-L	4.375	1	0.2	11	2.51	74	17	13	3	87
12-R	2.492	0	0	7	2.81	9	4	1	0	10
13-L	4.109	0	0	10	2.43	20	5	5	1	25
13-R	5.164	0	0	8	1.43	41	8	12	2	53
14-L	4.314	0	0	6	1.39	92	21	20	5	112
14-R	7.86	0	0	7	0.89	27	3	6	1	33
15-L	7.372	0	0	16	2.17	16	2	8	1	24
15-R	4.306	0	0	11	2.55	79	18	22	5	101
16-L	4.686	0	0	12	2.56	42	9	7	1	49
16-R	3.033	0	0	16	5.28	16	5	2	1	18
17-L	1.87	1	0.5	1	0.53	28	15	11	6	39
17-R	6.276	0	0	18	2.87	12	2	16	3	28
18-L	4.633	0	0	6	1.3	18	4	22	5	40
18-R	4.403	2	0.5	6	1.36	26	6	13	3	39
	84.616	5		194		549		188	26	737
Mean		0.3		10.8		31		10		41

	Words	who	Freq.	which	Freq.	a/an	Freq.	the	Freq.
Adols.									
2-L	2.313	1	0.43	0	0	26	11	60	26
2-R	3.681	2	0.54	0	0	52	14	63	17
3-L	1.978	0	0	0	0	30	15	40	20
3-R	2.985	1	0.36	0	0	61	20	90	30
4-L	2.42	1	0.41	5	2.07	51	21	109	45
4-R	4.149	1	0.24	11	2.65	74	18	138	33
5-L	2.703	1	0.37	0	0	34	13	24	9
5-R	1.724	1	0.58	0	0	23	13	15	9
6-L	1.827	0	0	0	0	26	14	38	21
6-R	2.528	0	0	0	0	41	16	89	35
7-L	2.356	2	0.85	0	0	42	18	59	25
7-R	4.608	2	0.43	0	0	31	7	70	15
8-L	3.43	0	0	0	0	65	19	128	37
8-R	3.284	0	0	0	0	52	16	101	31
9-L	1.754	1	0.57	2	1.14	49	28	54	31
9-R	1.306	1	0.77	1	0.77	20	15	48	37
	43.046	14		19		677		1,126	
Mean		9		1		42		70	
Adults									
10-L	4.582	8	1.77	4	0.87	116	25	157	34
10-R	7.265	17	2.34	7	0.96	126	17	303	41
11-L	5.195	17	3.27	9	1.73	165	32	252	49
11-R	2.681	9	3.36	5	1.86	72	27	107	40
12-L	4.375	10	2.29	9	2.06	130	30	130	30
12-R	2.492	5	2.01	4	1.61	61	24	90	40
13-L	4.109	0	0	0	0	75	18	177	43
13-R	5.164	0	0	1	0.18	122	24	209	40
14-L	4.314	0	0	0	0	83	19	145	34
14-R	7.86	0	0	1	0.13	147	19	262	33
15-L	7.372	0	0	1	0.14	173	23	333	45
15-R	4.306	0	0	1	0.23	75	17	151	35
16-L	4.686	4	0.85	16	3.4	112	24	233	50
16-R	3.033	3	0.99	13	4.27	84	28	139	46
17-L	1.87	1	0.53	2	1.07	34	18	77	41
17-R	6.276	1	0.16	6	0.96	165	26	343	55
18-L	4.633	1	0.22	5	1.08	105	23	202	44
18-R	4.403	0	0	4	0.91	102	23	198	45
	84.616	76		88		1,947		3,508	
Mean		4		5		108		195	

	Words	Adverbs in -ly	Freq.	very	Freq.	quite	Freq.	just	Freq.
Adols.									
2-L	2.313	13	5.6	0	0	3	0.86	21	9
2-R	3.681	38	10.3	0	0	18	4.89	29	8
3-L	1.978	5	2.5	0	0	8	4.04	18	9
3-R	2.985	8	2.7	0	0	1	0.34	17	6
4-L	2.42	38	15.7	3	1.24	2	0.83	39	16
4-R	4.149	50	12.1	9	2.17	18	4.34	46	11
5-L	2.703	17	6.3	2	0.74	3	1.11	11	4
5-R	1.724	16	9.3	0	0	1	0.58	18	10
6-L	1.827	15	8.2	0	0	0	0	11	6
6-R	2.528	4	1.6	1	0.4	0	0	11	4
7-L	2.356	11	4.7	0	0	0	0	22	9
7-R	4.608	12	2.6	0	0	0	0	50	11
8-L	3.43	12	3.5	0	0	0	0	37	11
8-R	3.284	15	4.6	0	0	1	0.29	22	7
9-L	1.754	4	2.3	1	0.57	0	0	9	5
9-R	1.306	6	4.6	1	0.77	0	0	15	11
	43.046	264		17		55		376	
Mean		16.5		1		3.4		23.5	
Adults									
10-L	4.582	30	6.5	18	3.93	8	1.75	13	3
10-R	7.265	70	9.6	7	0.96	19	2.62	58	8
11-L	5.195	67	12.9	10	1.92	14	2.69	25	5
11-R	2.681	40	14.9	4	1.49	18	6.71	13	5
12-L	4.375	59	13.5	48	10.97	22	5.03	15	3
12-R	2.492	28	11.2	18	7.22	6	2.41	13	5
13-L	4.109	31	7.5	0	0	8	1.95	15	4
13-R	5.164	15	2.9	0	0	7	1.25	22	4
14-L	4.314	20	4.6	0	0	17	3.94	47	11
14-R	7.86	27	3.4	0	0	2	0.25	61	8
15-L	7.372	41	12.2	5	0.68	6	0.81	90	12
15-R	4.306	29	6.7	3	0.7	10	2.32	26	6
16-L	4.686	61	13	27	5.76	18	3.84	27	6
16-R	3.033	44	14.5	16	5.28	20	6.59	17	6
17-L	1.87	2	1.1	0	0	0	0	5	3
17-R	6.276	32	5.1	4	0.64	1	0.16	23	4
18-L	4.633	31	6.7	3	0.65	8	1.73	26	6
18-R	4.403	16	3.6	1	0.23	1	0.23	23	5
	84.616	643		164		185		519	
Mean		35.7		9.1		10.3		28.8	

	can	could	may	might	must	should	will	would	need	going to	supposed to	All
Adols.												
2-L	6	0	0	2	0	1	16	11	0	2	2	40
2-R	12	1	0	2	2	7	11	15	1	8	0	59
3-L	3	5	0	4	0	0	0	6	2	1	1	22
3-R	8	4	0	0	4	0	8	19	0	7	1	51
4-L	21	3	0	0	0	1	21	2	4	3	0	55
4-R	24	9	0	0	0	2	24	4	0	5	0	68
5-L	6	4	0	3	0	0	22	16	2	7	8	68
5-R	3	2	0	1	0	0	13	24	0	5	1	49
6-L	6	5	0	1	1	0	10	7	4	11	0	45
6-R	6	6	0	2	0	1	21	8	0	15	1	60
7-L	13	1	0	0	2	1	36	7	3	11	1	75
7-R	13	7	0	1	4	3	33	10	1	17	2	91
8-L	12	3	1	1	4	1	25	19	1	14	3	84
8-R	7	7	0	0	1	0	18	8	0	9	0	50
9-L	16	3	0	0	1	2	20	0	5	8	1	56
9-R	11	7	0	0	1	0	10	3	1	4	1	38
	167	67	1	17	20	19	288	159	24	127	22	738
Adults												
10-L	19	7	0	0	5	5	18	19	2	12	0	87
10-R	14	13	1	0	4	3	26	15	4	18	0	98
11-L	20	10	3	7	6	3	22	23	1	9	0	104
11-R	3	2	1	1	1	6	11	6	2	1	0	34
12-L	10	4	1	0	11	1	11	12	2	6	0	58
12-R	6	2	0	3	1	2	4	12	1	1	0	32
13-L	17	3	0	0	1	3	20	10	4	11	3	72
13-R	24	11	1	2	7	6	45	20	4	16	2	138
14-L	12	16	0	2	5	4	19	39	3	4	1	105
14-R	15	23	0	6	7	8	63	37	14	15	5	193
15-L	20	14	0	0	1	3	35	90	9	9	4	185
15-R	11	9	0	3	3	2	25	31	3	10	1	98
16-L	15	9	0	2	0	0	6	10	0	2	0	44
16-R	2	3	1	2	3	1	1	5	0	1	2	21
17-L	4	2	0	0	1	0	3	4	0	0	0	14
17-R	22	12	2	0	4	3	23	14	8	0	0	88
18-L	15	21	0	1	2	5	18	16	1	2	0	81
18-R	17	19	0	0	1	0	12	7	0	1	0	57
	246	180	10	29	63	55	362	370	58	118	18	1,315

	Words	Adjectives	Freq.	Evaluative adjs.	Freq.	Highlight	Freq.	think/ thought	Freq.
Adults									
10-L	4.582	64	13.97	39	8.5	4	0.87	4	0.87
10-R	7.265	119	16.38	34	4.7	2	0.28	4	0.55
11-L	5.195	79	15.21	39	7.5	0	0	3	0.58
11-R	2.681	38	14.17	22	8.2	0	0	1	0.37
12-L	4.375	72	16.46	54	12.3	0	0	1	0.23
12-R	2.492	41	16.45	23	9.2	0	0	2	0.8
13-L	4.109	49	11.92	12	2.9	18	4.36	4	0.97
13-R	5.164	80	15.49	19	3.7	22	4.26	10	1.78
14-L	4.314	74	17.15	27	6.3	6	1.39	4	0.93
14-R	7.86	65	8.27	18	2.3	15	1.91	3	0.38
15-L	7.372	82	11.12	36	4.9	16	2.17	2	0.27
15-R	4.306	78	18.11	23	5.3	14	3.25	5	1.16
16-L	4.686	106	22.62	30	6.4	1	0.21	3	0.64
16-R	3.033	76	25.06	43	14.2	0	0	0	0
17-L	1.87	11	5.88	5	2.7	3	1.6	0	0
17-R	6.276	63	10.04	16	2.5	11	1.75	0	0
18-L	4.633	97	20.94	42	9.1	10	2.16	0	0
18-R	4.403	76	17.26	12	2.7	4	0.91	0	0
	84.616	1270		494		126		46	
Mean		71		27		7		3	

	Words	sort of	Freq.	maybe	Freq.	even	Freq.	Min. Resp.	Freq.
Adols.									
2-L	2.313	1	0.43	0	0	0	0	121	52
2-R	3.681	9	2.44	1	0.27	0	0	75	20
3-L	1.978	2	1.01	0	0	1	0.51	76	38
3-R	2.985	2	0.67	0	0	0	0	73	25
4-L	2.42	2	0.83	0	0	1	0.41	209	86
4-R	4.149	12	2.89	0	0	4	0.96	48	12
5-L	2.703	7	2.59	3	1.11	4	1.48	119	44
5-R	1.724	0	0	1	0.58	0	0	114	66
6-L	1.827	0	0	0	0	1	0.55	42	23
6-R	2.528	0	0	0	0	2	0.79	16	6
7-L	2.356	0	0	0	0	2	0.85	51	22
7-R	4.608	0	0	0	0	15	3.26	49	11
8-L	3.43	0	0	1	0.29	2	0.58	11	3
8-R	3.284	1	0.3	0	0	10	3.05	17	5
9-L	1.754	1	0.57	0	0	1	0.57	24	14
9-R	1.306	1	0.77	0	0	0	0	42	32
	43.046	38		6		43		1,087	
Mean		2.4		0.375		3		68	
Adults									
10-L	4.582	9	1.96	1	0.22	8	1.75	186	41
10-R	7.265	10	1.38	6	0.83	6	0.83	239	33
11-L	5.195	14	2.69	6	1.15	10	1.92	66	13
11-R	2.681	8	2.98	6	2.24	7	2.61	329	123
12-L	4.375	3	0.69	3	0.69	3	0.69	297	68
12-R	2.492	2	0.8	2	0.8	2	0.8	228	9
13-L	4.109	1	0.243	6	1.46	2	0.49	193	47
13-R	5.164	1	0.18	13	2.32	8	1.43	173	34
14-L	4.314	1	0.23	16	3.71	17	3.94	185	43
14-R	7.86	2	0.25	10	1.27	18	2.29	100	13
15-L	7.372	17	2.31	15	2.03	18	2.44	223	30
15-R	4.306	3	0.7	2	0.46	9	2.09	289	67
16-L	4.686	9	1.92	8	1.71	6	1.28	100	21
16-R	3.033	8	2.64	3	0.99	5	1.65	171	56
17-L	1.87	0	0	0	0	3	1.6	258	138
17-R	6.276	1	0.16	6	0.96	7	1.12	42	7
18-L	4.633	1	0.22	6	1.3	16	3.54	149	32
18-R	4.403	0	0	14	3.18	18	4.09	285	65
	84.616	90		123		163		3,513	
Mean		5		7		9		195	

	Words	he	I	it	she	they	we	you	all prons	Freq.
Adols.										
2-L	2.313	25	158	68	60	30	32	73	446	193
2-R	3.681	47	261	97	63	49	43	112	672	183
3-L	1.978	47	104	64	22	22	38	72	369	187
3-R	2.985	63	120	77	33	43	46	100	482	161
4-L	2.42	10	107	84	3	61	14	86	365	151
4-R	4.149	50	196	108	9	71	6	141	581	140
5-L	2.703	81	185	33	109	27	7	62	504	186
5-R	1.724	29	182	35	66	16	2	54	384	223
6-L	1.827	53	86	35	15	19	7	117	332	182
6-R	2.528	78	138	43	21	27	13	99	419	166
7-L	2.356	15	200	58	112	15	32	33	465	187
7-R	4.608	47	289	96	202	29	31	139	833	181
8-L	3.43	106	226	88	65	24	36	98	643	187
8-R	3.284	104	253	97	60	18	35	43	610	186
9-L	1.754	16	122	48	9	23	30	55	303	173
9-R	1.306	6	60	56	13	15	20	46	216	165
	43.046	777	2,687	1,087	862	489	392	1,330	7,624	
Mean		49	156	68	54	31	25	83	477	
Adults										
10-L	4.582	55	191	110	121	79	25	106	687	150
10-R	7.265	49	341	187	189	102	57	202	1,127	155
11-L	5.195	60	304	94	30	64	47	85	684	132
11-R	2.681	26	115	70	2	32	12	74	331	123
12-L	4.375	29	129	146	31	93	35	137	600	137
12-R	2.492	9	138	93	8	62	20	75	405	163
13-L	4.109	10	282	157	74	85	28	92	728	177
13-R	5.164	48	289	229	72	131	46	219	1,034	184
14-L	4.314	107	124	135	144	124	13	114	761	176
14-R	7.86	168	473	206	254	164	55	194	1,514	193
15-L	7.372	40	333	279	97	103	124	305	1,281	174
15-R	4.306	11	238	225	58	58	49	187	826	192
16-L	4.686	21	176	199	8	74	20	153	651	139
16-R	3.033	24	112	98	35	42	16	44	371	122
17-L	1.87	10	91	81	6	21	6	49	264	141
17-R	6.276	26	262	152	66	104	136	198	944	150
18-L	4.633	32	258	148	9	137	17	174	775	167
18-R	4.403	29	154	92	15	90	18	191	589	134
	84.616	754	4,010	2,701	1,219	1,565	724	2,599	13,572	
Mean		42	223	150	58	87	40	144	754	

	Words	she	Freq.	Named males	Freq.	Named females	Freq.	Named places	Freq.
Adols.									
2-L	2.313	60	25.94	7	3.03	14	6.05	4	1.7
2-R	3.681	63	17.11	5	1.36	19	5.16	5	1.4
3-L	1.978	22	11.12	19	9.61	4	2.02	13	6.6
3-R	2.985	33	11.05	45	15.08	13	4.36	21	7
4-L	2.42	3	1.24	1	0.41	0	0	4	1.7
4-R	4.149	9	2.17	11	2.65	0	0	9	2.2
5-L	2.703	109	53.69	44	16.28	116	42.92	7	2.6
5-R	1.724	66	38.28	12	6.96	74	42.92	5	2.9
6-L	1.827	15	8.21	19	10.4	11	6.02	12	6.6
6-R	2.528	21	8.31	54	21.36	14	5.54	33	13.1
7-L	2.356	112	47.54	9	3.82	26	11.04	5	2.1
7-R	4.608	202	43.84	44	9.55	173	37.54	10	2.2
8-L	3.43	65	18.95	43	12.54	40	11.66	9	2.6
8-R	3.284	60	18.27	39	11.88	34	10.35	13	3.9
9-L	1.754	9	5.13	2	1.14	5	2.85	6	3.4
9-R	1.306	13	9.95	6	4.59	0	0	5	3.7
	43.046	862		360		543		161	
Mean		54		23		34		10	
Adults									
10-L	4.582	121	26.41	21	4.58	37	8.08	32	6.98
10-R	7.265	189	26.02	27	3.72	71	9.77	38	5.23
11-L	5.195	30	5.77	6	1.15	13	2.5	31	5.97
11-R	2.681	2	0.75	11	4.1	1	0.37	16	5.97
12-L	4.375	31	7.09	6	1.37	12	2.74	58	13.26
12-R	2.492	8	3.21	3	1.2	1	0.4	21	8.43
13-L	4.109	74	18.01	10	2.43	38	9.25	32	7.79
13-R	5.164	72	12.83	10	1.78	16	2.85	52	9.26
14-L	4.314	144	33.37	8	1.85	29	6.72	8	1.85
14-R	7.86	254	32.32	57	7.25	65	8.27	73	9.29
15-L	7.372	97	13.16	17	2.31	51	6.92	19	2.58
15-R	4.306	58	13.47	2	0.46	23	5.34	12	2.79
16-L	4.686	8	1.17	0	0	5	1.07	140	29.88
16-R	3.033	35	11.54	4	1.32	3	0.99	49	16.16
17-L	1.87	6	3.21	7	3.74	1	0.53	47	25.13
17-R	6.276	66	10.52	12	1.91	9	1.43	213	33.94
18-L	4.633	9	1.94	4	0.86	0	0	33	7.12
18-R	4.403	15	3.41	7	1.59	0	0	68	15.44
	84.616	1,219		212		375		942	
Mean		58		12		21		52	

Notes

Chapter 5

1. There is an interesting parallel here to Robin Lakoff's (1973, 1975) claims about women's language. Although many of Lakoff's claims, which were based on her own observations and intuitions rather than on systematic research, have been discredited, her effective presentation of them stimulated a great deal of interesting research into gender differences in language use. Here, alas, the parallel ends, because Bernstein's claims tended to be accepted or rejected without a serious empirical attempt to replicate or refute them.

2. For those who find coincidences intriguing, there is a certain irony in the fact that Noam Chomsky and Basil Bernstein, who started from very different theoretical orientations in studying language, ended up being mainly concerned with abstract psychological processes that some people find rather distant from the subject of language.

3. This sounds more like Chomsky than Bernstein.

4. I drew attention to this problem in a comment on Rickford and McNair-Knox's (1994) analysis of two "interviews" by pointing out that the two recording sessions were actually rather different speech events (Macaulay 1999, 2001a).

5. Given the small numbers involved, even a difference of a few tokens might have affected the statistical significance. This seems to me a paradigm case of the misleading use of statistics. For example, Bernstein claims that the middle-class boys "use a greater proportion of passive verbs" (1971: 101) and that this is significant beyond the 0.02 level of confidence. The frequency of passive verbs that I have found in my corpora is between 3 and 4 per 1,000 words. If the frequency in Bernstein's sample was similar, he would have recorded between 24 and 32 tokens. While the results of the Mann-Whitney u test give Bernstein a significant result, the actual numbers might have revealed a rather slender basis for his claim.

6. Bisseret says much the same with a rather different emphasis: "His [i.e., Bernstein's] interpretation of the present social reality seems to be the following: the elaborated code, the language of his own class, is the result of slow evolution, of continual progress towards a superior state. He makes it seem as though one class has remained at the stage of restricted code, whereas the other was inventing a more perfect language, a language more adapted to the tasks to be accomplished, to the problems to be solved by man so as to dominate nature and constitute a corpus of scientific knowledge" (1979: 97).

Chapter 7

1. Elaine Andersen (2000: 243) found that by the age of six or seven children in several different language communities used discourse markers such as *well* appropriately in role-playing higher-status speakers.

2. The Ayr lower-class speakers also use a form (*you*) *ken* in this function with a frequency of 2.9, but this figure is distorted by the fact that one speaker (WR) is responsible for 78% of the examples in a relatively short interview. WR uses (*you*) *ken* with a frequency of 31.4. One other speaker (WL) is responsible for 17% of the examples, with a frequency of 2.15. The other four lower-class speakers have only 9 examples among them. If all the tokens of (*you*) *ken* are added to those of *you know*, the frequency of the combined forms for the working-class men in Ayr is 6.01 per 1,000 words, but without WR's exceptional use of (*you*) *ken* the combined frequency for the other working-class speakers is only 3.31, so the use of (*you*) *ken* does not greatly affect the overall picture. The form (*you*) *ken* does not occur in the Glasgow conversations. An example of WR's use of *ken* can be seen in Macaulay (1997: 155–56; 2002c: 761–62).

3. The gender difference might help to explain the lower overall frequency in Ayr, since there are only three women and nine men.

4. The London-Lund Corpus of Spoken English (LLC) consists of 500,000 words of spoken English, recorded from 1953 to 1987 at the University of London. The speakers are mostly middle-class.

5. The small difference from the figure of 4.49 provided by Svartvik and Stenström (1985: 346) may result from differences in the decision as what to count as tokens of *you know*.

6. The Bergen Corpus of London Teenage Talk (COLT) consists of 500,000 words, recorded in 1993, in which most of the speakers are teenagers.

7. This is perhaps the kind of use that Erman calls "metalinguistic" (2001: 1347).

8. Linell points out that the tendency to think of lexical items as having a fixed meaning is a significant example of "the written language bias" in linguistics: "Lexical meanings should not be seen as objectified items, static (paralysed, as it were) and stored in books or processed by computers" (1998: 119). This warning is particularly relevant when dealing with discourse features such as *you know*.

9. Edmondson calls this function "Let-me-Explain" and comments that "an utterance of the form *I mean* . . . cannot be said to *mean* 'I mean' . . . if it is to be accounted an instance of a Let-me-Explain" (1981: 154–155).

10. This pattern is also found in the London-Lund Corpus, where one all-male session (S. 1.7) has a frequency of 13.8 while the two all-female sessions with the highest use have frequencies of 12.2 (S. 1.3) and 10.6 (S. 1.8).

11. There is also the confounding factor of the form (*you*) *ken* used in Ayr. It obviously serves the same function as a discourse lubricant as *you know*, but their equivalence cannot be taken for granted.

12. Holmes (1986: 14) cites figures showing that women are more likely to use *you know* when expressing certainty and men when they are uncertain.

13. Oreström agrees that the use of forms such as *you know* is highly idiosyncratic: "Some people use them so often that even their intimacy effect seems to have been lost and the listener does not respond to them for some reason" (1983: 118).

Chapter 8

1. Examples of nonrestrictive relative clauses are:

> a. we looked at the dining room which is tiny (10L)
> b. it turned out her wee grandson who lives in Edinburgh was having problems (10R)

2. I have not attempted to distinguish different uses of the items I list as coordinate clauses, though clearly there are many. The term *coordinate* here simply applies to clauses beginning with *and*, *but*, or *so*.

3. In some cases it is clear that the speaker has pronounced both syllables, and in many cases it is clear that the speaker has used only the second syllable, but there are also many doubtful cases, so I have not separated them.

4. Examples of *get*-passives are:

> a. and every time he gets paid he goes and gambles it (7R)
> b. once they're at secondary school they get thrown in (10L)

Chapter 9

1. *Need* does not occur as a modal auxiliary.

Chapter 10

1. This figure is almost identical with that for the London-Lund conversations, 3.17 (based on Svartvik, Eeg-Olofsson, Forsheden, Oreström, and Thavenius 1982: 44).

2. The figures for the 34 conversations of the London-Lund Corpus are *very* 4.92, *just* 3.39, and *quite* 2.30 (based on Svartvik et al. 1982: 44). This is consistent with the middle-class status of the London-Lund speakers.

3. Bolinger (1972: 22) remarks that "the Middle English use [of *pure*] in the sense of 'very' . . . (e.g., *it is pure litille*) has evidently faded." Whether the Glasgow adolescents' use of *pure* in this sense is an innovation or a survival is unclear. Later investigation suggests that *pure* is replacing *dead* as the intensifier of choice. There is no sign yet that *weird, enough*, and *well* are used as intensifiers by Glasgow adolescents, as seems to be the case in London (Paradis 2000; Stenström 2000).

4. The middle-class Glasgow adults in general use more hedges than the working-class adults. For example, the middle-class speakers use *sort of* with a frequency of 1.84 instances per 1,000 words. The frequency for the working-class speakers is only 0.54, and this difference is highly significant ($p < .001$). There is no difference in the use of *kind of/kinda* (MC 0.49 versus WC 0.45).

Chapter 11

1. Bernstein claims that there are social class differences in the use of pronouns, but he includes the observation that working-class speakers infrequently use the pronoun *one*, which shows a rather old-fashioned view of middle-class speech.

2. The pronoun *it* was not included in figures 11.5 and 11.6 because *it* has other functions in addition to being an anaphoric pronoun. It is consequently difficult to draw conclusions about its referential function from the raw figures. For what they are worth, the frequencies of *it* are men 28.47, women 33.95, boys 26.55, girls 23.74.

3. In the Lancaster-Oslo/Bergen corpus of written English, forms of *he* are twice as frequent (17.6 per 1,000 words) as forms of *she* (8.2) (Johansson and Hofland 1989).

4. In tables 11.1 and 11.2, references to public figures such as footballers or actors are not included.

5. Nordenstam recorded all-male dyads, all-female dyads, and mixed-sex dyads, but even the same-sex dyads are not directly comparable with the Glasgow study because the all-male dyads contained several father-son pairs, thus introducing a generational difference in addition to the gender one.

6. In the mixed-sex pairs the wives mentioned almost four times as many people (30 vs. 8) as their husbands did, but it is impossible to calculate the frequencies because Nordenstam does not give separate word counts for males and females in the mixed sex dyads.

7. I first noticed this kind of difference in a stylistic comparison of interviews with a brother and sister (Macaulay 1996). The man used names referring to places with a frequency of 20.4 per 1,000 words, whereas in his sister's interview the frequency was only 3.2.

Chapter 12

1. Hickman (1993: 88) reports that in her sample of children aged 4 to 10, the proportion of *say* was 80% at 4 years, 91% at 7 years, and 87% at 10 years, compared with the adults' 56%.

2. Judging from some of the examples in Holmes 1997, *go* had reached New Zealand by then.

3. Interestingly, Winter (2002: 9) reports a different kind of hybrid example in Australia, such as those in (i).

(i)
    a. I *was like going* "I'm fine"
    b. my brother *kind of like goes* "Hmmm you've lost all your Chinese things"

She observes that these forms suggest "the newness of the form and may reflect some form of transitional stage of the form into the system".

4. Miller and Weinert 1995 examine the discourse functions of *like*, which has a long history in Scotland, but they found no examples of quotative *like* in conversations recorded in 1977–80.

Chapter 14

1. The following are some examples of the verb *nip* showing different contexts of use, showing that it can be arranged and also observed.

    a. she *nipped* him yesterday
    b. well she'll not be *nipping* him this year by the way
    c. and then the night after that I *nipped* her
    d. I would have asked to *nip* her
    e. she just *nipped* him for a one nighter
    f. so they just ended up *nipping* each other
    g. Tracey *nipped* Bryson and Mr Mitchell caught them he says "Did you enjoy that?" he says to her

References

Abraham, Werner, ed. 1991. *Discourse particles: Descriptive and theoretical investigations on the logical, syntactic, and pragmatic properties of discourse particles in German.* Amsterdam: John Benjamins.

Adamson, Sylvia. 2000. A lovely little example: Word order options and category shift in the premodifying string. In *Pathways to change: Grammaticalization in English,* ed. Olga Fischer, Annette Rosenbach, and Dieter Stein, 39–66. Amsterdam: John Benjamins.

Aijmer, Karin. 1985. Just. In *Papers on language and literature presented to Alvar Ellegård and Erik Frykman,* ed. Sven Bäckman and Göran Kjellmer, 1–10. Göteborg: Acta Universitatis Gothoburgensis.

———. 1987. *Oh* and *ah* in English conversation. In *Corpus linguistics and beyond: Proceedings of the Seventh International Conference on English Language Research on Computerized Corpora,* ed. Willem Meijs, 61–86. Amsterdam: Rodopi.

Albris, Jon. 1991. Style analysis. In *The Copenhagen study in urban sociolinguistics,* ed. Frans Gregersen and Inge Lise Pedersen, 45–106. Copenhagen: C. A. Reitzels Forlag.

Altenberg, Bengt. 1990a. Some functions of the booster. In *The London-Lund Corpus of spoken English: Description and research,* ed. Jan Svartvik, 193–209. Lund: Lund University Press.

———. 1990b. Spoken English and the dictionary. In *The London-Lund Corpus of Spoken English: Description and research,* ed. Jan Svartvik, 177–91. Lund: Lund University Press.

Andersen, Elaine. 2000. Exploring register knowledge: The value of "controlled improvisation." In *Methods for studying language production,* ed. Lise Menn and Nan Bernstein Ratner, 225–48. Mahwah, NJ: Lawrence Erlbaum.

Andersen, Gisle. 1997. *They like wanna see like how we talk and all that*: The use of *like* as a discourse marker in London teenage speech. In *Corpus-based studies in English,* ed. Magnus Ljung, 37–48. Amsterdam: Rodopi.

————. 1998. The pragmatic marker *like* from a relevance-theoretic perspective. In *Discourse markers: Descriptions and theory,* ed. Andreas H. Jucker and Zael Ziv, 147–70. Amsterdam: John Benjamins.

————. 2000. The role of the pragmatic marker *like* in utterance interpretation. In *Pragmatic markers and propositional attitude*, ed. Gisle Andersen and Thorstein Fretheim, 17–38. Amsterdam: John Benjamins.

Andersen, Gisle, and Thorstein Fretheim. 2000a. Introduction. In *Pragmatic markers and propositional attitude*, ed. Gisle Andersen and Thorstein Fretheim, 1–16. Amsterdam: John Benjamins.

————, eds. 2000b. *Pragmatic markers and propositional attitude*. Amsterdam: John Benjamins.

Argyle, Michael. 1994. *The psychology of social class*. London: Routledge.

Atkinson, J. Maxwell, and John Heritage, eds. 1984. *Structures of social action: Studies in conversation analysis*. Cambridge: Cambridge University Press.

Atkinson, Paul. 1985. *Language, structure and reproduction: An introduction to the sociology of Basil Bernstein*. London: Methuen.

Bäckman, Sven, and Göran Kjellmer, eds. 1985. *Papers on language and literature presented to Alvar Ellegård and Erik Frykman*. Göteborg: Acta Universitatis Gothoburgensis.

Baker, M., G. Francis, and E. Tognini-Bognelli, eds. 1993. *Text and technology: In honour of John Sinclair*. Amsterdam: John Benjamins.

Bahktin, Mikhail. 1973. *Problems of Dostoevsky's poetics*. Trans. R. W. Rotsel. Ann Arbor: Ardis.

————. 1981. *The dialogic imagination: Four essays by M. M. Bakhtin*, Ed. Michael Holquist. Trans. Caryl Emerson and Michael Holquist. Austin: University of Texas Press.

Bates, E., M. Masling, and W. Kintsch. 1978. Recognition memory for aspects of dialogue. *Journal of Experimental Psychology: Human Learning and Memory* 4:187–97.

Bauman, Richard. 1986. *Story, performance, and event.* Cambridge: Cambridge University Press.

Bell, Allan. 1984. Language style as audience design. *Language in Society* 13:145–204.

Berdan, Robert. 1978. Multidimensional analysis of vowel variation. In *Linguistic variation: Models and methods*, ed. David Sankoff, 149–60. New York: Academic Press.

Bernstein, Basil. 1958. Some sociological determinants of perception. *British Journal of Sociology* 9:159–74. Reprinted in *Class, codes and control*, 1:23–41. London: Routledge and Kegan Paul.

————. 1959. A public language: Some sociological implications of a linguistic form. *British Journal of Sociology* 10:311–26. Reprinted in *Class, codes and control*, 1:42–60. London: Routledge and Kegan Paul.

————. 1960. Language and social class. *British Journal of Sociology* 11:271–76. Reprinted in *Class, codes and control*, 1:61–67. London: Routledge and Kegan Paul.

————. 1962. Social class, linguistic codes, and grammatical elements. *Language and Speech* 5:31–46. Reprinted in *Class, codes and control*, 1:95–117. London: Routledge and Kegan Paul, 1971.

————. 1971. *Class, codes and control*. Vol. 1. London: Routledge and Kegan Paul.

————. 1997. Sociolinguistics: A personal view. In *Early days of sociolinguistics: Memories and reflections*, ed. Cristina Bratt Paulston and G. Richard Tucker, 43–52. Dallas: Summer Institute of Linguistics.

Biber, Douglas, and Edward Finegan. 1989. Styles of stance in English: Lexical and grammatical marking of evidentiality and affect. *Text* 9:93–124.

Bisseret, Noëlle. 1979. *Education, class language, and ideology*. London: Routledge and Kegan Paul.

Blakemore, Diane. 1987. *Semantic constraints on relevance*. Oxford: Blackwell.

———. 1988. *So* as a constraint on relevance. In *Mental representations: The interface between language and reality*, ed. Ruth M. Kempson, 183–95. Cambridge: Cambridge University Press.

Blyth, Carl, Jr., Sigrid Recktenwald, and Jenny Wang. 1990. I'm like, "Say what?!": A new quotative in American oral narrative. *American Speech* 65:215–27.

Bolinger, Dwight. 1972. *Degree words*. The Hague: Mouton.

———. 1977. *Meaning and form*. London: Longman.

Bourdieu, Pierre. 1977. *Outline of a theory of practice*. Cambridge: Cambridge University Press.

———. 1991. *Language and symbolic power*. Cambridge: Polity Press.

Brenneis, Donald, and Ronald K. S. Macaulay. 1996. *The matrix of language: Contemporary linguistic anthropology*. Boulder, CO: Westview Press.

Brinton, Laurel J. 1996. *Pragmatic factors in English: Grammaticalization and discourse functions*. Berlin: Mouton de Gruyter.

Brotherton, P. 1976. Aspects of the relationship between speech production, hesitation behaviour and social class. Ph.D. diss., University of Melbourne.

Brown, Colin, and Penelope Fraser. 1979. Speech as a marker of situation. In *Social markers in speech*, ed. Klaus R. Scherer and Howard Giles, 33–62. Cambridge: Cambridge University Press.

Brown, Gillian. 1977. *Listening to spoken English*. London: Longman.

Brown, Gillian, and George Yule. 1983. *Discourse analysis*. Cambridge: Cambridge University Press.

Brown, Penelope, and Stephen Levinson. 1987. *Politeness: Some universals in language usage*. Cambridge: Cambridge University Press.

Butters, Ronald R. 1980. Narrative *go* "say." *American Speech* 55:304–7.

———. 1982. Editor's note. *American Speech* 57:149.

Bybee, Joan, and Paul Hopper, eds. 2001a. *Frequency and the emergence of linguistic structure*. Amsterdam: John Benjamins.

———. 2001b. Introduction to frequency and the emergence of linguistic structure. In *Frequency and the emergence of linguistic structure*, ed. Joan Bybee and Paul Hopper, 1–24. Amsterdam: John Benjamins.

Campbell, Donald T. 1969. Reforms as experiments. *American Psychologist* 25:409–29.

Campbell, Donald T., and Donald W. Fiske. 1959. Convergent and discriminant validation by the multitrait-multimethod matrix. *Psychological Bulletin* 56:81–105.

Chafe, Wallace. 1982. Integration and involvement in speaking, writing, and oral literature. In *Spoken and written language: Exploring orality and literacy*, ed. Deborah Tannen, 35–53. Norwood, NJ: Ablex.

Chambers, J. K., Peter Trudgill, and Natalie Schilling-Estes, eds. 2002. *The handbook of language variation and change*. Oxford: Blackwell.

Cheshire, Jenny. 1982. *Variation in an English dialect*. Cambridge: Cambridge University Press.

Chomsky, Noam. 1965. *Aspects of the theory of syntax*. Cambridge, MA: MIT Press.

Cichoki, Wladyslaw. 1988. Uses of dual scaling in social dialectology: Multidimensional analysis of vowel variation. In *Methods in dialectology*, ed. Alan R. Thomas, 187–99. Clevedon: Multilingual Matters.

Clark, Herbert H. 1996. *Using language*. Cambridge: Cambridge University Press.

Coates, Jennifer. 1983. *The semantics of the modal auxiliaries*. London: Croom Helm.

———. 1988. Gossip revisited: Language in all-female groups. In *Women in their speech communities*, ed. Jennifer Coates and Deborah Cameron, 94–122. London: Longman.

————. 1996. *Women talk*. Oxford: Blackwell.

Coulmas, Florian, ed. 1986. *Direct and indirect speech*. Berlin: Mouton de Gruyter.

Coupland, Nikolas. 1988. *Dialect in use: Sociolinguistic variation in Cardiff English*. Cardiff: University of Wales Press.

————. 2001a. Age in social and sociolinguistic theory. In *Sociolinguistic theory and social theory*, ed. Nikolas Coupland, Srikani Sarangi, and Christopher N. Chandlin, 185–211. London: Pearson Education.

————. 2001b. Sociolinguistic theory and social theory. In *Sociolinguistic theory and social theory*, ed. Nikolas Coupland, Srikani Sarangi, and Christopher N. Chandlin, 1–26. London: Pearson Education.

Coupland, Nikolas, Srikani Sarangi, and Christopher N. Chandlin, eds. 2001. *Sociolinguistic theory and social theory*. London: Pearson Education.

Cowie, A. P., R. Mackin, and I. R. McCaig, eds. 1983. *The Oxford dictionary of current idiomatic English*. Vol. 2, *Phrase, clause and sentence idioms*. Oxford: Oxford University Press.

Crompton, Rosemary, Fiona Devine, Mike Savage, and John Scott, eds. 2000. *Renewing class analysis*. Oxford: Blackwell/The Sociological Review.

Crystal, David. 1966. Specification and English tenses. *Journal of Linguistics* 2:1–34.

Crystal, David, and Derek Davy. 1975. *Advanced conversational English*. London: Longman.

Dailey-O'Cain, Jennifer. 2000. The sociolinguistic distribution and attitudes toward focuser *like* and quotative *like*. *Journal of Sociolinguistics* 4:60–80.

Davis, Lawrence M. 1990. *Statistics in dialectology*. Tuscaloosa: University of Alabama Press.

Déjean le Féal, Karla. 1982: Why impromptu speech is easy to understand. In *Impromptu speech: A symposium*, ed. Nils E. Enkvist, 221–39. Åbo: Åbo Akademi Foundation.

Dines, Elizabeth R. 1980. Variation in discourse—"and stuff like that." *Language in Society* 9:13–31.

Dittmar, Norbert. 1976. *Sociolinguistics: A critical survey of theory and application*. London: Edward Arnold.

————. 1988. Foreword to the series "Sociolinguistics and language contact." In *The sociolinguistics of urban vernaculars: Case studies and their evaluation*, ed. Norbert Dittmar and Peter Schlobinski, ix–xii. Berlin: de Gruyter.

Dixon, R. M. W. 1982. *Where have all the adjectives gone?* Berlin: Mouton de Gruyter.

Docherty, Gerard J., Paul Foulkes, James Milroy, Lesley Milroy, and D. Walshaw. 1997. Descriptive adequacy in phonology: A variationist perspective. *Journal of Linguistics* 33:275–310.

Dougherty, Kevin A., and Stephanie M. Strassel. 1998. A new look at variation in and perception of American English quotatives. Paper presented at NWAV-27, University of Georgia, October.

Douglas-Cowie, Ellen. 1978. Linguistic code-switching in a Northern Irish village: Social interaction and social ambition. In *Sociolinguistic patterns in British English*, ed. Peter Trudgill, 37–51. London: Edward Arnold.

Dubois, Sylvie, and Barbara Horvath. 1993. Interviewer's linguistic production and its effect on speaker's descriptive style. *Language Variation and Change* 4:125–35.

Duranti, Alessandro. 1986. The audience as co-author: An introduction. *Text* 6:239–47.

Duranti, Alessandro, and Charles Goodwin, eds. 1992. *Rethinking context: Language as an interactive phenomenon*. Cambridge: Cambridge University Press.

Eble, Connie. 2000. It had to be *you, you know*. Paper presented at NWAV 29, Michigan State University, October.

Eckert, Penelope. 1990. Cooperative competition in adolescent "girl talk." *Discourse Processes* 13:91–122.

———. 1997. Age as a sociolinguistic variable. In *Handbook of sociolinguistics*, ed. Florian Coulmas, 151–67. Oxford: Blackwell.

———. 2000. *Linguistic variation as social practice: The linguistic construction of identity in Belten High.* Oxford: Blackwell.

Eckert, Penelope, and Sally McConnell-Ginet. 1992. Think practically and look locally: Language and gender as community based practice. *Annual Review of Anthropology* 21:461–490.

———. 1999. New generalizations and explanations in language and gender research. *Language in Society* 28:185–201.

Eckert, Penelope, and John R. Rickford, eds. 2001. *Style and sociolinguistic variation.* Cambridge: Cambridge University Press.

Eder, Donna (with Catherine Colleen Evans and Stephen Parker). 1995. *School talk: Gender and adolescent culture.* New Brunswick, NJ: Rutgers University Press.

Edmondson, Willis. 1981. *Spoken discourse: A model for analysis.* London: Longman.

Edwards, John. 1987. Elaborated and restricted codes. In *Sociolinguistics*, vol. 1, ed. Ulrich Ammon, Norbert Dittmar, and Klaus J. Mattheier, 374–78. Berlin: de Gruyter.

Eggins, Suzanne, and Diana Slade. 1997. *Analyzing casual conversation.* London: Cassell.

Ehrman, Madeline E. 1966. *The meanings of the modals in present-day American English.* The Hague: Mouton.

Eisikovits, Edina. 1989. Girl-talk/boy-talk: Sex differences in adolescent speech. In *Australian English: The language of a new society*, ed. Peter Collins and David Blair, 35–54. St. Lucia: University of Queensland Press.

Elifson, Kirk W., Richard P. Runyon, and Audrey Haber. 1990. *Fundamentals of social statistics.* 2nd ed. New York: McGraw-Hill.

Enkvist, Nils Erik, ed. 1982. *Impromptu speech: A symposium.* Åbo: Åbo Akademi Foundation.

Erickson, Frederick, and J. Shultz. 1982. *The counselor as gatekeeper: Social interaction in interviews.* New York: Academic Press.

Erman, Britt. 1987. *Pragmatic expressions in English: A study of* you know, you see, *and* I mean *in face-to-face conversation.* Stockholm Studies in English 69. Stockholm: Almqvist and Wiksell.

———. 1992. Female and male usage of pragmatic expressions in same-sex and mixed-sex interaction. *Language Variation and Change* 4:217–34.

———. 2001. Pragmatic markers revisited with a focus on *you know* in adult and adolescent talk. *Journal of Pragmatics* 33:1337–59.

Even-Zohar, Itamar. 1982. The emergence of speech organisers in a renovated language: The case of Hebrew void pragmatic connectives. In *Impromptu speech: A symposium*, ed. Nils E. Enkvist, 179–93. Åbo: Åbo Akademi Foundation.

Fasold, Ralph. 1972. *Tense marking in black English.* Washington, DC: Center for Applied Linguistics.

Feagin, Crawford. 1979. *Variation and change in Alabama English: A sociolinguistic study of the white community.* Washington, DC: Georgetown University Press.

Ferrara, Kathleen, and Barbara Bell. 1995. Sociolinguistic variation and discourse function of constructed dialogue introducers: The case of be+like. *American Speech* 70:265–89.

Fillmore, Charles J. 1979. On fluency. In *Individual differences in language ability and language behavior*, ed. Charles J. Fillmore, Daniel Kempler, and William S-Y. Wang, 85–101. New York: Academic Press.

Finegan, Edward, and Douglas Biber. 1994. Register and social dialect variation: an ntegrated approach. In *Sociolinguistic perspectives on register*, ed. Douglas Biber and Edward Finegan, 315–47. New York: Oxford University Press.

————— 2001. Register variation and social dialect variation: The register axiom. In *Style and sociolinguistic variation*, ed. Penelope Eckert and John R. Rickford, 235–67. Cambridge: Cambridge University Press.

Firth, John Rupert. 1935. The technique of semantics. *Transactions of the Philological Society* 36–72.

Fischer, John L. 1958. Social influences on the choice of a linguistic variant. *Word* 14:47–56.

Fischer, Olga, Annette Rosenbach, and Dieter Stein, eds. 2000. *Pathways to change: Grammaticalization in English*. Amsterdam: John Benjamins.

Fishman, Pamela M. 1978. Interaction: The work women do. *Social Problems* 25:397–406.

—————. 1980. Conversational insecurity. In *Language: Social psychological perspectives*, ed. Howard Giles, W. P. Robinson, and P. M. Smith, 127–31. Oxford: Pergamon.

Fleischman, Suzanne, and Marina Yaguello. Forthcoming. Discourse markers across languages? Evidence from English and French. In *Discourse across languages and cultures*, ed. C. L. Moder and A. Martinovic. Amsterdam: John Benjamins.

Foucault, Michel. 1980. *Power/knowledge: Selected interviews and other writings 1972–1977*. Ed. C. Gordon. Brighton: Harvester.

Foulkes, Paul, and Gerry Docherty, eds. 1999. *Urban voices: Variation and change in British accents*. London: Edward Arnold.

Fox Tree, Jean E., and Josef C. Schrock. 2002. Basic meanings of *you know* and *I mean*. *Journal of Pragmatics* 34:727–47.

Francis, Nelson W. 1983. *Dialectology*. London: Longman.

Fraser, Bruce. 1990. An approach to discourse markers. *Journal of Pragmatics* 14:383–95.

—————. 1996. Pragmatic markers. *Pragmatics* 6:167–90.

Gal, Susan. 1979. *Language shift: Social determinants of linguistic change in bilingual Austria*. New York: Academic Press.

Garfinkel, Harold. 1967. *Studies in ethnomethodology*. Englewood Cliffs, NJ: Prentice-Hall.

Giddens, Anthony. 1987. *Social theory and modern sociology*. Cambridge: Polity Press.

—————. 1990. *The consequences of modernity*. Cambridge: Polity Press.

—————. 1991. *Modernity and self-identity: Self and society in the late modern age*. Cambridge: Polity Press.

Giles, Howard, and Peter E. Powesland. 1975. *Speech style and social evaluation*. New York: Academic Press.

Goffman, Erving. 1974. *Frame analysis*. New York: Harper.

—————. 1981. *Forms of talk*. Philadelphia: University of Pennsylvania Press.

Golato, Andrea. 2000. An innovative German quotative for reporting on embodied actions: *Und ich so/und er so* "and I'm like/and he's like." *Journal of Pragmatics* 32:29–54.

Goldman Eisler, Frieda. 1968. *Psycholinguistics: Experiments in spontaneous speech*. London: Academic Press.

Goodwin, Charles. 1981. *Conversational organization: Interaction between speakers and hearers*. New York: Academic Press.

Goodwin, Marjorie Harkness. 1980. Directive-response speech sequences in girls' and boys' task activities. In *Women and language in literature and society*, ed. S. McConnell-Ginet, R. Borker, and N. Furman, 157–73. New York: Praeger.

Greenbaum, Sidney, Geoffrey Leech, and Jan Svartvik, eds. 1980. *Studies in English linguistics for Randolph Quirk*. London: Longman.

Gregersen, Frans, and Inge Lise Pedersen, eds. 1991. *The Copenhagen study in urban sociolinguistics*. 2 vols. Copenhagen: C. A. Reitzels Forlag.

Grice, H. P. 1975. Logic and conversation. In *Speech acts*, ed. Peter Cole and Jerrold Morgan, 41–58. New York: Academic Press.

Grimshaw, Allen. 2001. Discourse and sociology: Sociology and discourse. In *Handbook of discourse analysis*, ed. Deborah Schiffrin, Deborah Tannen, and Heidi E. Hamilton, 750–71. Oxford: Blackwell.

Gumperz, John J. 1992. Contextualization and understanding. In *Rethinking context*, ed. Alessandro Duranti and Charles Goodwin, 229–52. Cambridge: Cambridge University Press.

Habermas, J. 1972. *Knowledge and human interests.* Trans. J. Shapiro. London: Heinemann.

Haeri, Niloofar. 1996. *The sociolinguistic market of Cairo: Gender, class, and education.* London: Kegan Paul International.

Halliday, Michael A. K. 1987. Spoken and written modes of meaning. In *Comprehending oral and written language*, ed. Rosalind Horowitz and S. Jay Keyser, 55–82. San Diego: Academic Press.

Heath, Shirley Brice. 1982. What no bedtime story means: Narrative skills at home and school. *Language in Society* 11:49–76.

———. 1983. *Ways with words: Language, life, and work in communities and classrooms.* Cambridge: Cambridge University Press.

Heritage, John. 1984. A change-of-state token and aspects of its sequential placement. In *Structures of social actions: Studies in conversational analysis*, ed. J. Maxwell Atkinson and John Heritage, 299–345. Cambridge: Cambridge University Press.

Hickman, Maya. 1993. The boundaries of reported speech in narrative discourse. In *Reflexive language: Reported speech and metapragmatics*, ed. John A. Lucy, 63–90. Cambridge: Cambridge University Press.

Hjelmquist, Erland. 1984. Memory for conversations. *Discourse Processes* 7:319–34.

Holmes, Janet. 1986. Functions of *you know* in women's and men's speech. *Language in Society* 15:1–22.

———. 1990. Apologies in New Zealand English. *Language in Society* 19:155–99.

———. 1997. Story-telling in New Zealand's women's and men's talk. In *Gender and discourse*, ed. Ruth Wodack, 245–93. London: Sage.

Hopper, Paul J., and Elizabeth Closs Traugott. 1993. *Grammaticalization.* Cambridge: Cambridge University Press.

Horvath, Barbara. 1985. *Variation in Australian English.* Cambridge: Cambridge University Press.

Huang, Shuan-Fan. 1975. *A study of adverbs.* The Hague: Mouton.

Hunston, Susan, and John Sinclair. 1990. A local grammar of evaluation. In *Evaluation in text: Authorial stance and the construction of discourse*, ed. Susan Hunston and Geoff Thompson, 75–101. Oxford: Oxford University Press.

Hunston, Susan, and Geoff Thompson, eds. 2000. *Evaluation in text: Authorial stance and the construction of discourse.* Oxford: Oxford University Press.

Huspek, Michael. 1989. An analysis of YOU KNOW/I THINK variation in working-class speech. *Journal of Pragmatics* 13:661–83.

Hymes, Dell. 1974. *Foundations in sociolinguistics: An ethnographic approach.* Philadelphia: University of Pennsylvania Press.

———. 1996. *Ethnography, linguistics, narrative inequality: Toward an understanding of voice.* London: Taylor and Francis.

Ifantidou-Trouki, Elly. 1993. Sentential adverbs and relevance. *Lingua* 90:69–90.

Igoe, Matthew, Nel Lamb, Jon Gilman, and Ron Kim. 1999. The further grammaticalization of *be like* and some observations on *be all.* Paper presented at NWAV-28, University of Toronto, October.

Irvine, Judith T. 1990. Registering affect: Heteroglossia in the linguistic expression of emotion. In *Language and the politics of emotion*, ed. Catherine A. Lutz and Lila Abu-Lughod, 126–61. Cambridge: Cambridge University Press.

Jakobson, Roman. 1960. Closing statement: Linguistics and poetics. In *Style in language*, ed. Thomas A. Sebeok, 350–77. Cambridge, MA: MIT Press.

Jakobson, Roman, and Krystyna Pomorska. 1983. *Dialogues*. Cambridge, MA: MIT Press.

Jefferson, Gail. 1973 A case of precision timing in ordinary conversation. *Semiotica* 9:47–96.

Johansson, Stig, and Knut Hofland. 1989. *Frequency analysis of English vocabulary and grammar: Based on the LOB Corpus*. 2 vols. Oxford: Clarendon Press.

Johnstone, Barbara. 1987. "He says . . . so I said": Verb tense alternation and narrative depictions of authority in American English. *Linguistics* 25:33–52.

———. 1990. *Stories, community, and place: Narratives from middle America*. Bloomington: Indiana University Press.

———. 1996. *The linguistic individual*. New York: Oxford University Press.

———. 2001. *Discourse analysis*. Oxford: Blackwell.

Jucker, Andreas H., and Sara W. Smith. 1998. *And people just you know like "wow"*: Discourse markers as negotiating strategies. In *Discourse markers: Descriptions and theory*, ed. Andreas H. Jucker and Zael Ziv, 171–201. Amsterdam: John Benjamins.

Jucker, Andreas H., and Zael Ziv, eds. 1998a. *Discourse markers: Descriptions and theory*. Amsterdam: John Benjamins.

———. 1998b. Discourse markers: Introduction. In *Discourse markers: Descriptions and theory*, ed. Andreas H. Jucker and Zael Ziv, 1–12. Amsterdam: John Benjamins.

Kalton, Graham. 1983. *Introduction to survey sampling*. Beverly Hills, CA: Sage.

Kamp, Hans. 1990. Prolegomena to a structural account of belief and other attitudes. In *Propositional attitudes: The role of content in logic, language, and mind*, ed. C. Anthony Anderson and Joseph Owens, 27–90. Stanford, CA: CSLI.

Kiesling, Scott Fabius, and Natalie Schilling-Estes. 1998. Language style as identity construction: A footing and framing approach. Poster presented at NWAV-27, University of Georgia, October.

Kipers, Pamela S. 1987. Gender and topic. *Language in Society* 16:543–57.

Kretzschmar, William A., Jr., Charles F. Meyer, and Dominique Ingegneri. 1997. Uses of inferential statistics in corpus studies. In *Corpus-based studies in English*, ed. Magnus Ljung, 167–77. Amsterdam: Rodopi.

Kroch, Anthony. 1995. Dialect and style in the speech of upper class Philadelphia. In *Towards a social science of language: Papers in honor of William Labov*, vol. 1, ed. Gregory R. Guy, Crawford Feagin, Deborah Schiffrin, and John Baugh, 23–45. Amsterdam: John Benjamins.

Kroon, Caroline. 1995. *Discourse particles in Latin: A study of* nam, enim, autem, vero, *and* at. Amsterdam: Bieben.

Labov, William. 1963. The social motivation of a sound change. *Word* 19: 273–309.

———. 1966. *The social stratification of English in New York City*. Washington, DC: Center for Applied Linguistics.

———. 1969. The logic of nonstandard English. *Georgetown Monographs on Language and Linguistics*, 22, 1–31. Washington, DC: Georgetown University Press.

———. 1972. *Language in the inner city*. Philadelphia: University of Pennsylvania Press.

———. 1981. Field methods of the project on linguistic change and variation. *Sociolinguistic Working Paper*, no. 81. Austin, TX: Southwest Educational Development Laboratory.

———. 1984. Intensity. In *Meaning, form, and use in context: Linguistic applications*, ed. Deborah Schiffrin, 43–70. Washington, DC: Georgetown University Press.

———. 2001a. The anatomy of style shifting. In *Style and sociolinguistic variation*, ed. Penelope Eckert and John R. Rickford, 85–108. Cambridge: Cambridge University Press.

———. 2001b. *Principles of linguistic change: Social factors*. Oxford: Blackwell.

Labov, William, P. Cohen, C. Robins, and J. Lewis. 1968. A study of the non-standard English of Negro and Puerto Rican speakers in New York City. Cooperative research report 3288. New York: Columbia University.

Labov, William, and Joshua Waletzky. 1967. Narrative analysis. In *Essays on the verbal and visual arts*, ed. June Helm, 12–44. Seattle: University of Washington Press.

Laforest, Marty. 1993. L'influence de la loquacite de l'informateur sur la production de signaux backchannel par l'intervieweur en situation d'entrevue sociolinguistique. *Language Variation and Change* 4:163–77.

Lakoff, Robin. 1973. Language and woman's place. *Language in Society* 2:45–80.

———. 1975. *Language and woman's place*. New York: Harper and Row.

Lavandera, Beatriz R. 1978. Where does the sociolinguistic variable stop? *Language in Society* 7:171–82.

Lawton, Denis. 1968. *Social class, language and education*. London: Routledge and Kegan Paul.

Lee, David. 1987. The semantics of *just*. *Journal of Pragmatics* 11:377–98.

Leech, Geoffrey. 1983. *Principles of pragmatics*. London: Longman.

Lein, Laura, and Donald Brenneis. 1978. Children's disputes in three speech communities. *Language in Society* 7:299–323.

Li, Charles N. 1986. Direct and indirect speech: A functional study. In *Direct and indirect speech*, ed. Florian Coulmas, 29–45. Berlin: Mouton de Gruyter.

Linell, Per. 1982. *The written language bias in linguistics*. Linköping: University of Linköping.

———. 1998. *Approaching dialogue: Talk, interaction and contexts in dialogical perspectives*. Amsterdam: John Benjamins.

———. 2001. Dynamics of discourse or stability of structure: Sociolinguistics and the legacy from linguistics. In *Sociolinguistics and social theory*, ed. Nikolas Coupland, Srikani Sarangi, and Christopher N. Candlin, 107–26. London: Pearson Education.

Lippa, Richard. 1998. Gender-related individual differences and the structure of vocational interests: The importance of the people-things dimension. *Journal of Personality and Social Psychology* 74:996–1009.

Macaulay, Marcia I. 1990. *Processing varieties in English: An examination of oral and written speech across genres*. Vancouver: University of British Columbia Press.

Macaulay, Ronald K. S. 1976. Social class and language in Glasgow. *Language in Society* 5:173–88. Reprinted in Macaulay 1997, 85–99.

———. 1977. *Language, social class, and education: A Glasgow study*. Edinburgh: Edinburgh University Press.

———. 1984. Chattering, nattering and blethering: Informal interviews as speech events. In *Studies in language ecology*, ed. W. Enninger and L. Haynes, 51–64. Wiesbaden: Steiner.

———. 1985. The narrative skills of a Scottish coal miner. In *Focus on: Scotland*, ed. Manfred Görlach, 101–24. Amsterdam: John Benjamins.

———. 1986. Review of Atkinson 1985. *Language* 62:956–57.

———. 1987a. Polyphonic monologues: Quoted direct speech in oral narratives. *IPRA Papers in Pragmatics* 1:1–34.

———. 1987b. The sociolinguistic significance of Scottish dialect humor. *International Journal of the Sociology of Language* 65:53–63. Reprinted in Macaulay 1997, 61–69.

———. 1990. The essential meaningfulness of ordinary discourse: Evidence from mistranscription. Paper presented at NWAV-19, University of Pennsylvania, October.

———. 1991a. "Coz it izny spelt when they say it": Displaying dialect in writing. *American Speech* 66:280–91.

————. 1991b. *Locating dialect in discourse: The language of honest men and bonnie lasses in Ayr*. New York: Oxford University Press.

————. 1995. The adverbs of authority. *English World-Wide* 16:37–60. Reprinted in Macaulay 1997, 119–38.

————. 1996. A man can no more invent a new style than he can invent a new language. Paper presented at Sociolinguistics Symposium 11, Cardiff, September.

————. 1997. *Standards and variation in urban speech: Examples from lowland Scots*. Amsterdam: John Benjamins.

————. 1999. Is sociolinguistics lacking in style? *Cuadernos de Filologia Inglesa* 8:9–33.

————. 2001a. The question of genre. In *Style and sociolinguistic variation*, ed. Penelope Eckert and John R. Rickford, 78–82. Cambridge: Cambridge University Press.

————. 2001b. You're like *"Why not?"*: The quotative expressions of Glasgow adolescents. *Journal of Sociolinguistics* 5:3–21.

————. 2002a. Discourse variation. In *Handbook of language variation and change*, ed. Jack C. Chambers, Peter Trudgill, and Natalie Schilling-Estes, 283–305. Oxford: Blackwell.

————. 2002b. Extremely interesting, very interesting, or only quite interesting? Adverbs and social class. *Journal of Sociolinguistcs* 6:398–417.

————. 2002c. You know, it depends. *Journal of Pragmatics* 34:749–67.

————. To appear. *Extremely common eloquence: Some clear Scottish voices*.

Macaulay, Ronald K. S., and G. D. Trevelyan, 1973. Language, education and employment in Glasgow. Final report to the Social Science Research Council. Edinburgh: Scottish Council for Research in Education.

Markova, Ivana, and Klaus Foppa, eds. 1990. *The dynamics of dialogue*. Hemel Hempstead: Harvester Wheatsheaf.

Maschler, Yael. 2002. On the grammaticization of *ke'ilu* "like," lit. "as if," in Hebrew talk-in-interaction. *Language in Society* 31:243–76.

Mathis, Terrie, and George Yule. 1994. Zero quotatives. *Discourse Processes* 18:63–76.

McCafferty, Kevin. 2001. *Ethnicity and language change: English in (London) Derry, Northern Ireland*. Amsterdam: John Benjamins.

McCawley, James D. 1979. *Adverbs, vowels, and other objects of wonder*. Chicago: University of Chicago Press.

McConnell-Ginet, Sally. 1982. Adverbs and logical form. *Language* 58:144–84.

Meijs, Willem, ed. 1987. *Corpus linguistics and beyond: Proceedings of the Seventh International Conference on English Language Research on Computerized Corpora*. Amsterdam: Rodopi.

Menn, Lise, and Nan Bernstein Ratner, eds. 2000. *Methods for studying language production*. Mahwah, NJ: Erlbaum.

Miller, Jim. 1993. The grammar of Scottish English. In *Real English: The grammar of English dialects in the British Isles*, ed. James Milroy and Lesley Milroy, 99–138. London: Longman.

Miller, Jim, and Regina Weinert. 1995. The function of LIKE in dialogue. *Journal of Pragmatics* 23:365–93.

————. 1998. *Spontaneous spoken language: Syntax and discourse*. Oxford: Oxford University Press.

Milroy, James. 1979. Review of *Language, Social Class, and Education* by R. K. S. Macaulay. *Language in Society* 8:88–96.

Milroy, James, and Lesley Milroy. 1977. Speech and context in an urban setting. Belfast Working Papers in Language and Linguistics, 2:1–85.

Milroy, Lesley. 1980. *Language and social networks*. Oxford: Blackwell.

————. 2001. The social categories of race and class: Language ideology and sociolinguistics.

In *Sociolinguistics and social theory*, ed. Nikolas Coupland, Srikani Sarangi, and Christopher N. Candlin, 235–60. London: Pearson Education.

———. 2004. Language ideologies and linguistic change. In *Sociolinguistic variation: Critical reflections*, ed. Carmen Fought, 161–77. New York: Oxford University Press.

Munroe, Robert L., and Ruth H. Munroe. 1991. Comparative field studies: Methodological issues and future possibilities. *Behavior Science Research* 25:155–85.

Nordenstam, Kerstin. 1992. Male and female conversational style. *International Journal of the Sociology of Language* 94:75–98.

Ochs, Eleanor. 1979. Transcription as theory. In *Developmental pragmatics*, ed. Eleanor Ochs and Bambi Schieffelin, 43–72. New York: Academic Press.

O'Connell, Daniel C. 1988. *Critical essays on language use and psychology*. New York: Springer-Verlag.

O'Donnell, W. R., and Loreto Todd. 1980. *Variety in contemporary English*. London: Allen and Unwin.

Ong, Walter J. 1982. Oral remembering and narrative structures. In *Analyzing discourses: Text and talk*, ed. Deborah Tannen, 12–24. Washington, DC: Georgetown University Press.

Oreström, Bengt. 1983. *Turn-taking in English conversation*. Lund: CWK Gleerup.

Östman, Jan-Ola. 1981. *You know: A discourse-functional approach*. Amsterdam: John Benjamins.

———. 1982. The symbiotic relationship between pragmatic particles and impromptu speech. In *Impromptu speech: A symposium*, ed. Nils E. Enkvist, 147–77. Åbo: Åbo Akademi Foundation.

Overstreet, Maryann. 1999. *Whales, candlelight, and stuff like that: General extenders in English discourse*. New York: Oxford University Press.

Palmer, Frank R. 1986. *Mood and modality*. Cambridge: Cambridge University Press.

———. 1990. *Modality and the English modals*. London: Longman.

Paradis, Carita. 2000. *It's well weird*: Degree modifiers of adjectives revisited: The nineties. In *Corpora galore: Analyses and techniques in describing English*, ed. John M. Kirk, 147–60. Amsterdam: Rodopi.

Paulston, Cristina Bratt, and G. Richard Tucker, eds. 1997. *The early days of sociolinguistics: Memories and reflections*. Dallas: Summer Institute of Linguistics.

Polanyi, Livia. 1985. *The American story*. Norwood, NJ: Ablex.

Pomerantz, Anna. 1978. Compliment responses: Notes on the co-operation of multiple constraints. In *Studies in the oganization of conversational interaction*, ed. Jim Scheinkein, 79–112. New York: Academic Press.

Poole, M. E. 1973. Linguistic, cognitive and verbal processing styles: A social class contrast. Ph.D. diss., La Trobe University.

Powell, Mava Jo. 1992. The systematic development of correlated interpersonal and metalinguistic uses in stance adverbs. *Cognitive Linguistics* 3:75–110.

Quirk, Randolph, Sidney Greenbaum, Geoffrey Leech, and Jan Svartvik. 1985. *A comprehensive grammar of the English language*. London: Longman.

Rampton, Ben. 1995. *Crossing: Language and ethnicity among adolescents*. London: Longman.

———. 2001. Language crossing, cross-talk, and cross-disciplinarity in sociolinguistics. In *Sociolinguistic theory and social theory*, ed. Nikolas Coupland, Srikani Sarangi, and Christopher N. Chandlin, 261–96. London: Pearson Education.

Redeker, Gisela. 1991. Linguistic markers of discourse structure. *Linguistics* 29:1139–72.

Reid, Ivan. 1989. *Social class differences in Britain*. 3rd ed. London: Fontana.

———. 1998. *Class in Britain*. Cambridge: Polity Press.

Rickford, John R., and Faye McNair-Knox. 1994. Addressee- and topic-influenced style shift: A quantitative sociolinguistic study. In *Sociolinguistic perspectives on regis-*

ter, ed. Douglas Biber and Edward Finegan, 235–76. New York: Oxford University Press.

Roger, Derek B., and Willfried Nesshoever. 1987. Individual differences in dyadic conversational strategies: A further study. *British Journal of Social Psychology* 26:247–55.

Romaine, Suzanne, and Deborah Lange. 1991. The use of *like* as a marker of reported speech and thought: A case of grammaticalization in progress. *American Speech* 66:227–79.

Rosen, Harold. 1972. *Language and class: A critical look at the theories of Basil Bernstein.* Bristol: Falling Wall Press.

Sacks, Harvey. 1974. An analysis of the course of a joke's telling in conversation. In *Explorations in the ethnography of speaking*, ed. Richard Bauman and Joel Scherzer, 337–53. Cambridge: Cambridge University Press.

Sacks, Harvey, Emanuel Schegloff, and Gail Jefferson. 1974. A simplest systematics for the organization of turn-taking in conversation. *Language* 50:696–735.

Sanchez, Tara, and Anne Charity. 1999. The use of *be like* and other verbs of quotation in a predominantly African-American community. Paper presented at NWAV-28, University of Toronto, October.

Sankoff, David, and Gillian Sankoff. 1973. Sample survey methods and computer-assisted analysis in the study of grammatical variation. In *Canadian languages in their social context*, ed. Regina Darnell, 7–64. Edmonton: Linguistic Research.

Saussure, Ferdinand de. 1922. *Course de linguistique generale*. 2nd ed. Paris: Payot.

———. 1986. *Course in General Linguistics*. Trans. Roy Harris. La Salle, IL.: Open Court.

Schegloff, Emanuel A. 1982. Discourse as as an interactional achievement: Some uses of 'uh huh' and other things that come between sentences. In *Analyzing discourse: Text and talk*, ed. Deborah Tannen, 71–93. Washington, DC: Georgetown University Press.

Scheibman, Joanne. 2001. Local patterns of subjectivity in person and verb type in American English conversation. In *Frequency and the emergence of linguistic structure*, ed. Joan Bybee and Paul Hopper, 61–89. Amsterdam: John Benjamins.

———. 2002. *Point of view and grammar: Structural patterns of subjectivity in American English conversation*. Amsterdam: John Benjamins.

Schiffrin, Deborah. 1981. Tense variation in narrative. *Language* 57: 45–62.

———. 1987. *Discourse markers*. Cambridge: Cambridge University Press.

———. 1994. *Approaches to discourse*. Oxford: Blackwell.

Schiffrin, Deborah, Deborah Tannen, and Heidi E. Hamilton, eds. 2001. *Handbook of discourse analysis*. Oxford: Blackwell.

Schilling-Estes, Natalie. 1998. Situated ethnicities: Constructing and reconstructing identity in the sociolinguistic interview. Paper presented at NWAV-27, University of Georgia, October.

Schourup, Lawrence C. 1985. *Common discourse particles in English conversation:* Like, well, y'know. New York: Garland.

———. 1999. Discourse markers. *Lingua* 107:227–65.

Sinclair, John. 1995. From theory to practice. In *Spoken English on computer: Transcription, markup and application*, ed. Geoffrey Leech, Greg Myers, and Jenny Thomas, 99–109. London: Longman.

Smith, Jennifer. 2001. Negative concord in the Old and New World: Evidence from Scotland. *Language Variation and Change* 13:109–34.

Stenström, Anna-Britta. 1990a. Lexical items peculiar to spoken discourse. In *The London-Lund Corpus of spoken English: Description and research*, ed. Jan Svartvik, 137–75. Lund: Lund University Press.

———. 1990b. Pauses in monologue and dialogue. In *The London-Lund Corpus of Spoken English: Description and research*, ed. Jan Svartvik, 211–52. Lund: Lund University Press.

———. 1998. From sentence to discourse: *Cos* (*because*) in teenage talk. In *Discourse markers: Descriptions and theory*, ed. Andreas H. Jucker and Zael Ziv, 126–46. Amsterdam: John Benjamins.

———. 2000. *It's enough funny, man*: Intensifiers in teenage talk. In *Corpora galore: Analyses and techniques in describing English*, ed. John M. Kirk, 177–90. Amsterdam: Rodopi.

Strang, Barbara M. 1962. *Modern English structure*. London: Edward Arnold.

Stuart-Smith, Jane. 1999. Glasgow. In *Urban voices: Variation and change in British accents*, ed. Paul Foulkes and Gerry Docherty, 203–22. London: Arnold.

———. 2003. The phonology of modern urban Scots. In *The Edinburgh companion to Scots*, ed. J. Corbett, D. M. McClure, and J. Stuart-Smith, 110–37. Edinburgh: Edinburgh University Press.

Stubbe, Maria, and Janet Holmes. 1995. *You know, eh* and other "exasperating expressions": An analysis of social and stylistic variation in the use of pragmatic devices in a sample of New Zealand English. *Language and Communication* 15:63–88.

Stubbs, Michael. 1983. *Discourse analysis: The sociolinguistic analysis of natural language*. Oxford: Blackwell.

Svartvik, Jan. 1980. *Well* in conversation. In *Studies in English linguistics for Randolph Quirk*, ed. Sidney Greenbaum, Geoffrey Leech, and Jan Svartvik, 167–77. London: Longman.

———. ed. 1990. *The London-Lund Corpus of Spoken English: Description and research*. Lund: Lund University Press.

Svartvik, Jan, Mats Eeg-Olofsson, Oscar Forsheden, Bengt Oreström, and Cecilia Thavenius. 1982. *Survey of spoken English*. Lund: CWK Gleerup.

Svartvik, Jan, and Randolph Quirk, eds. 1980. *A corpus of English conversation*. Lund: CWK Gleerup.

Svartvik, Jan, and Anna-Britta Stenström. 1985. Words, words, words: The rest is silence. In *Papers on language and literature presented to Alvar Ellegård and Erik Erykman*, ed. Sven Bäckman and Göran Kjellmer, 342–53. Göteborg: Acta Universitatis Gothoburgensis.

Sweetser, Eve. 1990. *From etymology to pragmatics: Metaphorical and cultural aspects of semantic structure*. Cambridge: Cambridge University Press.

Tagliamonte, Sali, and Rachel Hudson. 1999. *Be like* et al. beyond America: The quotative system in British and Canadian youth. *Journal of Sociolinguistics* 3:147–72.

Tannen, Deborah. 1982. Oral and literate strategies in spoken and written narratives. *Language* 58:1–21.

———. 1984. *Conversational style: Analyzing talk among friends*. Norwood, NJ: Ablex.

———. 1986. Introducing constructed dialogue in Greek and American conversational and literary narrative. In *Direct and indirect speech*, ed. Florian Coulmas, 311–32. Berlin: Mouton de Gruyter.

———. 1989. *Talking voices: Repetition, dialogue, and imagery in conversational discourse*. Cambridge: Cambridge University Press.

———. 1996. *Gender and discourse*. New York: Oxford University Press.

Tao, Hongyin. 2001. Discovering the usual with corpora: The case of remember. In *Corpus linguistics in North America: Selections from the 1999 symposium*, ed. Rita Simpson and John Swales, 116–44. Ann Arbor: University of Michigan Press.

Thompson, Sandra A., and Paul J. Hopper. 2001. Transitivity, clause structure, and argument structure: Evidence from conversation. In *Frequency and the emergence of linguistic structure*, ed. Joan Bybee and Paul Hopper, 27–60. Amsterdam: John Benjamins.

Trudgill, Peter. 1974. *The social differentiation of English in Norwich*. Cambridge: Cambridge University Press.

————. 1975. Review of Bernstein 1971. *Journal of Linguistics* 11:147–51.

Underhill, Robert. 1988. *Like* is, like, focus. *American Speech* 63:234–46.

van Dijk, Teun A. 2001. Critical discourse analysis. In *Handbook of discourse analysis*, ed. Deborah Schiffrin, Deborah Tannen, and Heidi E. Hamilton, 352–71. Oxford: Blackwell.

Vincent, Diane, and David Sankoff. 1993. Punctors: A pragmatic variable. *Language Variation and Change* 4:205–16.

Voloshinov, V. N. 1986. [1929]. *Marxism and the philosophy of language*. Trans. L. Matejka and I. R. Titunik. Cambridge, MA: Harvard University Press.

Wales, Katie. 1996. *Personal pronouns in present-day English*. Cambridge: Cambridge University Press.

Warner, W. L., M. Meeker, and K. Eells. 1949. *Social class in America*. New York: Harper and Row.

Watts, Richard J. 1989. Taking the pitcher to the "well." *Journal of Pragmatics* 13. 203–237.

Weiyun He, Agnes. 2001. Discourse analysis. In *The handbook of linguistics*, ed. Mark Aronoff and Janie Rees-Miller, 428–45. Oxford: Blackwell.

Wennerstrom, Ann. 2001. *The music of everyday speech: Prosody and discourse analysis*. New York: Oxford University Press.

Wertsch, James V. 1991. *Voices of the mind: A sociocultural approach to mediated action*. London: Harvester Wheatsheaf.

Williams, Glyn. 1992. *Sociolinguistics: A sociological critique*. London: Routledge.

Wilson, John. 1989. *On the boundaries of conversation*. Oxford: Pergamon.

Winter, Joanne. 2002. Discourse quotatives in Australian English: Adolescents performing voices. *Australian Journal of Linguistics* 22:5–21.

Wolfram, Walt. 1969. *A sociolinguistic description of Detroit Negro speech*. Washington, DC: Center for Applied Linguistics.

Wolfson, Nessa. 1976. Speech events and natural speech: Some implications for sociolinguistic methodology. *Language in Society* 5:215–37.

————. 1978. A feature of performed narrative: The conversational historical present. *Language in Society* 7:215–39.

————. 1982. *CHP: The conversational historical present in American English narrative*. Dordrecht: Foris.

Woods, Anthony, Paul Fletcher, and Arthur Hughes. 1986. *Statistics in language studies*. Cambridge: Cambridge University Press.

Woods, Howard B. 1991. Social differentiation in Ottawa English. In *English around the world: Sociolinguistic perspectives*, ed. Jenny Cheshire, 134–49. Cambridge: Cambridge University Press.

Yaeger-Dror, Malcah. 1997. Contraction of negatives as evidence of variance in register-specific interactive rules. *Language Variation and Change* 9:1–36.

Index